Don Ameche

THE KENOSHA COMEBACK KID

BY BEN OHMART

PUBLISHED IN THE USA BY:

BearManor Media
PO Box 71426
Albany, GA 31708
www.BearManorMedia.com

LIBRARY OF CONGRESS CATALOGING-IN-PUBLICATION DATA:

Ohmart, Ben.
  Don Ameche : the Kenosha comeback kid / by Ben Ohmart.
      p. cm.
  Includes index.
  ISBN 978-1-59393-045-5
  1. Ameche, Don. 2. Actors--United States--Biography. I. Title.

  PN2287.A555O46 2007
  791.4302'8092--dc22
  [B]
                                        2006103487

Printed in the United States.

Design and Layout by Valerie Thompson.

Table of Contents

For my mother
For the years of love and devotion she continues
to heap upon me

Foreword

It was three weeks from principal photography on *Trading Places* when we were notified that Ray Milland did not pass his insurance physical. I had cast Ray to play opposite Ralph Bellamy as Mortimer and Randolph Duke, the elderly bad guys who set the picture's plot in motion. All of the lead actors in a movie must be insured, so Paramount insisted I replace Ray Milland. After a difficult phone call with Ray (who, by the way, lived to make several more films), we had to come up with an actor of Ralph Bellamy's age and stature, and quickly.

After much thought, I asked if Don Ameche had ever played a villain. I was told that Don Ameche was dead! I was sure that if Don Ameche had died, I would have known about it. After fruitless calls to the Screen Actors Guild, one of the secretaries at Paramount said, "Oh, I see Don Ameche all the time. He's always walking on San Vicente Blvd. in Santa Monica." And sure enough, there was a D. Ameche in the phone book listed in Santa Monica.

I called and the phone was answered in Don's unmistakable voice, "Hello. This is Don Ameche, may I help you?"

Don had been a major Hollywood Star, a Radio Star, a Broadway Star and a Television Star and, yet, he asked politely if I wanted him to read for the part. I just really wanted to meet him and see that he was fit. He drove himself to Paramount and we met that afternoon. His posture was perfect, his voice smooth as ever. All I wanted to do was to ask about Lubitsch and discuss the Bickersons and how I watched *International Showtime* as a kid, but instead I just offered him the role.

Once in Philadelphia, where we began shooting, Don and I became good friends and working with him was a pleasure. Don and Ralph impressed everyone with their professionalism and class. After the success of *Trading Places*, Don won an Oscar for his role in *Cocoon* and worked steadily until he passed away.

Don was a fascinating man. He was full of wonderful stories of Hollywood and Broadway. We worked together twice more; he played a priest in *Oscar*, and with Ralph they reprised their roles as the Duke Brothers in a delightful cameo in *Coming to America*.

Don had a magnificent career and one with a unique Second Act. I loved him.

JOHN LANDIS
LOS ANGELES, 2005

Introduction

My fascination with Don Ameche's talent had nothing to do with his impressive film career. For me, it all began with

BLANCHE: You hate that cat, don't you?

JOHN: I don't hate him at all.

BLANCHE: You do, too!

JOHN: I do not! I love the cat, I love the canary and I love you! I don't know which one of you I love the most . . .

BLANCHE: If the house ever caught fire, which would you save first? The cat, the canary or me?

JOHN: Me.

"Now here are Don Ameche and Frances Langford as John and Blanche Bickerson in . . . The Honeymoon Is Over . . ." This was the ultimate, over-the-top, never-stopping radio Valentine that put the word "Bickerson" into the English language and shocked the 1940s out of their lovey-dovey complacency. I discovered a cassette tape of this bubbling, acidic wit when I was 10 years old, and from then on I've been an intense fan of radio comedy (even BBC Radio 4, the only current haven for *new* radio comedy).

Don Ameche may have found everlasting financial and artistic success through his now-classic movies, but, like Peter Sellers, he acted foremost with his voice and never lost that subtle radio skill that could be all but understated when the shouting began. His was not the most expressive of faces, but his vocal ability was without question.

While his best friend during the Golden Years, Tyrone Power, was the handsome one, and his other Musketeer, Alice Faye, was popular enough to have her name above Don's (even if he had the starring role), Don's versatility outshone many of the bigger names with which he shared scenes. Not everyone was a radio star, Broadway star, singer, rogue, smiling & dashing leading man, inventor/thinker, and few have had 60-year careers and triple comebacks, topped off with an Oscar at the end.

The personal side of Don Ameche had shades of that maneuverability, as well. In 1986, Don stated, "There will be no *Mommie Dearest* in the lives of my children and no books like the one the Crosby boy wrote about Bing, or Bette Davis's daughter has written. My children love me very much and they are loved." Though there was an obvious distance placed between Don and his children, every one of his children I spoke with had a great deal of love and fondness for their father. I'm forever grateful to them all for being so open and trusting with me, giving me the facts as they knew them and instilling within this biography a sense of fairness and positive truth.

Don Ameche was a very private man. When assembling a biography on someone you've never met, with no true first-hand accounts to rifle (that is, from longtime friends, co-workers, or siblings), the writer's best friend is his research material. Foremost, I would like to thank a fan who (unfortunately) wishes to remain anonymous for sharing her *vast* and *impressive* collection of Don Ameche material with me. Most of the photos here came from her, and she unselfishly lent me all kinds of articles and material, including rare videos. Her generosity was incredible, and I honestly could not have written this book without her help. It was like having access to a private, personal Ameche library! *Thank you.*

And because of the very generous nature of the Ameche children (especially Connie, Bonnie and Don, Jr.), I was privy to the entire Don Ameche clippings collection from which to ween many facts. Yes, *every* time Don Ameche's name was mentioned in any newspaper or magazine in the world, whether it was just a snippet or a full five-page article, it was clipped by a professional service and sent to Don and his wife. Luckily for us all, Don did not keep the material himself— he kept virtually nothing his whole life—but entrusted it to his daughters.

These clippings, I realize, have to be taken with a shaker of salt since press releases are not delivered under oath, and from the sound of some of them (sappy; clashing facts; fictionalized studio copywriting), it's often obvious that certain "angles" were taken in order to get them into the papers or magazines. I hope this functions more as an explanatory note for the sometimes larger-than-lifeness of these contents rather than a disclaimer, but that's what comes of writing the life story of a great talent born almost 100 years ago today.

No book is an island, and without the help of many of these people, there would be a lot less between the covers:

Frances Langford, for putting up with a true fan and for just being Blanche; John Landis, for not just making *Trading Places* and giving Don Ameche his second, more permanent comeback, but for being a chronic and encouraging Ameche fan and for just being so damn *accessible*; John Dunning; Jay Hickerson (your *Ultimate History of Network Radio Programming and Guide to All Circulating Shows* is an invaluable reference tool); James S. Harris; Tim Hollis;

Ted Meland; Donnie Pitchford; Ed Reisner; Danny Sharples; Teri Seier; Sandy Singer; master collector and tireless benefactor Charles Stumpf; George Ulrich; a special thanks to Laura Wagner for helping at every stage, especially on my Bickersons book; and Nancy Wallen.

BEN OHMART
MAY 2006

Chapter One
The Kenosha Kid

Home to the first government lighthouse (1848), Kenosha, Wisconsin was established as the furthermost town before the Illinois border, facing the great Lake Michigan. The state was home to a massive settling of Native Americans, especially the Ho-Chunk tribe; and, in the Kenosha area, the Potawatomi. It is still known for its many tribal events, and fantastic charter fishing. And as the birthplace of Don Ameche.

Dominic Felix Amici (named for the Spanish Saint Dominic) was born in the Marche provinces of Italy (sometimes also given as Ascoli Piceno, a province northeast of Rome, Italy), where he joined the artillery in Italy's war with Abbysinia in the late 1890s. He came to the United States in 1898 and worked in coal mines, iron works and stone quarries all over the East, then in the coal fields of Springfield, IL. It was in Barkley, Illinois, working as a coal miner, where fell in love with the landlady's daughter, Barbara Etta Hertle, of German/Scotch/Irish roots. Both had only a third-grade education.

They married in Springfield, Illinois, when they'd saved enough money, and moved 36 miles from Milwaukee to set up house in Kenosha. There, in the Catholic faith, they raised a family of eight: Betty, Dominic (Don), Louis, Jimmy, Bert, Catherine, Mary Jane and Anne.

Times were lean and it took the Amici clan several years to settle into a lifestyle that would do well for their increasing family. Capitalizing on Barbara's profundity in the kitchen, they opened a small bakery, which did not last long. She once lost her wideband gold wedding ring during a particularly productive day and, after tears and prayers, it was returned to her by a customer who had found it in a loaf of bread she'd purchased. That event had a lot to do with getting out of the bakery business and into liquor.

Some news stories reported that it had actually been a small grocery store that the family ran. Moving into a more lucrative field, Felix sold the grocery store/bakery and opened a modest, orderly saloon to increase profits and be able to take care of his children and give them proper schooling. Business swelled so much, Felix soon had two saloons in Kenosha, later a third in La Salle, Illinois before Prohibition came and retired him.

Left to right: Don, Felix, Barbara, Betty, Jim, Bert, Louie.
Photo courtesy of Don Ameche, Jr.

Dominic Felix Amici, named after his father, was born on May 31, 1908, to a violent childhood. But only at the bar. In 1988 he told an interviewer, "My father ran a saloon in Kenosha, Wisconsin, which is just about as rough a living as I can think of. It was brutal; it scared the hell out of me. I was so petrified all the while I was a child, I didn't know what I was doing half the time. It was no fun living with someone who had a revolver in his trousers every day and a poison-tipped stiletto in the house.

"The lowest class people drank in his saloon. He had *three* revolvers in the back bars. A bartender got into an argument one day, reached for one of the guns and killed a guy, boom, just like that. Papa hid the bartender out for a while, then ripped him open with a pair of scissors and took him to court and got him off. Self-defense."

When Dominic was around seven years old, he saw his father throw two men out. The younger man savagely beat the older one, causing him to double over. All of a sudden the older man stood up with a five-inch knife in hand. With damaging force, he hit the younger man in the nose three times, then three times in the back as he went down. Blood was everywhere. Don called it par for the course.

To keep the peace, Felix kept a gun, baseball bats and a stiletto at strategic places in his saloon, and was never afraid to pull them out. The Italian temperament helped. And wasn't just manifested in the workplace. Felix once hurled a plate of pasta against the wall when his wife served it "imperfectly prepared." Don admitted, "That was the kind of man he was."

The Kenosha house.

There was also a certain distance in the Amici clan, a trait Don unfortunately seemed to inherit to an extent.

"Do you know," Don admitted in later life, "neither one of my parents ever told me they loved me. I never even heard them say they loved each other. I don't know what kind of a scar that left on me. I really hadn't thought about it until recently. But I just learned to live with it. When I got to be 40, I just thought things out and I said, 'This is what Mama is and this is what Papa is.' As I grew older, there came to me a tolerance and an understanding that they both did the best they knew."

When ruminating about his early life in the last years of his life, Don believed that his father had moved to America at age 25 and at 31 married a 16-year-old girl in a now nonexistent mining town near Springfield, Illinois. "I always thought that my father probably—possibly—bought her. My mother came from dirt-poor people. Maybe he paid $200, $300? It was a perfectly legitimate business deal, why not? She was of age and it was the custom of the day.

"It's been proven now that during the first year of a child's life, if they're not given the proper nourishment and proper love, they're irreparably damaged for all the rest of their lives. I believe that.

"I guess it goes to show that you're not totally damaged if that first year doesn't have all the things that it should have. But I'm sure that it has caused me to make mistakes. That's inevitable.

Little Dominic.

"Don't think that I hold anything against my mother and father. They did the absolute best that they knew how. My mother had migraines from the first time I ever had any memory of her. They'd last three, four, five days at a time. She couldn't move. And him? How could I hold anything against him? That was the way it happened. I don't know if I admired him, but I certainly didn't hate him. I have never hated anybody.

"My father, God bless him, couldn't see much of us in those days, but there wasn't any doubt that he was boss of our home. He had a voice that you could hear five blocks away when he was mad. He trained us mainly by voice. He beat my brother Louis once, and it frightened him—Pop, not Louis—so much that he let the voice and the look take care of us from then on. Believe me, when both were going good, well, you wouldn't want to be around him."

Naturally, his children had a great respect, mixed with a certain amount of fear, for their self-made father. Don: "Dad was the best saloon-keeper in Wisconsin. No man ever left his saloon drunk." He also served a great boiler-maker—the third one you drank (if you *could* drink a third) was on the house.

(After Don made it big, he bought his parents a place in the San Fernando valley, and Felix opened up another saloon. He liked the area so much that Don bought himself a nine-acre spread there, too.)

"I had more fights and lost more fights than any kid in Wisconsin," Don said. "They used to call me 'Wop,' and that burned me to a crisp. But after about eight years of black eyes and bumped noses I didn't care. And then they stopped calling me that. I thought, so that's the trick, is it? You just stop *caring* so much. It works like a charm."

It also helped little Don's early life when Felix went to a Minnesota lawyer to have the family name changed to the way it sounds: Ameche. Amici means "friend" in Italian. Around this time, Dominic began to go with the flow on his first name, as well. Though he was called Dom for short, most American kids were unfamiliar with the sound and usually called him Don. It stuck.

Don enjoys the simple life in Kenosha. Photo courtesy of Don Ameche, Jr.

Surprisingly, Don was not a tenacious movie fan, but he did like the occasional escapism it afforded. Given nickels for ice cream, sometimes he and his brother Louis would decide they would also like to go to a picture show. They would go downtown and tell Pop that Mother had sent them out for coffee, but had given them no money. With the quarter he hastily handed them (they were not allowed in his place of business), they would run off gaily to the movies, eating ice cream cones luxuriously in front row seats. When caught, Dad spoke of whipping, but Mom pleaded and they were sent to bed without supper, Felix eating their spaghetti himself. Don ran away from home only once, but found it better to return late for punishment than brave the world alone.

According to studio PR, Don was a destructive child, punished much by Dad, worried and cried for much by Mom, causing them to send him to Catholic kindergarten the second he was old enough. But from an early age, Don was taught supreme respect for all matters religious, and never cut up in church, where he sang in the choir.

When kids were put through an intelligence test—put in two subclasses, the less brighter ones sent into the cloakroom—Don was intrigued and faked deafness so he could assuage his curiosity for the darkened room. A week later, his father found out and showed up at school, where a teacher was loudly trying to get through to Don. Felix shouted, "Hey! Dominick!" and Don's hearing returned instantly, ending that game. A huge spanking loomed . . .

Another bad boy incident involved his least favorite task: minding the baby. One day, when there was a big marble game down the street, Don rolled his younger sister's baby carriage down a plank into a deep hole, where builders were excavating, so he could go join the game. His mother rushed out screaming, but the baby was unhurt and much amused with the trick. Don was a lucky kid, and was beginning to realize it.

Don was devoted to his siblings. So when he was age 11 and shipped off to Marion, Iowa, to St. Berchman's Academy, a boarding school, at least 9-year-old Louis was there to help him through the traumatic transition. Their folded, clean clothes sat in the living room waiting to be packed into the two large trunks. Also stacked around were bushel baskets of tomatoes, to be made into tomato paste. When Don started a tomato fight to "celebrate" going away, Louis joined in. The boys pasted the place: all over the walls, ceiling and carpet—and clean clothes. Into the night Don and Louis were made to take up the carpet, clean the stains and hang it outdoors, then put it back. They had to wash the walls and floors before going to bed. Mom and Sis washed and ironed all the clothes again, packing them for the train the next morning. But, still, Mom wept when her boys left.

Don and the boys of St. Berchman's. Photo courtesy of Don Ameche, Jr.

At St. Berchman's, they stayed with 140 boys who had gathered around the new kids to awe at their pairs and pairs of new socks. The others had been wearing socks so old they had to have new feet sewn in. Don also had his brand-new basketball with him, given to him for winning a local championship back home. Some kids called them rich kids and were prepared to hate them, but soon Don's wild side caught their attention; he could think up more crazy stunts than anyone. The nuns there, however, were strict—not so easy to get away with anything at a Catholic school. Disobedience meant public punishment there.'

The sisters of St. Berchman's were austere and exacting and Don's ingenuity for finding fun was taxed. He and his two classmates, Mark Tobin and Gabriel Vanden Dorpe, "made 'French beds' in the dorm so that no one could sleep." He took up smoking as a habit, knowing that if he were caught, it would mean instant expulsion. Still, he was a careful kid, and began a school "tradition" of betting desserts on who would win the World Series, with odds on ice cream.

For misdemeanors, St. Berchman students were assigned sums to do on paper: 2 and 2 are 4. 3 x 7 plus 4 x 11 plus 100 = 375. Don, in his spare study hours, copied out reams of these with a trick pen he put together that wrote five times at once. He sold these golden answer sheets to his friends and classmates, becoming the richest kid there by the end of his first year.

Don, the schoolboy.

During his second school year he turned very naughty, indeed, breaking rules left and right without on a cursory effort at concealing his crimes. The outraged Sisters gathered to plot his expulsion, but unfortunately realized they couldn't push him out. He was in every honor group there, plus the diploma class, the medal class—he had the medal for dramatics and elocution, he was in the orchestra, and had the lead in the school play. If they were rid of him, they would have no Commencement.

In the big dormitory there were all the beds, to be made up daily by the boys themselves; wrinkles on the sheets were not acceptable. Don and his best pal were sometimes the wrinkling instigators. For punishment they had to make every bed in the room before being allowed to go to sleep. No help from the Sisters, and no wrinkles allowed. After this exhaustive discipline, there were no more pillow fights for the Ameche boys.

Don later admitted that when Sister Cornelia checked in on them at night, "It was the first time I had ever thought about anything like love. Every time she'd stop by me, she never touched me or anything, but I felt *something*. I don't know that it was love she had, but it was something that I never, ever felt at home." It was there that he also began to develop his theatre skills, winning a statewide elocution contest with his arm-waving talk, "The Going of the Swan."

He also sang in the choir, played piano in the orchestra and took part in religious plays. For his first bit of acting, Don said, "I played the part of the Blessed Mother in the Christmas play the boys put on. One of my duties was to help put the smaller boys to bed. That involved considerable rough-housing before the lights went out. And three days before the play was to be given, what should happen during one of those sessions, but that I should get kicked in the eye. I developed a beautiful shiner.

"By the day of the play, it was hardly noticeable. Then, that day, we had a fire drill. I ran down the fire escape and tore around the corner of the building. As I

Don, front row center, on the basketball team. Photo courtesy of Don Ameche, Jr.

rounded the corner, I bumped into the janitor, who was coming toward me with a pipe in his mouth. The pipe hit me in the eye. The same eye was blacked all over again. I'm probably the one and only actor who ever played the Blessed Mother with a black eye!"

He was also one of eight boys caught smoking off the school grounds. There was talk of expelling them, but Don was about to be presented with his special medal for elocution, as well as an award for excellence in Latin. Severe reprimands were given to all instead. As press releases would usually state, Don Ameche continued to milk his lucky streak.

Two of his best friends were Mark Tobin of Chicago, and Gabriel Van der Dorpe, a Belgian boy who could hardly speak a word of English before Don took the youngster under his wing. Gabe became right-hand man at Don's Hollywood home years later. He also had a deep affection for his teacher, Sister Cornelia, and afterwards Mother Cornelia at Mt. Mercy in Cedar Rapids, where two of Don's sisters were later enrolled.

Mom often came to visit, sending huge boxes of food between times, which the Ameches would share with roommates. Their vacations were spent at home where spaghetti with anchovies and steaming bean soup were served on Christmas Eve.

Don, far left, first row, on the baseball team. Photo courtesy of Don Ameche, Jr.

Reports indicate that at the age of 13, Don completed his freshman high school work at St. Berchman's and moved on to Columbia Academy in Dubuque the next fall. He spent four years there and two years at Columbia College, where he was cast in several plays staged by Father Semper, his English teacher: *Shepherd in the Distance* in 1922, *Dress Rehearsal* in 1923, *Captain Applejack* and *The Lamp Went Out* in 1924, *Finders Keepers* in 1925, and *Game of Chess* in 1926.

It was at Columbia that Don began pre-law classes, and began wrestling with Latin, though he already had a jump start on it due to his Catholic upbringing. He had promised his father he would become a lawyer, but his obvious thirst for extra activities in and out of school, and his wanderlust for no one university, proved Don Ameche was not happy with his life's plan.

Very athletic, Don played on the football team, was guard on the basketball team, and was the catcher on the baseball team. He swam and played tennis, and was among the first-string players in the national basketball tournament of Catholic schools, held in Chicago in 1924. He also came in second in a national oratorical contest.

At Columbia, the master of discipline was the Rev. Father Kucara, who later became a bishop in Lincoln, Nebraska. Kucara had a deep baritone speaking voice, which Don practiced until he could imitate it. Often he would imitate his teacher, causing the master to say, "Ameche, what's to become of you? You're doing the devil's work!"

The Rev. Maurice S. Sheehy, D.D. was another of his instructors. "There may have been some opportunities for mischief which escaped Don during his days at Columbia Academy, but if so, I do not recall them. The mischief, however, was never malicious. And he won professors to him by his smile, which melts the strongest defenses of the heart. During fifteen years' association with students I have never met anyone more honest and fearlessly frank, at all times and under all conditions, than Dominic Ameche.

"Was there anything in Don's school days which presaged his success as a motion picture actor? He never walked, he always ran. One day to my horror I saw him playing tag along the ledge of the roof of a five-story building. Fear of danger, physical danger, was something to which Don was ever a stranger."

Elmer Layden, later a Notre Dame coach, was athletic instructor at Columbia and taught Don all he knew about football. All his teachers liked him, though they thought him something of a hellion.

It was there at Columbia University that Don met the love of his life, Honore Prendergast. "Don and I were fourteen. We were sophomores. He was going to Columbia and I was at St. Joseph's Academy. We had a terrible crush on each other and went together four years. I was his first girl and he was my first fellow.

"Then he left for Marquette College. Our correspondence dwindled to less and less, until it amounted to marking off birthdays and such. During the next six years we saw each other exactly three times. The third time was on September 2, 1932."

Every summer vacation Don would return home to Kenosha, assuredly keeping enough free time during the Depression to earn extra money for college; he did not want to depend fully on his family, though Felix always kept enough ravioli and red wine on the table for his kith. The solidly-built young Ameche had a strong enough back for his first job: laying cement walks. Through his college years he would work as a bolt-tightener in an automobile plant, and even dug ditches. "One of my first jobs was working with a shovel gang in Wisconsin. Digging ditches never hurt any man, and it's fine for the shoulder muscles. But I lost that job, because the foreman had a quick Irish temper, and he punched me in the eye one day. Then, I worked with a group of city workmen. Our job was to make square street corners round, which must have been an early form of boondoggling."

One July he had brief employment as a messenger boy for the Simmons spring factory, but was impatient with it and found it beneath him. He moved on to an assembly line at the Nash Company, hating the harsh noise and relentless monotony of the four precise movements he had to perform on the moving belts.

The motto he kept above his bed was GRIN AND BEAR IT! Saving a little money each week, he always held out a few dollars for gambling. He usually won. His father cautioned him to "brush your teeth every day, bathe, watch your manners and go to mass every Sunday." These instructions he took with him to Marquette College in Milwaukee, Wisconsin, transferring for "a change of scenery. I went from one college to another in the hope the next would have a more exciting law course." It was 1925 and Ameche was 18, sharing a room with

The college Don. Photo courtesy of Don Ameche, Jr.

four other guys. They made gin by mixing alcohol with juniper juice and played poker, winning Don an average of $40 a week. The collegian benders of drinking too much gave him a taste for alcohol that stuck with him (in alternating moderations) the rest of his life.

The drive to succeed in a calling that was not his came in fits and starts. Some weeks he was determined to achieve his goal, in lieu of anything better. Energetically, he took on 19 hours of schoolwork a week immediately, but it was overtaxing. Soon he cut it to 12 hours a week, struggling through Latin and the meaning of equity, habeas corpus and all the other dull terms. "I had discovered that it was more fun to play than to work. Dancing was my specialty. I managed to pass my examinations at Marquette, but it took a lot of fast talking to get by."

Switching to Washington's prestigious Georgetown University at age 19 didn't help matters much. "I was developing into the world's worst student. Bridge and poker demanded a lot of my personal attention, and I attended only about twenty classes during the first semester. With football games [he was on Georgetown's team] and races taking a lot of time, too. I knew there was no use of taking my examinations. So I pulled out just ahead of them and entered the University of Wisconsin."

There he met two people who would shape and change his career: Bernardine Flynn, later of *Vic and Sade* fame, and Prof. Troutman. Right on the brink of flunking out, Don was discovered by Professor William C. Troutman of the School of Speech (later, director of dramatics at Kansas State College), who was seeking "a gay young blade" to portray Dick Dudgeon in George Bernard Shaw's *The Devil's Disciple*, which was being staged by The Wisconsin Players. The year was 1928.

In an article written by Don during his career in early television, he wrote:

"All this time, my grades were passing. But I could have done better. The truth is that I wasn't interested.

"This particular afternoon my friend had a suggestion.

"'If you're not doing anything,' he said, 'take a walk with me.'

"The walk led us to the college theater where he had a date to try out for a part in a campus play. I curled up in a seat as he stood on the bare stage and auditioned for director Bill Troutman.

"But then I got a sudden impulse. As soon as my friend finished, I hopped onto the stage and began reading the same part.

"'Where'd you come from?' demanded Troutman.

"'Well, I was told to try out, wasn't I?' I bluffed.

"It was a kid's cocky trick. But as it turned out, it couldn't have been better-timed. The part was the cock-sure lead in *The Devil's Disciple*. I got it!

"After *Disciple* came roles in five more plays and the realization that acting was the one thing I cared for!"

Another version of Don's introduction to legitimate theatre went thusly:

Auditioning with his roommate for *The Devil's Disciple*, Don casually took the script and ran through the lines. "You didn't try," his roommate accused. But the director was of a different mind. "You sensed that character perfectly. It's a conceited, bullying, what-the-hell kind of character and no one else has been able to do it. Can you come to rehearsal tomorrow?"

"No," Don said shortly. "First year students aren't allowed to do extracurricular things like this." The director replied, "It's the lead. And it pays. Think it over, kid. We'll get you a dispensation or something. You were terrific."

Still another version ran:

Finding no lead in his School of Speech after three days of tryouts, on that third day luck was with Troutman and Ameche. Some of Don's friends had dared him to try out for the Dudgeon part. Being the gambler that he was, Ameche agreed, and read. After only a few lines in that booming voice of his, which caught the empty back rows of the Bascom Theater as well, Troutman snapped, "Where have you been keeping yourself?"

Don thought he was kidding and answered, "Oh, I've been around," before walking off the stage. But Troutman grabbed him quickly. "The part is yours!" So ended a possibly great law career.

Troutman next put him in *Liliom*, opposite Bernardine Flynn. Together, the three considered themselves the "Triumvirate." Don recalled: "After rehearsals the three of us would go over to Bern's house to empty the Flynn icebox . . . I was trying to swing over from law to dramatics, but the dean wouldn't stand for it. However, as the time neared for the University's big spring production, *Liliom*, they didn't have anybody to play the lead and began to put pressure to have me permitted to play it. Finally it was fixed and I was cast to play *Liliom*. I performed with the University Players during the next fall and winter and with the stock company in June. There was a summer session with the

Honore and Don. Photo courtesy of Don Ameche, Jr.

University Players at Wisconsin in which anyone can play, so I got fifty dollars a show for four shows that summer. By this time I was thoroughly inoculated with the acting virus."

Troutman was also supposedly Don's roommate in his first year at Wisconsin. Having a mentor literally in residence did not help his grade point average; the more dramatic roles he attained, the more comic his legal class work became.

In one particular class, Professor of Law, William Herbert Page, called on Don first in Constitutional Law class. Page, who hated to hear a student say he was unprepared, received just such a reply from Ameche, who was burning the candle at both ends with various productions around campus; he had just performed in a student production the night before.

"Unprepared," said Ameche.

After a moment of uncomfortable silence, at last Page remarked, "Well, Mr. Ameche. I enjoyed your play last night. You did a fine job. But I think the time has come for you to decide whether you want to be a lawyer or an actor."

Don Ameche stood up and said, "Mr. Page, you're right," and walked out of the room and out of the law school into a long successful career as an actor.

He had probably attended a total of twelve classes altogether once the acting bug bit. But it wasn't all stage work for Ameche. He'd briefly pledged into the P.A.D.'s, a law fraternity, where he lived in-house, and found time to chat up the ladies. Don: "Sometimes I had as many as four separate dates with different girls in a single week." Yet Honore was still on his mind.

With school sagging and performances in *Captain Applejack, Officer 666, Cradle Song, Outward Bound,* and *A Game of Chess* taking up most of his waking hours, Don was getting the experience. What he needed was a professional break.

In March of 1929 the Al Jackson Players came to town about to stage Jack McGowan's *Excess Baggage,* but their leading man met with an accident. The director called Troutman on Sunday night, as the play was advertised to start on Monday. "Is there an actor in town?" he pleaded. Troutman helped Don into his overcoat and hurried him to the Garrick Theater where the company was rehearsing. Don stayed up all night learning his lines, and the show went on without a flaw. They signed him to a 20-week contact with the company as a result.

In *Excess Baggage* he made $35 a week while still going to college. In the midst of the Depression, it was a good time to have a professional acting job. Prohibition was quickly sinking Papa Amici's saloon, so he could send no more money to Don, who just then barely got by his midterm exams. Nearly ready to chuck it all and get a job, it was then that Troutman took Don into his apartment. They cooked their own meals. Don also leased out his luck and gained a few bucks in some on-campus poker hands.

That summer Don and Troutman decided it was time for the young man to take the next step in his career, so the two of them went on a trip to New York City "with hilarious stop-offs" in Canada. It's uncertain whether or not Ameche actually graduated from college (one report states he did so in 1926), but when the Big Apple beckoned, Don had to take his bite.

Chapter Two

Radio Star

"I went to New York," Ameche said in a later interview, "and I played bits in shows there for the next year. I was there in the spring of 1930 when the Depression was bearing down on us. I was completely broke all the time."

That, plus a city full of creditors, gave Don ample reason to return home to be the best man at his sister's wedding. He just needed the plane ticket, and called collect for it. He spent a few weeks there admiring his brother-in-law's admirable wine cellar, then looked up Mark Tobin, a friend from St. Berchman's, and they drove to Chicago in Mark's vintage Pontiac. Don had learned that a big oil company there was offering willing young men positions in South America at pretty good salaries. Bewildered with his own starving acting career, he had to try. Luckily for Hollywood all positions were taken. Gloomily chain-smoking, he and Mark discussed the situation on the drive back to Kenosha. Mark knew Don would've been a fool to take a job like that. Don thought it over, and decided to trust in the luck which had propelled him this far.

One summer Sunday afternoon, while playing golf with Mark, Don collapsed from exhaustion. He didn't want a hospital, so Mark drove him to Marion, Iowa to St. Berchman's, where he requested a three-day stay with the Sisters to have "a little time in the chapel. I want to settle some things with myself." The following Thursday he withdrew and went to a doctor, who told him he had a curious ailment and was on the verge of a fatal collapse. A second opinion said the opposite. He had a tooth that was bothering him pulled, and was back at health's peak within 24 hours.

At times, Ameche also found solace in alcohol and could, say some friends, out drink anyone. It was never a problem, especially where work was concerned, merely a crutch to rest on during the hard times. Times were particularly difficult when he returned to New York City where the Great Depression was eminently grim.

When he couldn't get a job on Broadway, he took a job "tearing down an overhead railway." The crew foreman asked, "You're not a laborer, are you?" Don said he was an actor. The foreman advanced him his wages so that he could find time to look for another stage job, and knew someone who was producing a show called *Jerry for Short*, starring Fisk O'Hara. It was to be Don's first Broadway role—as a butler.

Jerry for Short, written and staged by William A. Grew, survived the Crash and ran through the 1929-30 season, though only for 64 performances. Living on his own, playing out the role of struggling, starving, wannabe actor with perfect realism, there was one pocket on which Don could count. Troutman's dwindling professorial accounts may have had only a mere $10 to spare on occasions, but when Don needed it, he would meet his friend at a discreet, though slightly posh, tearoom on 52nd Street and slip him the money. As the orchestra, camouflaged by potted trees, played, Ameche complained at length about *his* butler in the play.

An early Ameche.

"Worse butler I ever saw in my life. Stinks. And he's got a big hunk of every scene, too." But the part paid $60 a week, so there was no way out of it.

He also wired home for money. "I know that's one of the things you're not supposed to say you did, you're supposed to be too proud to let the folks know you're down and out. But let me tell you that after a couple of days with nothing to eat you get powerfully hungry." Al Jackson (of the Al Jackson Players) also wired him $50 a few times. And his landlady of the cheap boarding house in which he lived would let him go weeks at a time without worrying about the rent.

Don was a proud man and for the rest of his life would make independent almost a religious part of his nature. But for now, if he *really* wanted to make it as an actor—and he did—there was no way around accepting favors. He made the rounds with fervor. "I wore the patience of theatrical agents thin. My soles got thin too. I put cardboard in my shoes. Eventually I took the bean course for dramatic talent. The bean course consists of eating beans every day. I had the advantage over some of the fellows in my school: I could afford a plate of ten-cent beans at noon and a nickel apple at night. As my studies became more involved, I found a beanery where I could load up for a nickel."

Troutman returned to his university job in Madison, but kept in touch with his favorite student through a series of notes and telegrams. Don was soon eating two apples and a can of beans a day when an agent's letter brought word of a role in Chicago for $150 a week. Good timing, since Mom could only send $5 in her recent letter.

The show was *Illegal Practice*, which lasted all of two weeks. "The notices were all right—not raves, but all right. Yes, I guess I was pleased. But I wasn't making enough to live on. I'd get money, when I needed it, from home and from my friend Troutman. So in 1930 I decided to give the family a break, and spend the summer with them."

He had no choice but to return home and shave off some difficult living expenses. It was temporary; he had to keep making the audition rounds or be locked out of the profession. Poppa Felix dug into his shallow pockets to give Don the train fare back to New York, where Don lived on agents' invitations to dinner for the next few months. At one of these meetings, he met Texas Guinan, infamous skirter of prohibition laws and owner of the 300 Club in New York City, who had conceived a parody version of her recent arrest and trial as a part of a floor show. Don was signed on to act as the prosecuting attorney who frolicked with Tex and her half-naked girls on the variety stages of Manhattan and Brooklyn. One night during the finale of the riotous act things got rough and a lady patron was hit in the eye with an artificial snowball. The lady, digging borax out of her face, threatened suit, making Texas quite angry. So she cancelled the act and Don's contract. He protested, but his heart wasn't in it. He knew he'd thrown that snowball a little too hard.

Another report claimed that Texas Guinan let Don go in Chicago because he was too stiff and thought he'd never make it as a popular singer. It's also difficult to say which came first, this show or *Illegal Practice*, but the starving was at least consistent. After the Guinan play, Don said, "At this point, you had better give Professor Troutman plenty of credit. When I was down to a plate of beans a day,

I'd wire him, collect. The money always came by return wire. But I seemed headed for Kenosha and the Ameche spaghetti."

Times and roles could be lean. Troutman recalled, "Luckily I had a professor's income and was a bachelor. I could always wire him $50 the same day, then send the less important letter telling him to keep his chin up, because there were people who believed in him."

Luckily, Don found himself cast as a lead in a play with the Brown Stock Company in Greenwich, Connecticut. The show opened in Chicago and *un*luckily, the critics lynched it. It wasn't a good time. Patron Troutman also felt the Depression's squeeze and found himself in financial difficulties (along with everyone else) and had to discontinue Don's much needed monetary assistance. It was perhaps Don's most depressing state of affairs. Troutman stated, "He had allowed himself to become serious about one thing, acting, and it had failed him."

The 1930s soon turned around. "The first of June of 1930 I went up to WMCA in New York and took an audition as a singer. I sang a couple of numbers for them—and after I gave up hope of hearing that I was a second Caruso I wrote home for money and got it. Then I returned to Kenosha. I stayed at home until late August, when Bernardine Flynn, who had played in a college show with me, phoned me to come to Chicago for a radio audition." Bernardine Flynn had found the New York acting life difficult, too. After a failed attempt at conquering Broadway, she was beaten, and ended up in Chicago, where she'd heard that actors were making a decent living in radio, with no impossible rehearsal hours and lines to learn. She found that an advertising agency was holding open auditions for an NBC dramatic series entitled *Empire Builders*. She decided to try out, and learned that they needed a leading man too. She phoned Don. Ameche continues: "I took that audition and while waiting did another audition, getting *that* job on a sustaining (i.e., not sponsored) program called *Evening Star* and made one broadcast for $22.50." A week later, NBC called again about the previous audition. After two or three further days of auditioning against hundreds of other actors (as Bernardine had done), he got a lead part in *Empire Builders*.

Empire Builders ran from 1928 to 1931, when the Great Depression finally killed its lavish production: a large cast, a 23-piece orchestra, seven sound-effects men (five in the studio, two on the roof of the Merchandise Mart). It was a "variety" show that, while technically not commercial, did weave its stories to the benefit of its sponsor, the Great Northern Railway (which ran from Chicago to the Pacific Northwest). It was "variety" in the sense that there were no recurring characters save the deep-voiced, sympathetic Old Timer who got along with everyone, encouraging strangers to open up and tell him their problems, providing the comedy, drama or adventure for the week. The half-hour series aired Mondays at 9:30 to 10:00 p.m. (Central Time) over the NBC Blue Network. Ameche appeared on *many* episodes as different characters.

Don called *Empire Builders* "one of the most realistic and gripping radio dramas ever produced, because the sound effects were authentic. The clickety-click of a train on the rails was timed to the fraction of a second. If the producer wanted the sound of marching feet, he'd hire a small army of men to tramp about the building when the show was on the air. That was real radio production—but it was expensive." He was earning $60 a week, and learning how to be a different kind of actor.

Don: "In radio drama makeup, facial expression and gesture—great aids on the stage—are of no use at all. While on the stage comedy can be created by a look, a position, a gesture, over the air the best comedy is situation comedy. The radio theater must present in one-half hour a play that is allotted two and a half to three hours on the stage.

"The trick is to have your eyes trained on words that are ahead of what you're actually saying. In that way you don't get tripped up, and you can throw in expressions that aren't in the script to heighten the naturalness of your work.

"If you've got a clear picture in your mind of the sense of a series of speeches, you can transplant it to your listeners and use the words in the script merely as a guide. Photographic memorization gives you the chance to forget the script at times and actually listen to the other actor who is working with you." Some stage actors, he said, sound stilted when having to read a performance, while others might overact when put before a studio audience, when their real audience couldn't see them at all.

Once he'd broken the network barrier, Ameche's career was made. Beans became a thing of the past when he began guesting on shows like the *Rin-Tin-Tin* show (1931). Then, in April of 1931, he got his first starring series.

The First Nighter Program was another dramatic anthology series first broadcast over the Blue Network on November 27, 1930. By the time Ameche came on board opposite June Meredith, it was a well-established hit that lasted all the way to radio's demise, ending on September 13, 1953. Its magic stemmed from a sincere love for the theatre and replicated its opening night excitement with the traffic sounds and bristling 42nd Street pedestrians of New York City. "Have your tickets ready, please!" An usher would show Mr. First Nighter to his box and from a fourth-row center seat, he would introduce the week's play, complete with cast and author, amid the "famous First Nighter orchestra." From announcements that "smoking is permitted in the lobby only" to narration that the lights are dimming to the applause at the end, *The First Nighter Program* was one of the most elaborate, meticulous deceptions ever to broadcast out of Chicago.

Charles P. Hughes had been the original Mr. First Nighter, followed by Macdonald Carey, Bret Morrison and Marvin Miller. When Ameche stepped into the genial host role, he "became radio's first sex symbol," according to John Dunning, author of *On the Air: The Encyclopedia of Old-Time Radio*.

The dashing, leading man image would follow Ameche through the 1930s. Anderson C. Chanin called him the Don Juan of radio: "He's straight and tall, a six-footer, lean, lithe, alert and vital. There's a hint, too, of Valentino about him, dark eyes, olive skin, black hair." But as few fans could ever see him, Chanin admitted that it was the voice listeners were falling for. "His eager, often ecstatic words are music; his speed flows in rhythmic cadences, soft and undulating. It is capable of fire and fury, too."

First Nighter made Don a national/network star. It broadcast at 10 p.m. EDST on Fridays over stations WEAF, WEEI, WTIC, WJAR, WTAG, WCSH, WLIT, WFBR, WRC, WGY, WBEN, WCAE, WTAM, WWJ, WSAI, WMAQ, KSD, WOC, WHO, WOW, WDAF, KGO, WTMJ, KSTP, WEBC, WSM, WSB, KVOO, WSMB, WKY, KPRC, WOAI, KOA, KDYL, KFI, KGW, KOMO, KFSD, KTAR, KHQ, WMC, WRVA, WWNC, WJAX, WIOD, WFAA, and WFLA.

He enjoyed one particular recurring role, that of Beau Bachelor (a singing Frenchman), but told an interviewer: "The players themselves have nothing to do with the actual selecting [of plays]. This is relegated to a committee. I imagine that the studio receives between twenty-five and forty plays each week. The best of these we read for the committee and they make the decision. Each play requires about five hours' rehearsal." Most of his fan mail came from elderly ladies and shut-ins, the radio giving them relief from pain of body and mind for a bit.

One of the two scripts that Don kept all his life was the December 6, 1935 episode of *First Nighter*, "That's My Baby." Written by Carolyn Clarke, it starred Don, as "a young, proud, unemployed and very worried father," and Betty Gerson as his wife.

When Don later won his movie contract, the press assured everyone that it wouldn't distract Don from his radio work. *First Nighter* would move to Hollywood, produced by Charles P. Hughes who had ambitious dreams to take the show on a forty-city tour. One reporter aptly wrote of the show: "The worthwhile object of *The First Nighter* is to embody all of the glamour, excitement and romance of the theater for isolated listeners and city folk who cannot afford the real thing, yet seek to realize its thrill."

At some point Don starred in *Milligan and Mulligan* on WGN. The 15-minute mystery series was heard at 10:15 every night except Sunday. Don starred as Ed Milligan of the Milligan Detective agency, and Bob White as Mickey Mulligan, his goofy assistant. Together they solved crimes, such as their first case, "Back Stage Murder," about the death of matinee idol and Don Juan, Ronald Fortescue. White was best known to listeners as Dr. Petrie on *Fu Manchu*, also heard over WGN. As with many detective stories of the era, there was comedy mixed up with the plot.

When *Betty and Bob* began on October 10, 1932, Don found himself with another success in the title role of producers' Frank and Anne Hummert's first hit network soap opera. Playing opposite Elizabeth Reller as Betty, Bob was the attractive heir to a fortune which was withdrawn when he fell for his secretary. It was a situation fraught with turmoil and melodramatic zeal, especially when Betty and Bob found themselves with a child, Bobby, in the hungry Depression.

All the typical TV soap fodder coursed through its veins: death, jealousy, quick-tempered decisions, murder, more jealousy. The series lasted until 1940, but was hard-hit in the ratings twice: first, when Bobby was born (which some say slowed the show), then when Don left for a film career in the mid-1930s. Les Tremayne would half-joke in interviews that he owed his career to Don Ameche. Indeed, Les was the actor to take over for him on both *Nighter* and *Betty and*

Bob when Hollywood called.

Around this time Don's younger brother Jim Ameche (born August 6, 1915) had his first taste of national stardom himself at the age of 18 in the lead role (1933-38) of *Jack Armstrong, the All-American Boy*, possibly the biggest hit adventure serial ever devised for the youth of radio. The hero of Hudson High School had many adventures with his friends around the world, from the 1933 Chicago World's Fair (the opening show) to Easter Island to batting guerrillas in Casablanca; it was a serial kids voraciously ate up for nearly twenty years.

Betty and Bob.

Jim Ameche went to Kenosha High School, where he did well, won the state oratorical contest for debating and played tennis in his spare time. Jim wasn't active like the other brothers (Don and Lou being on the same basketball and football teams in school), he was frightened of sports and fights. But when he was eight years old driving with his father, an accident threw Jim out of the car and he lost consciousness. He wasn't badly hurt—a cut on his forehead required stitches. For two years Jim didn't step inside a car, afraid of them. But when Don returned home from school for the summer, he tried to teach Jim self-reliance, and boxing, and got him to conquer his fear of cars by backing the car out of the driveway and just driving around the block.

It's been reported that Don filled in on radio for Jim occasionally, and vice versa, as their voices sounded so much alike. He once took over Don's parts in *First Nighter* when the star vacationed in Hollywood. Radio child actor Sandy Singer remembered that "every now and then, when both Don and Jim Ameche were together at the BLUE studios, we would play Ameche Roulette. All the staffer's and actor's would meet in a studio, throw a dollar in the pot, turn the lights out, and listen to one of the Ameches speak a line. When the lights came on, we voted on which Ameche spoke, and the winner's divvied up the cash."

Jim was later heard on several series, including *Win Your Lady* over the NBC-Blue network. Don was a firm supporter of his brother's career, even helping pay for his acting lessons, though Don would become somewhat estranged from his family as the pressure of further work and stardom increased.

Jim (and naturally Les Tremayne, though in differing roles) would also take over for Don in the dramatic anthology, *Grand Hotel,* which ran from 1930 to 1945. Like the famed Garbo film, its plot wove a collection of problematic visitors whose lives romanced, fell apart or were reborn in the glorious Grand Hotel.

Later, (notoriously fictionalized) fan magazines told of Don's "brief but torrid romances" with a blues singer, then "a glamorous lady with brass-colored hair"—and nights spent in white tie and tails dancing at the Blackstone, the Palmer House, the Edgewater Beach Club, then dashing for a bit of sleep before his early morning broadcasts.

Don Ameche was Chicago's star. He became a regular as a forest ranger on The *National Farm and Home Hour*, a 60-minute variety series catering to the farm community and giving an ambrosial taste of rustic life to the rest of America. Don would often do other shows in the week and was making good money. Good enough to think about having a family.

He and Honore Prendergast had kept in touch during his difficult, though brief, years of struggling. Honore was then dietician at Michael Roese Hospital in Chicago, having finished her college courses. One romanticized tale of their courtship told of their rekindling: during a *First Nighter* rehearsal one evening, Don's friend Terry Yore called to set him up with an old friend for a double date. It was Honore. They danced that night, and the next week, he and his friend Mark drove to see her in an old Pontiac that made them arrive a day late. Other weekends followed. Two months later, Don thumped on her door at five in the morning while Mark slept in the rumble seat of the Pontiac. Honore was in her robe when Don announced that they were getting married, while he fumbled for a solitaire ring which he just got the previous morning.

They had gone steady until Don graduated in 1926 and their courtship continued by letter and once-a-year meetings until 1932, when they were finally married at 8:30 a.m. on November 26, 1932 by Rev. Maurice S. Sheehy (of Catholic University of D.C.) at the Church of Nativity in Dubuque. Leona Heim played Lohengrin's "Wedding March" as Honore strode down the aisle in a floor-length gown of pearl luster satin with large sleeves. She carried calla lilies and wore a veil trimmed with orange blossoms, which fell from a lace Dutch cap, fashioned with a chin strap. *Photoplay* claimed the event had "more incense and more solemnity than any other wedding had ever had."

Miss Clare M. Predergast was maid of honor, Mrs. Robert White was matron of honor, with bridesmaids Esther Nash Myers and Mary B. Prendergast. The bride's brother, Jerome G. Prendergast, was Don's best man. Don's parents were unable to attend, as they were recuperating from injuries in a recent auto accident. After the ceremony a breakfast was served to 30 guests at the bride's home. They spent their honeymoon "motoring in the west." One fan magazine wrote the following description:

> Their honeymoon was an evening's drive along the Lake Shore, as Don was too busy to get away just then. But he promised her they would manage a trip in a few months, perhaps to Bermuda. They sat in the car at the edge of the road as the ceaseless rain beat on the canvas top, when Don turned serious. "Just for a minute I'm going to be serious. You have to know about me."

The Ameche wedding.

Honey (he always called her Honey) settled comfortably against Don's shoulder. "I came into this with my eyes open. I know what I'm in for, and I'm glad. You're my kind of people."

He said, "From the usual standpoint, I'll probably make the worst husband a girl ever had. I've never been a responsible guy. Things will happen and I'll have no answer when you ask why they happened. If there's any need for economy I'll save on bread and butter to buy poker chips. We may get rich and we may have to live in hovels—I don't know. Only understand this. I'll always love you. And I'll be honest."

"You dope, do you think I'd have you any other way?"

Another version of the fur coat story went:

Don and Honore only had $100 to their names on their wedding day, and spent it foolishly on a fur coat. Don had little conception of the value of a dollar, especially during his Hollywood heyday. When he slipped a magnificent solitaire on Honey's hand, he was broke. "I don't care if we are broke, you gotta have a wedding present. He steered Nora [nickname for Honore] through the frozen slush of the Chicago gutters and across icy sidewalks to a furrier's window. "There. Pick it out."

Later, freezing by the curb in front of the hotel, Honey shivered and wanted her new coat, but it wasn't among the packages they bought. They stared at each other. Slowly Don said, "Maybe when we both went back to get your purse you left it on the counter . . ."

That afternoon Don answered the phone in his suite. He ran out, returning an hour later, tossing the coat on the sofa. He sat wearily down by the window and said, "That was the thief who phoned. He said to come to the Central Hospital lobby and bring $250 with me."

"You didn't!"

"I got it for $150."

Honey was furious, wondering why he didn't call the police. Don's instructions had been that if he made any trouble, they'd get it back, but the thief would get it again—with his wife inside it. When she finished crying Honey said, "But now you can't pay for the thing anyway. How silly."

Like an exhausted John Bickerson, he stolidly claimed, "I'll pay for it."

They made it back home at 532 Sheridan Road in Evanston, Illinois on

January 1, 1933 due to Don's rigorous radio schedule.

Honore was a simple girl; a tragic flaw that made her and Don instantly and ultimately incompatible, though they would remain married for 50 years. She wanted an ordinary life and had little conception of what his current stardom would mean, and certainly not of the mega-stardom that lay ahead. She was happiest to stay in the background and play the ordinary wife who baked, made dinner for a hard-working man, and raised children. She got her wish for a few years, and was certainly very proud of his accomplishments, especially what he was accomplishing in the early 1930s with that booming voice of his.

Don and Honore on the town.

Their daughter, Connie Ameche, recalled, "My mother was born in America—Lincoln, NE, of an Irish American father and a Swedish-American mother. She had no accent. As a matter of fact she had a wonderful voice that was free of even regional accents. She sometimes had a hint of a Mid-Western accent, but only on certain words."

Early on Don was quoted as wishing he'd quit school earlier to be further along in his career by the mid-'30s. By that point, he was looking toward Hollywood as his next step, urged on by industry professionals who knew it was the only step up from where he was.

It was also a risk. Honey was pregnant with their first child; it was a difficult time for her. She had trouble eating, even drinking a glass of water. During the delivery, she was fed at the hospital with hollow glass needles. Don was meanwhile working from 8:00 a.m. to midnight, snatching naps in cabs from the Loop to the studios.

In October of 1933, they moved. Don had signed a rental lease quickly before dashing off to another rehearsal. He woke the next morning to find that he'd taken a 14-room house miles from the center of town. Mary, Honey's sister, helped with the moving, and Don had taken her for a tour of the town that kept them both up too late. Minutes after the movers had left, Mary crumpled in a chair, exhausted. Suspicious, Honey called an ambulance. It was appendicitis. Honey threw a comforter over her snoring husband and set to work unpacking trunks, scrubbing closets, but the activity was too much. They called the doctor again, and Honey was in the hospital having her baby.

Their first son, Don, Jr., was born in 1933. The child was delivered by Bernardine Flynn's husband, a doctor, and was baptized by old friend Father Sheehey in St. Luke's Church in River Forest, Illinois. Don read Latin over the priest's shoulder, and was corrected just once on pronunciation.

That same year Honore, Don and his brother Jim had come to River Forest, Illinois and rented a large residence on Franklin Avenue, north of Lake Street. They lived two years in River Forest, where the family attended mass at their regular parish, St. Luke's, and sometimes at St. Catherine's in Oak Park. On May 12, 1935, Don helped raise funds for a new building for St. Luke's by donating his services in an act called "Chatter" when the church choir presented a festival of songs. After the birth of Don, Jr., the Ameches moved to a home with an enclosed yard on Edgewood Place.

Ameche's fan mail and salary kept on the rise, and Hollywood was interested. According to Troutman, "Don wanted to be in the movies more than anything else in the world. The microphone restrained his never-ending energy. But, as is characteristic of him, he did very little about it. He was doing all right in Chicago: money to burn almost, a wife and two children over whom he was wildly enthusiastic, plenty of good poker playing, his name a household word coast-to-coast, radio work as easy for him as rolling off a log."

During the *First Nighter* stint, he had begun receiving offers from Hollywood through his new agent, George Frank. Frank had come to Hollywood in 1930 as an agent with Maurice Small and then established his own agency in partnership with Scotty Dunlap. Among the stars that he brought to pictures and radio were Don Ameche, Clara Bow, James Cagney, Carmen Miranda, Peggy Shannon, Allen Jenkins, Joan Blondell and Lowell Sherman. He also helped his good friend Oscar Hammerstein II with his musical projects to get heard and produced.

Another adventurous account of the Hollywood breakthrough had Don himself taking the initiative: "I've always waited for things to happen to me, and always they have. Until now. For two years everything's been coasting—and I can't have that. Radio has its limitations. I want to get into the big time." He and Honey discussed going for a screen test in Hollywood. "It's September, getting cold. How'd you like a little trip to California?"

She shook her head. "Thanks. But you'll do better alone." He was off within the hour, the cottage a mess from such hasty packing.

Don made the test, but received a polite refusal. Some stories state that it was at this point that he caught the eye of agent George Frank, but Frank was obviously helpful in Don's radio career several years before this.

Don made a second test, which also lit no fires with producers. Troutman speculated on both failures. "I think I know what was wrong with those first screen tests. The same things that were wrong in Don's first picture, *Sins of Man* with Jean Hersholt. In five years at a microphone, using only his voice, Don had forgotten motion. As a result, he energized too much, smiled too much, turned in a much too eager personality. Those mistakes almost killed his motion picture career."

The third time, they say, is the charm. As always, there are several versions of Ameche's Hollywood discovery. 1. Fox producers were interested in the screen test of a certain young lady, and they viewed Don's old one by mistake. 2. While Don resumed his radio duties, Darryl Zanuck, head of Fox, was shown Don's first test by "an enterprising Chicago insurance man." 3. In December of 1934 George Frank flew east, stopping in Chicago to pick up Don to take him to New York to make another test, the first one for Fox. A year later, Zanuck asked Don to come to New York for a second test to appear with a young actress they were testing for Hollywood.

Regardless of the cause, the effect was an offer from Zanuck that came just before Christmas. With the Ameches' second child, Ronnie, born on December 30, 1934, it was indeed a time for celebration.

The Ameches.

Chapter Three
Movie Star

In 1935 Fox Film Corporation merged with Twentieth Century, and a new producer, Darryl Zanuck, had been hired to retrieve Fox out of its mounting debt. The new 20th Century-Fox was to produce 55 pictures a year, 29 of which were to be personally supervised by Zanuck. Unfortunately, while its 96-acre lot and huge production budgets gave Zanuck and Fox a good shot at assembling moneymaking projects, the studio did not have many bankable stars. Will Rogers, always relied upon to bring in box office receipts, had just died in a plane crash, and their only other major star, Shirley Temple, some said was already past her prime at age seven. Janet Gaynor and Warner Oland (who played Charlie Chan in Fox's popular mystery series) were also there, but Zanuck had to build a sturdy stable of studio talent—and fast.

And he did. Loretta Young, Warner Baxter, Victor McLaglen and Ronald Colman were brought in, and then a charming radio performer, who stood 5'11.5", 170 pounds, with hazel eyes and brown hair, by the name of Don Ameche.

Zanuck was a tough boss, often thought to be rude and thoughtless, but the studio machine he had built, and the constant activity and work that that haven provided, attracted the many people he would call in for jobs. He also shared Don's loved for practical jokes, though his were notoriously meaner than any a star might chance to make, such as inserting cheese into the lunch of a subordinate who was allergic to dairy products. When the man began wheezing and showing a blotchy complexion, Zanuck would laugh merrily.

Ameche came to Hollywood alone again in early March 1935, Honey staying behind because Ronnie was ill. He soon used his college-honed gambling skills to score bigtime. Lifelong friend Richard Frank, son of Don's agent George, recalled: "I met Don Ameche in 1935 when I celebrated my first birthday at my house in Beverly Hills. I was told that we would be moving to Encino, which was a drive over the hill to the San Fernando Valley. We would be living right next to the Ameche boys and would be able to play together all of the time. Daddy had made a deal with Mr. Hays, who owned a big 10-acre spread which he would cut in half and sell to Don Ameche. The deal was a good one, according to my daddy George, who was Don's personal representative and agent. We were taking an acre for ourselves. We started to have our builder and architect draw up plans and get us into our new abode.

"That same year Mr. Ameche got into a card game with Al Jolson where he was able to bet and win the lovely ranch house in Encino that Mr. Jolson used for his vacation get-away. It was a wonderful ranch house located in Encino about 15 streets away from the Havenhurst Avenue property that Ameche was supposed to buy. Anyway, the deal was canceled for that little spread. The difference was that the Frank Boys would have to travel a few streets to hook up with the Ameches. My father bought 2 acres [from the original Ameche deal] and built our house there. It was designed by the famous architect and designer of the Art Deco period, Paul Frankell. The Ameches were always able to play with us over there and we went to the old Jolson house to play with them.

"In those days there were musical giants in Hollywood—Al Jolson, Eddie Cantor, Ed Wynn and Don Ameche. They all needed a place to relax and eat what was then their favorite food, barbecue spareribs, thus was born Southern Pit Barbecue in 1936. At a certain hour every night an unemployed piano player named Harry Rosenthal sat down at the piano to play the popular song 'Give My Regards to Broadway.' All over Hollywood heads lifted and hopes revived as one by one Jimmy Cagney, Pat O'Brien, Spencer Tracy, Frank McHugh and Don Ameche would take their seats around the piano and break into song starting with 'When Irish Eyes Are Smiling.'"

Whether winning the Jolson home with cards was a Hollywood myth or not, the move to bigger quarters was perfect. It allowed Don to bring his whole family—father, mother and brothers, Jim, Louie (who bought a small ranch house in the San Fernando Valley near Don) and Bert—out to California. Later, Don hired Columbia College friend Gabriel, age 27, as a jack of all trades; he became Don's secretary after Donny (Don, Jr.) was born. They'd first met when Gabriel came as a Belgian refugee to the Catholic grammar school Don attended. Anna, the young Wisconsin farm girl whom Honore brought from Chicago to look after the children, also lived with them. Anna would hum a Polish folk song while hanging diapers amidst the green and gold orange trees that stretched toward the boulevard.

"It was such a good life, such a fruitful one," Don later said. "We had the five-acre ranch in Encino, some twenty miles out of Hollywood, with cows and chickens, citrus trees and a truck garden. Above all, and best of all, there were the babies who came along, in fairly rapid succession. Dominic Felix, Jr. was the firstborn. Two years later, Ronald John bowed in. A lapse of four years and then, with only a year between them, Thomas Anthony and Lawrence Michael were born. Familiarly known as Donny, Ronny, Tommy and Lonny, all four boys were born by Caesarian section."

Brother Jim was enrolled by Don in Paramount's training school, then moved to Chicago to appear in various network shows. Bert was sent to study architecture at Catholic University (in Washington, D.C.), where he made the Dean's List. Don also set his parents up in a little farm/ranch of their own.

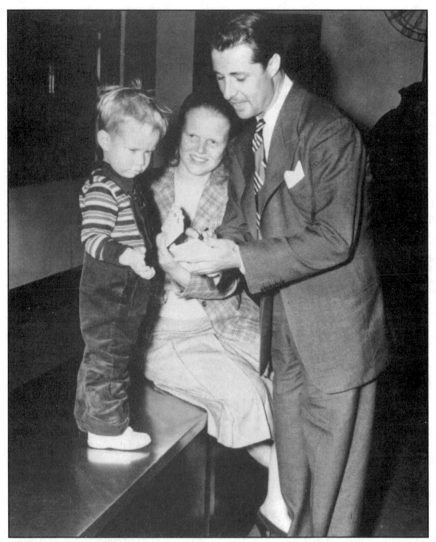

Don, Jr., Honey and Don

The Don Ameche homestead in the green rolling hills of Encino in San Fernando Valley was paradise: a large, rambling spread filled with trees and rose trellises all around, a swimming pool in the back, and those fresh oranges picked for the family's breakfast. The picturesque ramada, showcasing a tree-lined driveway, led to a spacious lawn, and a badminton court nearby. Gabriel was kept busy pruning the crimson ramblers and planting a new bed of zinnias, which he would try to protect from the curious claws of Donnie and Ronnie's Irish Setters, Sheila and Lady.

For all their apparent luxury, the Ameches would always strive to keep a semblance of regularity about their lives. In January 1939's **Woman's Home Companion**, Honore admitted that Don hated to shop, but ordered brown, blue and gray suits from the tailor when he must. Honore bought the rest of his clothes—silk black, brown or white socks. His shirts were mostly white but also tan, blue and gray, and he kept a supply of imported "gay and giddy" French ties on hand. She made his monogrammed ("Don" mostly) handkerchiefs herself: white monograms for the day, black for night. She even made camel's-hair coats with box pleats down the sides of the front for Donnie and Ronnie to match Daddy's, which they adored. When around the house, Don dressed in sports clothes all the time. Honore, still roaming the place in braided, thick yellow hair, preferred to do most of the household chores and all of the cooking herself. (One reporter wrote that Honore "looks and reasons like Ann Harding and has the wit of Myrna Loy.")

She told *Modern Screen*, "Well, we haven't any formula. We just try to take things as they come. We don't look on Hollywood as a strange, fantastic place in which we must also be strange and fantastic. We don't look on Don's work as something which must necessarily change and make over our personal lives. It is just a job which he enjoys and at which he can make a living.

"We believe you can earn your livelihood in Hollywood without being a part of the Hollywood which is forever in the limelight—of Hollywood, the Playtown. We really have very little time to play. Don has two jobs most of the time—radio and pictures—and I work, too. Besides running the house, I handle his personal mail, much of which is from friends we both of us knew in school. This, naturally, is mail which he wants answered personally. Also, I handle the family finances. I really could abscond with the family fortune and he wouldn't have a cent. But I don't plan to do that quite yet. Instead, I am buying annuities and insurance. I know, we both know, that you can't count on the future.

"We've had a good many ups and downs but we've never had a quarrel. I mean that. I suppose we have been near to it sometimes but I always think: What's the use? You'll only start something you perhaps can't finish. Besides, no one could quarrel with Don. Anyway, he's sweet, really sweet. He has his faults, of course. He forgets things, for instance. He'd forget his head, as his mother says, if it weren't fastened on, just as he forgot his keys this morning. But he doesn't forget some things. Not anniversaries nor birthdays nor Mother's Day nor the meaning of honesty and truth. And I always say as long as your husband is like that, well, things can't go so awfully wrong."

There are great stories of Don Ameche stepping off an airplane immediately after a Sunday afternoon radio broadcast, and three hours later he was in front of the camera, caked with makeup, starring in *Sins of Man*; that night, Zanuck saw the rushes and ordered Don to change his makeup the next day for an additional role. But the road to stardom is potholed with bit parts, and the great smiling Don was not immune to that hard-hoed road.

He was reportedly in *Clive of India*, detailing Ronald Colman's epic rise from mere clerk to the most powerful white military leader India has ever known. But Don is almost impossible to locate in the film's many crowd scenes.

Don had actually made his screen debut with lifelong friend Tyrone Power and Forrest Tucker, at the Century of Progress World's Fair in Chicago in 1933.

The short film, *Beauty at the World's Fair*, may have been a filmed radio broadcast with no sustained plot, cashing in on Don's high radio popularity. He and Power had met when the latter had some minor roles in *The First Nighter*. According to Power's biographer, Dennis Belafonte, Ameche was the one who talked Power into both the short film and radio work. At that point, the struggling actor-friends were bunking together, along with Forrest Tucker, but split up when Power headed for Broadway and Ameche for the Hollywood coast.

Don: "I first met Tyrone at a radio studio in Chicago. I had just been assigned to a part in a radio sketch, when Tyrone came bursting into the studio, full of high hopes and ambition, to apply for the job. After that, practically the same thing happened several times in connection with other programs. Tyrone was always just a bit too late, and he began to look upon me as his Nemesis. When he came to Hollywood, he was pretty much annoyed, as he's since told me, to learn that I was under contract to the same studio. The poor kid actually became convinced that he'd never get anywhere as long as I was around. But he got even with me when it came to the role in *Lloyd's of London*. We were both being considered for the part. I knew it was one of the best parts of the year, and, of course, I was anxious to do it. But when I heard that they'd decided on Power, I was almost glad. I was beginning to think that maybe I *was* standing in his way, and I knew that Power deserved all the breaks in the world.

"I'm thankful that there proved to be room enough for both of us in Hollywood. I'm glad for Tyrone's sake as well as my own, and I have an idea that he'd win out if it came right down to an acting competition."

In 1938 Power told the *Cleveland Plain Dealer*: "In order to boost me, some of the reporters are comparing me to Ameche, and I feel pretty terrible about it. You see, my rise has been spectacular, while his has been slow but steady. But only a couple of years ago he was a star on the radio in Chicago, and I was just a bit player. The reporters play up the fact that now I am ahead of him. I'm fond of him and I know this hurts, because the truth is that I've had the breaks but he is a more consistent player than I am—I mean he always turns in a good performance."

In Jane Lenz Elder's book on Alice Faye, she states that Don was signed to Fox the same day as Tyrone Power and Tony Martin (Alice Faye's soon-to-be-husband).

Don Ameche's assent to stardom, however, certainly flew on the wings of *Sins of Man*. The story:

In 1900 Christopher Freyman (Jean Hersholt) is a simple man who lives in Zenbruck (on the Austrian-Italian border in the Alps) and rang his church bells with pride. His wife dies after giving birth to Gabriel (Mickey Rentschler), who is born deaf. When Christopher and Karl (Ameche), his eldest son, quarrel over his wanting to be a scientist, the young Freyman leaves for America, where he secures work as an aeronautical engineer. Christopher disowns him, burning Karl's unopened letters. When Gabriel begins to show signs that he could be cured, Karl arranges for father and son to come to America where Gabriel can receive treatment. Karl and Christopher are finally reunited, and just in time; the next day, Karl is killed test flying a new airplane. Days later, World War I begins, stranding Christopher in America. He learns that Zenbruck has been bombed and Gabriel is listed as dead. Christopher toils for years in menial labor jobs, but, as an old man, his life finally turns around when he meets Mario Singarelli, a famous symphonic bell player, who has recorded a variation on the tune Christopher used to play on the old church bells. Mario turns out to be Gabriel, cured of deafness from the bombs that fell and raised in Italy as one of Zenbruck's few survivors. Father and son are overjoyed, and Christopher realizes his dream by playing the bells in the symphony's next concert.

Jean Hersholt and Don in *Sins of Man*, 1936.

Working titles for the film included *Job* and *Turmoil.* (It was announced after *Turmoil* that Don would work opposite Myrna Loy in the tentatively titled *Love to Mary*, with songs by Irving Berlin. It was one of many projects that failed to materialize.) Hersholt had to spend nearly three hours each day getting into makeup to play the old man who significantly ages throughout the picture. For $10,000 Zanuck had bought the movie rights to the three-year-old novel held by Gregory Ratoff, who had wanted to produce it in England.

"While it is uncompromisingly tearful," wrote *The New York Times* of *Sins of Man*, "it happens also to have been splendidly performed, honestly directed and handsomely produced." They went on to encourage that "Mr. Ameche gives a likeable and straightforward performance which amply justifies Darryl Zanuck's announced intention of featuring him in several of the new Twentieth Century-Fox films this season."

Another review pointed out that "you will either find this the most unforgettable picture you have ever seen, or you will consider it the most dismal whodunit you ever sat through—depending entirely upon your mood of the evening." *The Hollywood Reporter* praised the film and performances highly. "It is a picture that once seen will never be forgotten . . . Don Ameche makes a really auspicious screen debut in a dual role." And rightly admits that the film title is not wholly appropriate.

Most critics flattered the film, one calling Jean Hersholt's performance "the best role of his career" and Ameche "a real find." One press release stated that Don originally had a small role in the film, but after seeing the rushes, an executive ordered him in the dual role. He wasn't an overnight sensation, but Ameche was on his way.

Father and son reunited in *Sins of Man*, 1936.

When the film previewed, Don and Honore decided not to sit together. She said later, "I was afraid that Don might turn and ask me something. I didn't want to add to the nervous strain. But neither did I want to tell him it was good if I thought it wasn't. So I sat alone." She later said, "I went to his first picture with him. He wants me to be honest. Until the middle of that effort I thought we'd pack the next day and go back to Chicago and the radio alone. In the last half he overcame his greenness, though. But then and there I decided I wouldn't go to any more of his pictures with him."

When Troutman went out to Hollywood a few years later to visit the new star, he "saw his name on posters and billboards halfway across the United States. I saw his picture in magazines and newspapers as I traveled west. I wondered what the person with that name was now like.

"It didn't take long for me to find out. My visit was a whirlwind. There was still the boy about Don, as if the studios, the publicity, the great network show were all something he had received for Christmas, something great to play with. Acting, that's the life. Fun from the word go. Interesting and famous people around all the time. No one dull. Everything fascinating.

"Yet Don was working hard, using every ounce of that tremendous eagerness of his. Once, during the making of a picture, he didn't get to his ranch home for three weeks. He didn't have time to drive home nights. There was so much work to do."

Don's first few films came in quick, assembly-line order. His name may have been Ameche, but with his dark hair and tanned skin, Don looked Indian enough to play the tragic role of Loretta Young's husband, Alessandro, in *Ramona*, based on Helen Hunt Jackson's 1884 novel. Pietro Gentili, Phillip Reed, Gilbert Roland and John Boles had also been considered for Ameche's role, but Zanuck was eager to put Don in a major role (Jean Hersholt had been the true star of *Sins of Man*). With a few songs by William Kernell and L. Wolfe Gilbert & Mabel Wayne, the 1936 Technicolor drama was not the first filmed *Ramona*. That honor went to D.W. Griffith's 1910 "Biograph film" starring Mary Pickford and Henry B. Walthall. A popular story, there were then two other versions before the Ameche rendition.

Ramona told the tale of Senora Moreno's beautiful ward, Ramona (Loretta Young), who learns that her real mother was an Indian. This actually pleases her because she never did feel the love for Felipe (Kent Taylor), who wants her, but was always more drawn to his friend, the Indian leader, Alessandro (Ameche), even though in 1870's California Indians were still very much outcasts. She runs away with her new love, has a daughter with him, but just as life looks good, White Men, as usual, ruin everything. The government has given the Whites title to Alessandro's land, making the couple travel through storms and rocky roads to find and make a new home. On the way, their baby develops a sickness she cannot shake. Though they find temporary refuge in the house of good Aunt Ri (Jane Darwell), the baby's health does not improve, causing Alessandro to run quickly to fetch a doctor who does not come, but sends Alessandro returning with medicine instead. His horse becomes lame as he rides, so that he has to steal a horse from a nearby farmer (John Carradine). who gives chase and shoots him for the crime once they arrive at Aunt Ri's. Broken by the injustice, Ramona finds hope in her child, who is now better, and in the visiting Felipe who comes to offer his love.

It was a fine role for Ameche, who not only was able to demonstrate his able singing voice, but was the picture of propriety and pride in the role of leader, lover and father. The film was set to start in July of 1935 but was postponed several times due to Loretta Young's illness. In October she had been replaced by Rochelle Hudson, but by the time shooting began on May 11, 1936 (in order to avoid the rainy season in San Diego County, as most of the film was exterior), Young was back in the cast. The film's opening also had to be delayed since Technicolor couldn't supply enough prints in time.

The dashing Alessandro in *Ramona*, 1936.

Many reviewers made a fuss over the beauty of *Ramona*'s Technicolor, though some reviews were mixed, writing that sometimes its color was the only thing worth looking at, besides some of the supporting players. One reviewer wrote: "In photographic beauty this picture has never been equaled on the screen . . . Though color is not 'natural' yet, the early California outdoor setting of this film lends itself to the Technicolor process with hardly a jarring note." The main filming was done on a 55,000-acre ranch in the Mesa Grande area of the San Jacinto Mountains between Hemet and San Diego, 140 miles south of Los Angeles. It was chosen after many color tests, though the extreme brightness of the sun in the clear mountain air made it necessary to film many scenes under a scrim (a fragile bobbin netting that softens light and helps eliminate glare). Unfortunately, the high winds often ripped the nets to shreds. And because of the color process, they found that the lighting was only best for filming between 6:00 a.m. and 3:00 p.m.

Months before filming began, a cherry orchard and an apple tree had been selected for use when both bared full fruit. As they ripened on schedule, Indian boys were hired to guard them from the swallows with shotguns. More than 3,000 people were involved with the filming, most living in tents and cabins, except Loretta Young and Kent Taylor, who had rented special two-room trailers with electric refrigeration and shower baths. Don and Loretta both wore wigs made from human hair bought from peasants in the remote villages of the Tyrol, where often a woman could be paid several hundred dollars for her lovely head of hair.

Don told a reporter, "You should have seen my prized critic when I was about to go into my first important movie love scene. We made *Ramona* on location, and Honey and I slipped off to the beach at La Jolla to swim. In the Atlantic the stingrays float, so you can see them coming; in the Pacific they lurk where you can step on them. Yes, I stepped!"

Honore: "The doctor didn't believe he could go on working, but I bathed his foot most of the night, and we split his moccasin so he could get it on for a 'take.' Two men carried him down a wooded hill. He was in terrible pain, but he joked, 'All I need now is a snazzy rattlesnake!' Well, I raised my head and I saw a rattlesnake several yards long. I ran like fury." She screamed for someone to get it; luckily the snake was interested in another direction. Actually, the stingray wound kept Ameche away from the cameras for less than a week.

Loretta Young, recovering from her recent illness, required a stand-in. Her regular for pre-filming work was Dorothy Tunney, and her riding double was Betty Hager. Don's stand-in for some of the harder riding scenes was stuntman Clint Sharp. The small chapel built on location was blessed by one of the Franciscan fathers who helped make sure the picture was authentic and was used for masses during filming by cast and crew; Honore was on set and went to mass. It was reported that when the director got stuck at the Mass part in the filmed marriage ceremony because the altar boys couldn't recite Latin, Don offered to stand off stage and recite the prayers.

London's Sunday Graphic wrote: "The film contains no outstanding acting performance, but it gains by its simplicity of story, acting and direction . . . The film is a pleasant pastoral." Another London paper, the *Daily Telegraph*, preferred Dolores Del Rio's original version, but admitted that "Don Ameche makes an impressive debut as the red-skinned but highly polished hero." The paper didn't find him particularly good-looking, but "he has quite uncommon poise, and a speaking voice of extraordinary resonance and masculinity. I should like to see more of him." Many admitted that, if properly used, Don might become a major star. Louella Parsons in her review wrote: "Young Ameche is a definite find, restrained, human and completely without self-consciousness."

The studio pushed *Ramona*, and Don Ameche especially, hard. They put up a contest for theater managers and publicity directors showing the picture, offering $1,000 in cash prizes "to get over to the public, with the greatest effectiveness, that Don Ameche—star of the famous Italian Balm *First Nighter* Coast-to-Coast broadcast—has come to the talking screen in the 20th Century-Fox Corporation's picture—*Ramona*." The main theme they wanted to see aggrandized was that "these millions of fans will want to see Don Ameche in *Ramona*. Remember that they know him only as a voice on the air." Fox gave theater managers ideas: write to Campana (*First Nighter* sponsor) for some 22.5 x 28-inch 4-color lithographed display cards which contained blank space for theater imprints; run a contest in their local paper with a question like "What was Ameche's most outstanding role in a *First Nighter* play?" The contest, which closed December 31, 1936,

The athletic Ameche.

wanted more and better ideas for publicity. "Play up Ameche in your newspaper publicity releases and in your advertising. Tune in the *First Nighter* on Friday night at 10 o'clock Eastern Time yourself. You'll get plenty of original angles by listening in. Give the radio tie-in a 'run for its money' on the marquee, in the lobby—in all forms of advertising including displays in local stores—and watch the stampede at the box office!" First prize was $350, all the way down to the tenth prize of $25.

It was announced during *Ramona*'s release that Jim Ameche was to marry Betty Harris of Rochester, NY. Movie work kept Don from attending the service, and started a dangerous precedent in the battle of film career vs. Ameche's private life. While making *Ramona* Don read of his good notices on *Sins of Man* in his hometown *Kenosha Evening News,* which also ran a notice on the social page that his sister Mary Jane had the leading part in the play *Evangeline.*

However, it was soon after this that Don told *Radio Mirror* "Why I'm Quitting *First Nighter*." After months of indecision, he simply had to leave the program. "The people who make up the radio audience brought me whatever success I've had and I shall be eternally grateful. Whatever else you write, please make that clear.

"Have you ever broken up with a close friend you've known for a long time? Then you know the funny feeling it gives you inside. I lost just about the oldest friend I had. I would never have done it, if it could have been helped. It couldn't.

"First of all, I'm sure I've been with the program too long. All winter I felt that I had given it all I could. And then when I saw, according to surveys, that the program was more popular than ever before, I knew it was time to step out and let a new voice come in to bring the show still greater popularity.

"There were other reasons. In six years' time, I have had just four weeks' vacation. Two of those were during my second year on the program and the other two over a year ago. No matter how much you like your work, you get pretty tired of it with only two brief vacations in six years." He also wasn't happy with some of the weekly stories he had to appear in. Bags of fan mail corroborated his feelings that his roles were sometimes unsatisfactory; one report stated that in 1937 his fan mail was rivaling Shirley Temple's. He also wanted to broaden his radio work with other roles and genres.

"*The First Nighter*, naturally, will continue. I have a hunch you'll like the new leading man. In fact, I suspect you'll like the whole program all over again."

He was enjoying movie stardom. "I was never frightened, nervous. They're such grand people to work with. They're *big*. Maybe it's because they've arrived, because they don't need to worry about their own positions, I don't know. But anyway, they seem to be real and sincere and friendly—I love working with them. And there doesn't seem to be the pressure, the driving urge to lead, to dominate, that you find in other fields. Of course, if one actor outplays another, that's different. But there is no mean rivalry."

Only practical jokes. April 19, 1940's *Photoplay* told some of the craziness that went on between best friends Alice Faye, Tyrone Power and Don Ameche.

In 1936, on the set of *Sing, Baby, Sing*, starring Faye, Don was a frequent visitor to the set, first arriving with an army of combs, flowers, folding chairs and powder puffs. Whenever Alice moved, he popped up to make a mock fuss over her, which annoyed her greatly. This went on for two weeks, with neither side giving in, so Don brought Ty into it. When Alice got a class A super-deluxe dressing room, she called them in to show it off. The men waited for their opportunity to be alone with the Victorian lamps with pink shades, white satin-covered chairs, dressing tables, and mirrors that reached from floor to ceiling.

When Alice was finally called away, Ty and Don wrecked the joint: lamps overturned, gowns lay limply over everything, mirrors smudged with greasepaint, except for a single mirror on which was written HELLO, DEAR. The guys weren't around to be murdered, but when Alice realized how much to heart she'd taken all the luxury, she just began to laugh. And plot revenge.

She rushed to Don's dressing room. It was locked. Ty hadn't thought that far ahead: his was open. Inside, Alice took a hammer and nails and pounded Ty's imported English shoes (he boasted paying a grand $35 for them) to the floor.

There was no stopping them after that. It was always two against one, in differing combinations. Once, Alice had planted garlic in Ty's dressing room, but he got an early whiff and shoved her in the reeking room first, locking the door. The day Don was to die in *In Old Chicago*, his two Musketeers kept sending him dead flowers all day, "to get him in the mood." Don retaliated by sending Alice a necklace made of empty gin bottles before doing her hysterical lost-in-the-fire scene. When Ty's regeneration scene came up, the other two planted a load of garbage in his car.

But times weren't all frivolous. Don visited Alice on the set of *Sally, Irene and Mary*, where she wasn't feeling well at all. She thought it was just a cold, but Don was concerned and immediately called for his doctor who came over and pronounced her on the verge of pneumonia. Ordered to bed, her life may have been saved that day.

Of course, his joke time wasn't confined to the Faye-Power connection. Don would frequently phone Honore with an altered voice or an accent. He'd rib her father a lot, too; said Don, "he could become a wild Irishman so easily."

Don Ameche was the only guy to get the girl in *Ladies in Love*, Fox's 1936 episodic love story involving three women—Martha Karenye (Janet Gaynor), Susie Schmidt (Loretta Young) and Yoli Haydn (Constance Bennett)—who share an apartment in a fashionable neighborhood in Budapest, Hungary. The film mostly follows the love lives of Susie as she is thrown over by Count Karl Lange (Tyrone Power) for a Countess; and poor Yoli, who tells herself and John Barlett (Paul Lukas) that they could just have fun and not worry about taking their affair too seriously, but he ends up in love while another, younger girl (Simone Simon), who spirits John away to South America and the altar. It's Martha who strikes it lucky at the end with Ameche, who plays young Dr. Rudi Imri, and, as is sometimes his usual screen persona, is engrossed with experiments, finding it difficult to display his true emotions. It is only after thinking he's lost her twice—once to the egocentric magician Paul Sandor (wonderfully played by the stiffly comic Alan Mowbray), and finally to almost being killed by drinking Susie's suicide-laced champagne by mistake—that Rudi comes to his senses and asks the cute girl (who used to take care of the rabbits he used for experiments) to marry him. The girls move out of the ritzy apartment in a rather downer ending for this Depression-era film. Still, the two women who have lost their loves have gathered a kind of strength from it, determined to face life, come what may.

Of *Ladies in Love* one reviewer wrote: "The production is marked by a singular lack of movement and by an obvious overplay of hackneyed sentimental tricks."

One in a Million fared *much* better and shot ice skater Sonja Henie into a different kind of mega-stardom at the top of 1937. Having won Olympic gold medals for figure skating in 1928, 1932 and 1936, she knew her box-office worth, and requested $75,000 per film, which every studio shunned. The Esther Williams of ice merely rented a rink for a few New York shows, which raised $28,000 (she gave $8,000 to charity), then made $28,000 in just three nights in Hershey, PA. Zanuck agreed to her terms, which by then had gone up to $100,000 (plus extra, if the filming went over schedule).

Sonja Henie and Don in *One in a Million*, 1937.

Supreme supporting talent zoomed *Million* to become a huge hit. Jean Hersholt played the father of Swiss beauty Greta Muller (Henie), while the underused Ritz Brothers played themselves, with Don Ameche as Bob Harris, reporter for *The Paris Herald*, as the love lead who ultimately saves the day.

The story could have been autobiographical: Greta has been training for the Olympics since age 12, egged on by her father who had lost his own gold medal due to a scandal in which he'd taken money for teaching before the big Games. Shifty promoter Thaddeus Spencer (Adolphe Menjou) ultimately puts his daughter in the same predicament, until Bob Harris explains to the Olympic committee (who gave her the medal after a grand performance near the film's end) that she never profited from Spencer's lying trick of having her perform previously at a St. Moritz exhibition.

Borrah Minevitch and his Gang of Harmonica Rascals stole the show with their hilarious comedy number. The film did much to popularize ice skating in the United States, and was also the first film to show Don's trademark pencil-thin mustache.

Famed newspaper columnist Louella O. Parsons proclaimed the HENIE FILM DEBUT AUSPICIOUS and that Sonja "not only gives an amazing ice-skating exhibition but proves that she has a screen personality and that she is indeed a valuable addition to motion pictures." She equally raved Don's role as his "best work to date. We can see him, with the right roles, carrying on as one of the leading musical comedy actors."

Were it not for Don's previous commitment to *Love Is News,* he would have found himself the third star in *Seventh Heaven,* a 1937 romance with Simone

DA, Loretta Young and Tyrone Power in *Love Is News,* 1937.

Simon and James Stewart. He was considered for the part of Father Chevillon, which was slated for John Carradine but finally ended up in Jean Hersholt's lap. That same year he also tested for the lead of Jonathan Blake in the historical drama *Lloyd's of London*, but at the insistence of director Henry King and editor Barbara McLean, Zanuck changed his mind in favor of Tyrone Power after Power's subsequent screen test.

Love Is News was worth getting. Ameche played barking *New York Daily Express* editor Martin J. Canavan, who is almost driven crazy by his ace reporter, Steve Leyton (Tyrone Power), and his inability to get the simple news story of which he is the star:

Rich, perpetually-engaged Tony Gateson (Loretta Young) is sick of the scandal treatment she's getting from one Steve Leyton, and after being tricked by the guy into giving him a story, she decides to wreak revenge by making *him* part of the story. She announces her engagement to Steve to his rival newspaper buddies and proceeds to give all papers but his the scoop on their blossoming romance. Steve hates all the attention he's getting from the press and the hundreds of hawking salesmen who think he's loaded now. Canavan is beside himself with rage at every turn; he's told one thing by Steve (who believes it himself), then finds alternate, story-blasting headlines in all the other rags in town. As time and the war rages on, Steve and Tony fall for each other, and Canavan finally gets the scoop of all scoops: they're getting married.

Picturegoer Weekly's December 4, 1937 review of *Love Is News* gave it three stars and called Don Ameche "brilliant as the hard-bitten city editor." It was clearly Tyrone Power and Loretta Young's film, though.

Don Ameche had not forsaken radio, nor vice versa. He became a regular on *The Chase and Sanborn Hour* from July 25, 1937 to November 5, 1939, playing additional straight man (and Master of Ceremonies) roles to the greatest dummy of them all, Charlie McCarthy. Old-time radio historian, Martin Grams, Jr., wrote: "Like Rudy Vallee's program, *The Chase and Sanborn Hour* was constantly presenting new acts, comedians and singers, hoping some of the rising stars would become national celebrities soon after their appearances."

Ameche was also a part of radio's most infamous shows: the Adam & Eve sketch on the December 12, 1937 *Chase* broadcast starring Mae West. The following is an excerpt from a Bergan article by Martin Grams, Jr.:

When the producers of *The Chase and Sanborn Hour* offered the sex goddess the opportunity to appear on the program—then currently the highest-rated program of the year—she accepted if only to promote her latest film, *Everyday is a Holiday*. West often wrote her own scripts and even produced her own movies, so she did have a financial interest among her radio appearances.

When one listens to a copy of the recording of this program, one can hear Don Ameche [in the lead as Adam] hesitate and even try to improvise to West's lines. (Ameche even repeated the same line twice, the second with a slight hesitation!) But even when Mae West went up against the wooden dummy later in the program, exchanges such as "So good-time Charlie's going to play hard-to-get" and "You're all wood and a yard long" didn't help matters any.

What Mae West said wasn't so bad as how she said it. Telling the serpent that "I feel like doin' a big apple" was one comment ad-libbed, but when the serpent got stuck between the picket fences in an attempt to fetch the forbidden fruit, West exclaimed with the emotion of a woman going through an orgasm, "There! There! Now you're through!"

Hollywood columnist Hedda Hopper was in the audience during that broadcast, and later wrote in her column that she had "never seen anyone as embarrassed as Don Ameche. And I understand when they first showed him the sketch he absolutely refused to do it. They assured him Mae would play it straight and not indulge in any of her Westian nuances and if he refused to go on they would keep him off the air. Mae was wearing a black evening gown, a long silver-fox cape, orchids and lilies of the valley, black eyelashes, the longest I've ever seen."

Even his old friend Troutman admitted in a lengthy interview, "In religion he has always put great faith and trust. Priests have been his counselors at all times. I am sure that his participation in the notorious Mae West radio skit hurt him

Don, Charlie McCarthy, Edgar Bergan and tenor John Carter. March 1938.

deeply, for his own Catholic Church started the wave of disapproval. It was the first time the theater, a second-love in this case, had come into conflict with something he placed first, his religion."

The New York Times headlined, "Mae West Script Brings Sharp Rebuke from FCC," stating that not only NBC but its 59 substations "violated the ethics of decency." After carefully reading a transcription and listening to a recording of the broadcast, the Federal Communications Commission decided that it was "vulgar and indecent," claiming that the show fell "far below even the minimum standards which should control in the selection and production of broadcast programs.

"We commend your company for having apologized over the radio and through the press for these features and again in your letter to the commission. We are unable, however, to accept the view expressed in your letter that the broadcasting of these features was only 'a human error in judgement.' The care with which the public has a right to expect, and which is, as we understand, the practice, in the writing and editing of the manuscripts and in the rehearsing of such features would seem to exclude the elements of accident and surprise."

Writer Arch Oboler caught the most hell, including several lawsuits for indecency. Also, Jane Storm, author of the play *Love and Applesauce*, filed a $10,000 copyright infringement suit against Ameche, West, writer Oboler, NBC and others, claiming they lifted the "offending" piece from Act 1, Scene 2 of her play. Her attorney at the time claimed, "Miss Storm thought she had a clean play until she heard it over the radio."

Apart from this racy incident, Don vivaciously enjoyed filling his off-hours from movies with radio. He enjoyed being a star, even though the hours and days were far too long to pay complete attention to his work *and* family. Even his weekends were filled up: Saturdays he would have a radio rehearsal from 7:30 p.m. to 2:00 a.m. On Sundays, he reported to the broadcasting studio at 11:00 in the morning and rehearsed until four, when he went on the air. Honore supportively said at the time, "It relaxes Don to run away from routines, to eat in a popular restaurant. He likes the bustle, the sense of being in the midst of things; he likes to be with friends."

Career-wise, his dual-end candle burning was paying off. In 1938, he told *Modern Screen*, "It's a sacrifice for me to be in pictures and on the air. I can think of at least half a dozen other businesses that would be easier on me. This work is hard, don't let anyone tell you different. It's nervous work. We're always at high emotional tension. We ourselves don't realize at what tension we work until we crack up one line, and then that's that.

"Honore and I always eat dinner out, you know. Not that I don't like to eat at home, but simply because I've gone at such a tempo all day that I can't relax, can't go where it's quiet, can't go to bed before one or two in the morning, because I'm too keyed up to sleep. It's not exactly soothing syrup, working in pictures."

But he was certainly enjoying it.

"Honestly, I don't know what people mean when they speak about the 'hard heart of Hollywood.' It's a big country, this California, it's a big industry, this movie business, and the people in it are big, too, big of heart and generous of spirit. I mean every word I say. I'm not theorizing. I can give you facts.

"Take Tyrone Power and me, for instance. Tyrone and I should certainly be rivals if any two men in this business would be. We are on the same lot. We are often tested for the same role in a picture. Sometimes Ty gets it, sometimes I do. But we never get out our Boy Scout knives, whichever way it falls. We play together, our parts fairly comparable in importance, as in *In Old Chicago*, and now in *Alexander's Ragtime Band*. Yet I feel nothing but friendliness for Tyrone. I'd do anything I could to help if he needed help. I know that he'd do the same for me. We often given each other 'tips' we think might help one another's performance. We clown together on the set, lunch together, play golf together. We are friends.

"I don't mean that we all are too good to be true, like angels in Arcadia. Certainly not. It's our business to look out for ourselves, and we do. But I mean that we are not forever going about with knives in our make-up kits, just waiting for a fellow actor's back to be turned. You often read that an actor has 'stepped out of a picture' because he didn't get as good a part as some other fellow. The chances are that if you could read the script, you would know why the actor had stepped out. A million to one it had nothing to do with the other actor.

"Jack Benny and Mary are among our best friends out here. And I mean friends. Do you know what Jack did a few weeks ago, when I was ill? He drove out to see me one Sunday morning, a drive of some thirty miles from his house in Beverly Hills to our place in the San Fernando Valley. When he got there, I was asleep, and Honore had gone to church. He wouldn't let Annie or Irene, the girls who work with us, disturb me. He said, 'I'll just sit in the parlor and wait.' And that's just what he did, for an hour. Then he strolled into the kitchen, asked if he could have a cup of coffee, and sat there at the kitchen table, drinking it. When I finally work up, an hour and a half later, he came up and sat with me for another hour, and then drove home again. Now, the thing is that Jack had two radio broadcasts to do that day, his own, and a guest appearance he was making. He was also leaving for New York early the next morning. But he took all that time to come out and see me, because he is a friend.

"Jack and Mary, George Burns and Gracie, Lum, of *Lum and Abner*, and his wife, Harriet, Honey and I, we're all so happily married that we all go places together, talk about our homes and our kids, and are as plain folksy as old shoes. Take Bing Crosby and Dixie, and their well-known four boys, or Eloise and Pat O'Brien. They certainly don't hide their family life under any bushel of glamour, and certainly it doesn't decrease their popularity. I've never known people to care so much for children as the folks in Hollywood do. The bigger they are, the more precious they seem to find that 'patter of little feet.' If they haven't children of their own they take children into their hearts and homes, which seems to me to be the height of unselfishness."

His radio work also increased his circle of stars well past that of a "mere" studio contract player. His comic and dramatic flair was put to the test as lead, MC and straight man to weekly listeners. He even held his own against the anarchic

W.C. Fields on Bergen's show. *Radio Daily*, in their May 11, 1937 review of *The Chase & Sanborn Hour*'s May 9 show, loved all the W.C. Fields comedy, Bergen's "consistently fine material," and wrote "the versatile Ameche handled most of the continuity as the master of ceremonies, also ably singing a ballad and playing opposite Miss [Ann] Harding in a scene from Molnar's *The Guardsman*."

In J.E. Doyle's May 25, 1937 newspaper column, *Dialing with Doyle*, he too loved W.C., calling Fields "the 1937 discovery" and "Ameche is probably radio's outstanding actor." The show "is entertainment which will cause people to hurry home Sunday nights." The previous week he had written that Ameche "is probably the best actor on the air, a most gracious fellow to meet, a splendid master of ceremonies when he limits his laughter to a point where it doesn't interfere with his program." Even Don Foster in Chicago's *Daily Times* wrote that "Don Ameche should do something about that giggling of his. It keeps getting away from him in his chatter with Fields and sometimes almost drowns out some of Fields' lines." At first Don backed away from the microphone when the giggles (scripted or real, it's hard to say) began, but then it was permanently kept, complementing the ribbing Fields would always give him.

Said Ameche, "Although I am prepared at all times to ad lib and to take care of any emergency, I have so far been extremely fortunate in not having had to do so. We have had only first-rate personalities for our guest stars, and no one has ever yet failed to show up, no one has ever been late, or visibly afflicted with mike fright, or become jittery, or otherwise acted irregularly."

One fright to Bergen himself came when Charlie was stolen, as Don explains. "Yep, it's true. It seems that last night after we finished the rehearsal and Bergen had put Charlie to bed in his own little case, dirty work was afoot. We all went out and I left them a little early and returned to the hotel. Well, it seems someone called Bergen's hotel and convinced them it was Bergen and, with a tear in his voice, insisted he was sending for his old friend Charlie! Along came a midget pageboy and collected C.M. and the snatch was complete. Bergen didn't know a darn thing about it till he got in and saw the vacant stare on Charlie's kisser. Seriously, it was a bad moment, for Bergen can't work as well with any of the doubles. He says none of them have any personality. Charlie alone possesses this attribute. However, before the broadcast rehearsal, Charlie was chuckling to himself on Bergen's knee and telling the darndest version of his incarceration you can imagine."

Queues formed early outside the modernistic entrance to NBC's Studio B in Hollywood from which *Chase* broadcast. At the appointed hour, street noises began, and tall, blond announcer Don Briggs stepped up to the microphone to begin the latest revue, then Don Ameche would step up and flash the audience a smile before putting his highly polished black shoe tip against the base of the mike.

For his elegance and eloquence on radio, he received many honors, including a beautiful silver plaque, mounted like an easel in hardened wood, for polling the most votes for a male star during the four consecutive years in *Radio Guide*'s Star of Stars contest.

Audiences loved watching their movie stars. Studios often flexed their shooting schedules around stars' live radio broadcasts, knowing one complementedg the

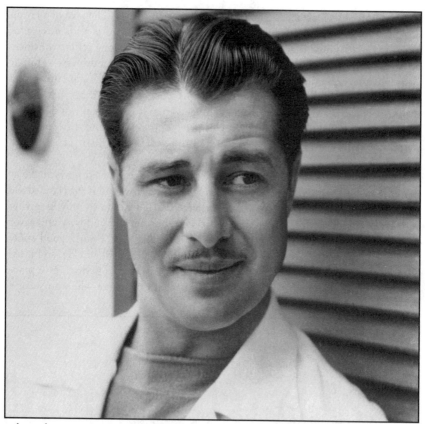

other when it came to publicity. But there were occasions when Don just couldn't make it to a broadcast. On one particular show, both Ameche and W.C. Fields were off the air, with Herbert Marshall filling in for Don. Most of the reviews that week in 1937 mourned the loss.

"I am enthusiastic over pictures," he said at the time, "but I try not to let my enthusiasm overcome me. A happy medium, that's what one must strive for out here—moderation in everything. And I admit it takes some figuring to be moderate in this town. But as I have a five-year contract, with yearly options, I won't worry too much.

"I'm sure that, without radio I would never be where I am today; and it is also because of radio that I never starved in the show business—as many others have. I still feel I need the constant stimulation which the radio gives any actor with the public. With that and films they can't forget me because if they go to a movie there I am, and if they stay at home, I catch them via the radio. They can't possibly escape me.

"I have it in my contract that I am to get off every afternoon I broadcast at 4 p.m. There is not time to go home, as the radio show goes on at 7 o'clock Hollywood time. So I just go into town, rehearse and do the show—and have my dinner after the broadcast.

"Naturally I like the money and the thrills that go with it. The idea of a group of people living glamorous lives appeals to me. But, back of it all is a sense of unreality and I know that unless we actors run our lives along strictly business lines, we will eventually come to grief. This is an abundant business—while it lasts, which is not as long as any other business career. And here's something else. I don't think that ability is so important in this game. I'm sure that what we call the breaks have more to do with it than ability. Often it is personalities that crash through, rather than talent. And camera personalities are quite different than stage personalities—people who succeed in one might not hit it at all in the other, and vice versa.

"To tell the truth, I'd probably be better on the stage. But I'd never make as much money there as out here. And as fate, or whatever we call it, has landed me here, I'm going to try to hang on. But I realize that I shall do so only by giving consistently good performances. Even in this unbusinesslike industry any actor who can be depended upon to always come through with a fairly good show becomes an asset to a producer. I mean merely that I'll never skyrocket, so I must be someone on whom they can always depend. I feel there will always be a place for the man of whom the director says, 'Get what's-his-name—he's no second Booth but he won't let us down.'"

Ann Sothern and DA in *Fifty Roads to Town*, 1937. Courtesy of Laura Wagner.

Fifty Roads to Town, based on the novel by Louis Frederick Nebel and again directed by Norman Taurog, was a pleasant 1937 semi-screwball comedy which gave Don Ameche ample opportunity to skirt between romantically menacing and farcically comic. Ann Sothern was his perfect foil and fool for love, sparking a chemistry between them that made this a delightful, if inexpensive (most of it takes place in a single set), film.

In the opening scene, Peter Nostrand (Ameche) is tipped off by a friend that a warrant has been issued for him. "Your friend Winship threatens to shoot you on sight," is all Nostrand has to hear before packing up liquor, a gun and a few clothes. He races off in a speeding car down a lonely road on which wealthy young Millicent Kendall (Sothern) finds herself racing off to marry a man of lower social standing. Followed by a cop for speeding, the two eventually wind up at the same hotel, shortly closing before the heavy snow comes, and then a cabin. Millicent thinks Peter is a gangster because of the gun he keeps waving around (since he, at first, thinks she's a sexy server of warrants), but soon the real gangster, Dutch Nelson (Douglas Fowley), arrives to stir up trouble. The police are looking for Dutch, so he takes Peter's car and strands them at the cabin by shooting out the tires on his own car. Left with nothing to eat but caviar, Saltine crackers, hearts of artichokes and French jelly, the two slowly fall for one another as a blizzard rages outside. They don't care. Peter chops up the furniture for firewood as Millicent cuddles up in the full-length fur coat (with only a nightgown underneath) she almost never takes off.

Edwin Henry (Slim Summerville), a trapper, stops in with his still-live catch, a rabbit, but Millicent is adamant about not killing the poor thing. Good thing, too; she gives birth to a small litter of fuzzy ones. Peter smiles and admits, "The triumph of mother over menu." The trapper gets away from Peter, who still delights in playing the gangster for his love, telling her of his target practice in his basement on a team photo of the St. Louis Cardinals. But when the trapper brings the law down on them, the cabin is shot to pieces. Only poor aim from the cops' tear gas bombs (throwing them *outside* the cabin, and when the wind changes, gives it back to them in the puss) allows the cooing couple to give up without bloodshed. All's well in the end when, at the police station, Peter learns that the warrant (issued to bring him in as a divorce witness for two close friends) has been withdrawn since his friends have reconciled and are now on their way to Bermuda.

The New York Times didn't care for Nebel's novel being rehashed "with its original melodramatic content washed out and an inlay of gibbering farce put in its place." *The Standard* called *Fifty Roads to Town* "a laugh-spiced romance pungent with danger" and acclaimed Don and Ann Sothern as "two delightfully thrilling young stars."

The film's working title had been **50 Roads Back**, though neither title was referred to in the movie nor seemed to have had anything to do with the plot. Since director Taurog believed in realism, during the course of filming, Ameche and Sothern consumed fourteen large jars of caviar and twelve bottles of artichoke hearts, plus the many pounds of salt, gypsum and untoasted cornflakes that simulated the snowstorm. A very food-filled picture.

Last Year's Kisses, later retitled *You Can't Have Everything*, was one of Don Ameche's best pictures, and the first to team him up with his favorite leading lady, Alice Faye. He plays successful, famous musical comedy writer George Macrae who meets up with Judith Poe Wells (Faye), the great-granddaughter of Edgar Allan Poe, in an Italian restaurant. She's a starving playwright suffering from youth and ego who thinks true art must be *real*, not fun and frivolous. Macrae feels sorry for her and options her play so she won't have to go back to her old hometown. When he finds that Judith has a great voice, he quickly puts her in his latest show in place of the temperamental star, Evelyn Moore (Phyllis Brooks), who has just quit. Trouble rears when Macrae's old girlfriend Lulu (Louise Hovick) informs him, and the eavesdropping Judith, that they were married one night when he was too drunk to remember. Judith runs back home on opening night, canceling the show. Macrae gets the brilliant idea to turn Judith's stinker of a play into a musical comedy; that'll get her back. And it does. Once it's found that the judge never signed the marriage license and that Macrae is off the hook, the singing show ends with smiles all 'round.

The cast for the 1937 film was stellar, containing one of the Ritz Brothers' longest and finest performances throughout the 100-minute film. Singer Tony Martin, violinist Rubinoff, extraordinary dancers Tip, Tap and Toe and others highlighted this tuneful Mack Gordon/Harry Revel score. The original casting would've been quite different: Joan Davis and Frances Drake had been signed on, and Zanuck himself had wanted to feature Jimmy Ritz on his own, but Al and Harry strongly protested, so all three brothers were used. Their "Boots! Boots!" was especially and intensely zany. Louise Hovick—better known as stripper Gypsy Rose Lee—made her screen debut in this film. Alice Faye and Tony Martin were married right after the picture wrapped, though they divorced a mere three years later.

Directed by Norman Taurog, the script by Harry Tugend, Jack Yellen and Karl Tunberg was based on an original story by Gregory Ratoff. A hit in Kuala Lumpur, the *Malaya Tribune* excitedly wrote that *You Can't Have Everything* had it all: "rhythm, sweet trembly and low-down; heavenly song hits by Gordon and Revel; scrumptious girls; a parade of personalities . . ." It was "a well-rounded gem of fun and amusement."

Loretta Young was back, again opposite Ameche, in the romantic semi-mystery, *Love Under Fire*. Detective from Scotland Yard Tracy Egan (Ameche) is on vacation in Spain where he meets and falls for Myra Cooper (Young) before being set on her trail as a suspected jewel thief. They are both pursued and threatened by Lt. Chavez (Harold Huber), who must return the jewels to the new military government for which he works, or lose his life. Egan tricks him at the end with fake jewels and admits he loves Myra, but still has to do his duty. She also loves him and succumbs to his custody, though they both know she's innocent. It is that fact that makes Egan sure that no jury in England will convict her, and she takes solace in his belief and love.

Film Weekly said in their January 29, 1938 issue that *Love Under Fire* was "entertaining, if you don't take it seriously . . . a film of no consequence, which

Clowning with wrestler "Hangman" Howard Cantowine during a break from
*You Can't Have Everything***, 1937.**

you'll enjoy while you're seeing it."

Ameche's next film was a classic. *In Old Chicago* fictionalized the great fire accidentally started by the O'Leary clan. Dion O'Leary (Tyrone Power) is in love with stage singer Belle Fawcett (Alice Faye), enraging his mother Molly (Alice Brady), a washer woman, who wants so much more for her son. Dion is an ambitious runner of a gambling house, while brother Jack (Ameche) ultimately winds up as Mayor of the town. Jack loves Chicago and vehemently and eloquently fights for a new town, one made of brick and stone, not the wooden gambling, etc., slums that infest it now. Because of this, the brothers are on opposite sides, but when the fire begins to rage (started by the O'Leary cow kicking over a lantern in the barn), they make their peace before Jack dies trying to save his beloved city by lighting a dynamite fuse in order to stop the deadly inferno's spread.

During the filming, Don had to fly back to the coast due to Honore's sudden illness. (Another report claimed that Don raced back from Bermuda to be at his wife's bedside at Cedars of Lebanon where she miscarriaged their third child.)

The director, Henry King, thought that Alice, Ty and Don should all take flying lessons, to cement their friendship with a common love. Ty was the only one to continue on with flying, but it did help the three of them feel close enough to hold off playing pranks on each other for a while. Alice and Ty felt closer, perhaps because they shared a birthday, with Alice feeling it was more of a brother-sister relationship.

The fiery climax took about two weeks of night shooting to complete, beginning at 8:00 or 9:00 p.m. and lasting until dawn, interrupted at five or six in the morning. Stuntmen in dresses did the fire scenes—the only injury in the film was to Alice, who fell down a flight of steps and bruised her back.

A foreign premiere of *In Old Chicago*, 1938.

Chicago's own *Daily Times* newspaper hailed that "Darryl Zanuck, its shrewd producer, has created a vivid and lifelike picture of the young city." The New York Post concluded its praise of *In Old Chicago* with "the only thing lacking in the picture is the heat on your face and the smoke in your eyes and nostrils." *The New York Times* stated that "Troy was a bonfire, Rome a false alarm, compared" with Zanuck's production. Its greatest compliment was that "the film achieves the lusty, amoral quality of the original city. At the first cry of 'Fire' the screen suddenly flowers into beauty, violence and terror."

The regal opening of the film at the Four Star Theater on Wilshire Boulevard was populated by, among others, Mr. and Mrs. Ameche (wearing a black velvet gown and mink coat), Power and Zanuck. For the Zanucks it was a double celebration, being their 14th wedding anniversary. Thousands of fans lined the streets, giving the greatest ovation to the studio head. After the premiere guests attended a supper dance at Joseph M. Schenck's home.

The film was nominated for six Oscars, including Best Picture, winning two: Alice Brady for Best Supporting Actress, and Robert D. Webb for Best Assistant Director.

Don got the girl—Sonja Henie—in his next (her third) picture, *Happy Landing*, which was shot between October and December of 1937, and had its New York premiere on January 21, 1938. The musical comedy lacked the Ritz Brothers deranged touch, but had everything else going for it that

Don Ameche on ice.

One in a Million did. The big song pushed was "A Gypsy Told Me," one of several ballads written by Walter Bullock and Harold Spina, though the hot standout dance number, "War Dance of the Wooden Indians," was written by Raymond Scott. Cesar Romero as Duke Sargent was actually the focus of the plot, with Ethel Merman, playing Flo Kelly, given nearly as much "performing" time as Sonja.

When Duke Sargent and his publicity man, Jimmy Hall (Ameche), lose their way while flying to Paris for Duke's nightclub gig, they land in Norway where dancing with a girl twice means you want to marry her. Duke, a woman-crazy flirt, never has the sense to keep his mouth shut when turned on by the next dame. Jimmy had already saved him from a previous girlfriend, Flo, whom he described as having "alimony in one eye and breech of promise in the other." Indeed, Flo has a habit of keeping a blank record recording under the bed, the couch, etc. for capturing marriage proposals; you have to be careful with that brunette singer.

Trudy Ericksen (Henie) has no inkling of the strange world and lying men outside her native Norway, though she keeps wishing for a dashing young man to come take her away. A gypsy told her that the first man she sees in her special mirror would be the man she marries—unfortunately for everyone, Duke walks through the door before Jimmy. Duke woos her like every other girl he's ever known, mostly to get inspiration (he says) for penning new music, but runs away after he realizes what happens after a second dance. Trudy follows him ultimately to New York, where he continues his words of love, for publicity purposes, but when Flo steps back into his life, Trudy realizes the truth. Jimmy feels sorry for her, but then sees how well she skates and builds her up into the biggest act ever on ice. Jimmy falls for her, but finds out that she's still sweet on Duke. It's only when Jimmy steps out of the picture that Trudy realizes where her heart truly lies. After some misunderstandings instigated by a vengeful Flo, both couples wind up getting married before ice skating off at the movie's end.

The New York Times was dazzled. "*Happy Landing* is not so much a variation of the old musical comedy formula as a successful realization of it." *The Republican* echoed that "Don Ameche never misses; his portrayal is natural, free and winning." A reporter for Britain's *Film Weekly* (Feb. 12, 1938) was impressed with Don's ability to do a scene in which he had to say 350 words in 90 seconds. The scene was shot six times and Ameche never tripped over a syllable.

By this point in her career, Sonja Henie was ranked as the eighth (some reports state third) biggest box office attraction. It was merely her third film, which had early working titles of *Bread, Butter and Rhythm, Hot and Happy,* and *Happy Ending*. Funnily, Ameche had originally been suggested for Romero's role, which was then rewritten for the unused Adolphe Menjou. Ameche could have usurped the starring role of "Larry Taylor" opposite Sonja Henie in her fourth picture, *My Lucky Star*, from 1938, but he was replaced by Richard Greene. Luckily, he did not appear in 1939's *Second Fiddle*, with Tyrone Power opposite Sonja that time. Had Don not been previously committed to *The Story of Alexander Graham Bell*, Power may have invented the telephone while Don fell flat on his ice.

He was to have been loaned out to Paramount in 1938 for *Sing, You Sinners,* to support Bing Crosby in this comedy-drama about three singing brothers, but he was replaced by the usually non-singing Fred MacMurray. Besides, Ameche *much* preferred 20th Century-Fox to being loaned out.

Next up for the Fox home team was *Gateway,* based on a story purchased from "Prince" Michael Romanoff, the famous imposter who claimed to be part of the Romanoff dynasty and later became wealthy with a string of Romanoff restaurants. The story and original film title: *Ellis Island.* It starred Ameche as

Ameche and Whelan in Gateway, 1938.

tired war correspondent, Dick Court, who meets the beautiful Catherine O'Shea (Arleen Whelan), a true innocent from Ireland, who is forced into staying at Ellis Island after defending herself against the lecherous advances of Mayor McNutt (Raymond Walburn). The scandal ruins her life, causing a distance from her stuck-up fiancé; so much the better for Dick, who finally manages to wrangle her out of all the trouble others have landed her in, and the two are married.

Don reunited again with Tyrone Power, Alice Faye and director Henry King for the semi-biographical *Alexander's Ragtime Band,* "based" on Irving Berlin's early years as a bandleader in San Francisco. This Fox musical starred Power as Roger Grant, a promising young classical violinist who forsakes his studies to lead his newly-formed jazz band, which includes Charlie Dwyer (Ameche) on piano and Davey Lane (Jack Haley) on drums. The band doesn't click until hooking up with the tough singer Stella (Faye), but together, though there are many riffs between Roger (now called "Alexander" after their first hit song) and Stella, they begin headlining all the way to the top. Along the way, opposites attract and Stella and

Don and Alice Faye in *Alexander's Ragtime Band*, 1938. Photo courtesy of Laura Wagner.

Alex fall for each other. That is, until Stella is offered a trip to New York and the promise of stardom, which infuriates the neglected Alexander who orders her to leave. She and Charlie reluctantly go to New York and ultimately marry. After his stint in WWI, Alex visits New York and Charlie sees the old love between his friends and bows out of the picture with the offer of divorce (an anti-marital act that Ameche himself would never dream of committing).

Irving Berlin received the rare distinction of having *his* name above the film's title. He also took an Alaskan vacation with his family where he composed additional music for the film. The film cost about $2 million, the same as *In Old Chicago*, because of its nostalgic production numbers. One news article reported that it took two years to make, overlapping the two productions (*In Old Chicago*) at once so that the stars made several films at the same time. Like *Chicago*, *Band* was also nominated for a few Oscars, winning for Best Scoring. According to *Variety*, it was the top moneymaking picture of the first nine months of the year. (For promotion, theaters could buy 500 "novelty oblong balloons that emit a musical note as the balloon deflates" for $7.50.)

The New York Times called it "a long, elaborate, handsomely-produced musical review, a pictorial trip down Memory Lane with one of this generation's most competent ballad-makers." They thought the film overlong, but worth it to hear Berlin's melange of hits again.

During their time together, Don found Alice a very nervous and insecure actress, but recalled that she seemed more natural and relaxed when she sang.

Incredibly, an energetic, expensive number called "Time Marches On," sung by Ethel Merman, was cut from this picture, along with the sportive ballad "Some Sunny Day," sung by Don. He was supported by a harmony-chorus of beautiful girls who come in to surround him, as Tyrone continues to conduct the huge band. Don was in fine voice for this one. Too bad it was cut. It was, after all, Fox's biggest musical success of the year.

Like baseball players, actors were often traded between studios, though they usually came back home. Ameche was not immune. Fox traded Ameche to Paramount for Randolph Scott, who starred opposite Shirley Temple in 1938's *Rebecca of Sunnybrook Farm*. Don was scheduled to star in Paramount's musical *Ensenada*, taking place in Mexico, with Arthur Hornblow, Jr. producing, but he did not make the film.

In 1938 it was reported that French actress Annabella would star with Don in *Her Masterpiece*, a romantic mystery about "bogus oil paintings masquerading as old masters." She didn't make the picture, but soon it was announced that Don would star opposite Simone Simon in the same film, with Gregory Ratoff directing. Instead:

A cute couple in *Josette*, 1938.

The 1938 romantic comedy *Josette* was a little fluffier than usual for Ameche, but at least he got the girl, knockout Simone Simon. She sang several Mack Gordon/Harry Revel songs, in between being chased by brothers David Brossard, Jr. (Ameche) and Pierre Brossard (Robert Young). It was a farcical story based on the play *Jo and Josette* (also the film's original title) by Paul Frank and George Fraser, itself based on the Ladislaus Vadnai short story.

The brothers Brossard know that their father (William Collier, Sr.) is a fool over women. His latest stupidity is becoming engaged to the famous French singer, Josette (Tala Birell), now performing in New Orleans. They send him away on a business ruse, determined to buy or bully her off, little realizing that he's taken the little lady with him. Renee Le Blanc (Simon) is an ambitious singer who goes on in Josette's place, much to the high-blood pressure of club owner Barney Barnady (Bert Lahr). Only he and Josette's maid, May Morris (Joan Davis), know the truth. Pierre falls for the doll, but she falls for the more serious-minded David. He gets the girl while Pierre gets a broken leg after a complex pass at her on board his yacht fails.

If Ameche had not needed an emergency appendicitis operation while on vacation, he would have followed this up with *Kentucky*, filmed over September and October of 1938. Richard Greene replaced him opposite Loretta Young in what was essentially the basis for Don's musical, *Down Argentine Way*, coming a mere two years later.

The Ameches had crossed over in the *Queen Mary* with other actors, including Eddie Cantor, on their way to The Hague, Netherlands, at the Hotel De Witte Brug. The ailment struck Don while taking time off in Holland with Honore for that neglected first honeymoon they'd always meant to take before his career got in the way, on a Dutch train while en route from Amsterdam to Paris. She summoned a doctor at Utrecht, who ordered Don's admittance to St. Anthony Hospital there. The Saturday operation by Dr. G. H. de Kleijn was a success, with Darryl Zanuck, whom Don was to have met in Paris, noted to have been in attendance during the operation. Zanuck cabled the Vice President of Fox, William Goetz, to postpone the start of Kentucky, but as Don still wasn't ready in time, filming went ahead with a cast change. Don left the hospital on the morning of July 27, 1938. His brother Louis had come over from Paris and traveled by car to Amsterdam with his wife. From the aerodrome Schiphol they all took a plane to Paris, Honey and Don continuing on to the Riviera to complete recovery.

He didn't need *Kentucky*. Filmed from November 1938 to January 1939, under the early title of *Careless Rapture*, the now-classic *Midnight* was born. With a clever and quick-paced script by Charles Brackett and Billy Wilder (Oscar-winning writers of *The Lost Weekend* and *Sunset Blvd.*), and Mitchell Leisen directing, the Paramount picture told the story of American Eve Peabody's rise from a poor showgirl to poor cabbie's wife.

When Eve (Claudette Colbert) arrives in Paris in evening gown but penniless, a friendly taxi driver, Tibor Czerny (Ameche), befriends her with a night of cruising to cafes to find a job as a singer. Tibor offers her the use of his apartment, but being a worldly but good girl, she declines and secretly departs from his cab when the guilt for what she's cost him in cab fare starts to mount. She lucks into admission to a ritzy charity concert, and with the aid of jaded Georges Flammarion (John Barrymore), steps into another world as the supposed Countess Czerny. Georges' wife, Helene (Mary Astor), is in love with Jacques Picot (Francis Lederer), but when Jacques starts to fall for Eve, Georges, who is still in love with his wife, knows he can use that wedge to break up the affair. Eve loves living the rich life, but when Tibor finally finds her, after rallying all the cabbies of Paris for a citywide search, she's confused about whom to love. He appears as her husband, which she can't

Hail, Ameche in _Midnight_, 1939.

deny, and farcical times ensue when Eve makes everyone believe he's crazy. It only works in his favor at the end when, during Eve and Tibor's divorce proceedings, he begins shaving in front of the judge. Eve is relieved—she didn't really want Jacques—so she and Tibor head down the hall to get _properly_ married.

Of Ameche's performance, one reviewer asked, "Don't you love his laugh?" Another applauded, "Of all the zippy, zany, sparkling little gems of monkey business to come out of Hollywood, _Midnight_ wins the gold cup. The cast, one of the best ever assembled for the purpose of fun making, turns in individual performances that are wows."

For his cabbie role Don was taught piloting techniques by "southern California's safest taxicab driver," Earl Riggs. He was instructed on the proper conduct of a driver, signals used, advice on when to expect tips, etc. The L.A. cabbie had driven a million miles since 1924, with nary a dented fender.

Production had to be divided into two film units to make sure Don would finish in time enough to start his next picture, which is why Ray Milland had also been considered for his part. Marlene Dietrich was reported to have been the original desire for the lead, with Fritz Lang directing. Loaned to Paramount, it was Ameche's first picture away from Fox.

Apparently, the wrap party for *Midnight* roared on until 4:00 a.m. and Don had an 8:00 a.m. call to begin shooting *The Story of Alexander Graham Bell*. He still hadn't memorized the six pages of dialogue that would be called for . . .

Don Ameche wanted it all: family *and* career. But being a movie star unquestionably took more time and effort than a 9 to 5 father and husband needed to exert. He wore his wedding ring in films, when possible, as in *Ramona* and *Ladies in Love*. One incident reported in December 1936's *Photoplay* told of the director of his last picture wanting him to take off the ring. Don gave a shrug that seemed to suggest he'd just as soon tear up his contract. The director didn't press the point.

In interviews, he always put his wife and children first. Whereas other stars, such as Tyrone Power, were single and gave girls a rush to read about them in the great fictional fan mags of the time, the studio and press had a more difficult job trying to sell the idea of Ameche, the beloved family man, to teens and still retain a semblance of sex star quality. It wasn't easy to walk that tightrope, but because of it, we have some detailed insight into the Ameches' homelife during their Golden Age.

At their Beverly Hills home the family had an Irish setter named Sheila, whom he spoke of to a Hollywood paper: "She's a fun-loving companion when I want to frolic, she'll go away and leave me alone when I'm busy studying a script or doing other work, and she feels as though she were personally responsible for the house and everyone in it. In addition she is simultaneously a gentle playmate and a formidable guardian for my two children."

Don was puzzled over the studio's decision to try to soft-pedal his marriage because they thought fans wouldn't like him as much if they knew he'd been happily married for five years.

"We have known one another since we were high-school age," Don explained. "Neither of us ever cared for anyone else. And she's an integral part of me, of whatever I have or can achieve. She's a wonderful mother; but more, she's a wife who's an ideal companion. I have more fun with her than with any woman or man I've ever known.

"Frankly I don't believe people who like my work will resent my personal luck in getting a girl like I got. Of course, I'm new at the picture game; I acknowledge that I'm a novice out here. Still, when I stood before an altar and exchanged vows I wasn't fooling. And it's my own opinion that my wife deserves to share every break, every privilege I can earn. I'm proud as punch of her."

Honore remained Don's biggest fan. "It isn't that Don is better or stronger than other men. Or that I'm cleverer than other women. It isn't even that he and I are more in love with each other than others have been who have come here and then separated. We're both human. But we have one protection—Don's radio work, his attitude toward it. His devotion to it is almost a religion."

She reported to *Radio Mirror* that once the radio money started rolling in, Don sent his mother in for some much-delayed medical treatment and sent his siblings through school. "Don will never forget. He knows he must repay the beneficence of that Providence. That is why his attitudes toward his radio work and his movie work are so different. He feels that in his radio work he can, in a

small way, bring comfort and cheer to the sick, the shut-ins, the blind, the aged—people who cannot go out of their own homes to seek entertainment and pleasure.

"And you know, much of his radio fan mail comes from just such people. He reads and answers every bit of his radio mail himself, but his movie fan mail is altogether different. Most of it comes from gushing girls.

"Of course, Don enjoys his movie work. But he enjoys it because it's more a matter of personal gratification as an actor. And of course there is the financial angle. Anyone likes to feel he can make money—a lot of money."

Don put more faith in God than cash, strongly sticking to the strict moral code he'd been brought up to respect. He believed he owed a lot to his faith, as he told one magazine in the late '30s: "I wasn't discouraged when I was ignored in New York, for I hadn't pinned my hopes explicitly on the stage. I gradually saw the futility of despair. I realized that success in work, and with friends, and in love, was a natural thing also. God isn't purposeless. He didn't make me, nor anyone else, for failure. If I followed His laws of cause and effect I would get the success, the all-around success I wanted.

"I made myself learn to trust—I didn't know how I could climb, where I was to climb. But the minute I began to trust, wholly, my good luck began to unfold. I didn't plan. I exercised my faith that what I needed for a normal, full life would come to me somehow, exercised it by constantly being optimistic and certain of my good future, though there was no girl and no keen job at the time."

To "de-square" the religious family man, one tact the press took was to push how hard Don, with or without Honey, lived the Hollywood life with vigor. Honore was once quoting as saying: "Cook, indeed! He may be living out here like a gentleman farmer, but don't let that deceive you. Every evening Dom wants to go into Hollywood for dinner. But any man who maintains the extraordinary work schedule he does is deserving of a whim once in a while." In another interview, she admitted that they eat at the Brown Derby frequently, sometimes joined by bachelor Ty Power, who might bring Sonja Henie or another pretty lady. "He has only one idiosyncrasy, only one trait which might be called temperamental. He can't eat his dinners at home! He doesn't like to know what he is going to eat. He likes to have a choice. He likes to have lots of people and lots of talk and noise around him."

When asked by Gladys Hall in a magazine article, "Are Hollywood Wives Jealous of Women Stars?," Mrs. Annabella Power answered, "When Tyrone goes on location I go with him—always. You see, on locations they usually finish the shooting at four in the afternoons, because the light goes. There is a lot of living to be done between four in the afternoon until it is time to go to bed. I see to it that we have that living—together."

Honore Ameche had more to say. "Jealous of Don? Quite the contrary. I glory in his popularity and, being of a practical nature, my worrying would begin when it ceased. I don't see how anyone can be jealous of anything so general as a career, or of the fans, or even of the girls he plays with in pictures. If it were *one* girl, and one only, picture after picture, that might conceivably be different. Or if it were

one girl and he was alone with her, in an office, in private—but in a huge factory like a *studio*, no.

"Besides, I am a hero worshiper myself so I can understand the hero worship of others. Both how ardent it is, and how innocuous. Not only that, but I am just as much an Ameche fan as anyone else so the more gallantly he makes love, the better I enjoy his portrayals. It's funny, perhaps, but this is the way it is with me: when Don is not working, when he is at home, he's just Don, my husband and the boys' Dad. I certainly have neither cause nor occasion to be jealous of him then. When he is working, he is, to me as to others, the Movie Star and I am one of his fans, one of his audience myself. I certainly have neither cause, right nor occasion to be jealous of him then, when I am just one of his fans—and there it is!"

The Ameches wanted their homelife as separate from the Hollywood life as possible, regardless of what the press claimed. But to spice up the couple's image, much was made of the couple's love for nightlife. "They dine and dance every Sunday at the Trocadero," wrote *Photoplay*, "where Don has a thick rare steak and an entrée of spaghetti. He hates lettuce and tight collars."

One magazine report gave the following adventure: Don invited Maddox (a reporter) to dinner and asked Honore to invite Toughy ("Abner" from radio's *Lum and Abner*) and wife Liz to join them; they were next door neighbors, and had been chums since the Chicago radio days. They went in one car to the city, to the Beverly-Wilshire Hotel, but were wearing no ties. The head waiter was stern about ties, but Honore melted him. They ate. Over coffee Don suggested they go to Venice (California). "Honey wants to ride the whip." They collected Claire Trevor and Billy Bakewell, and Polly Ann (sister of Loretta) Young and her husband en route. They rode the roller coaster three times, shot rifles, raced rabbits and chased goldfish with paper nets. Then the nickel dance hall. Maddox stated, "A lot of people were on the verge of recognizing Don, but evidently they concluded he couldn't be a celebrity. No one enjoying himself so much could be!"

Then Don exclaimed, "The Bublichki!," and they moved to the Russian nightspot on Sunset Blvd. "There's a marvelous fiddle player there. He's taught many of the finest violinists!" They had midnight supper there. The proprietor played the guitar and everyone sang, including Don.

"He doesn't take voice lessons," Honore told Maddox. "Back in Chicago he went to a man who knows much about singing, and Dom was advised not to spoil his natural tones as long as he wasn't aiming for opera. That teacher is partly blind, and Dom thinks a lot of him. Every week Dom looks forward to the letter of criticism he gets from him about his radio program."

They left the club at 3:00 a.m. and went to Abner's house for some penny poker. Don said, "I guess I had my fill of routine when I was in boarding school. Now my working hours are comparatively irregular, and so are my non-working hours. I like it this way!"

After poker with the neighbors, there were ham and eggs for breakfast, after which Maddox went back to his car where the Ameches saw him off.

The great thing about early Hollywood was that if you had black hair, you got more work. You could play Italian, Latin, Indian, etc., etc. One 1937 press release, picked up by several papers pronounced DON AMECHE FIRST LATIN TYPE TO APPEAL IN TALKIES, and went on to say, "Don Ameche, in spite of American birth and an American accent, is primarily a Latin. His name is boldly so. His attitude is in the Valentino tradition." The key elements that Fox wanted brought out on Don were his easy-going nature, his natural and serene homelife, his intrinsic smile, his bold voice, and his agreeableness to fit into any kind of role.

So, he invented the telephone.

Chapter Four

"You're wanted on the Ameche!"

Production for Ameche's most famous role began on January 5, 1939. Some critics consider *The Story of Alexander Graham Bell*, which Darryl Zanuck personally produced, one of the finest historical biographies Hollywood has ever filmed. It's easy to see why, until *Cocoon*, it was the film most associated with Don Ameche. His impassioned performance as the inventor of the telephone combined fevered drive with the tenderness of a man moved by love and ideals, and hope.

Bell, a teacher of deaf mutes, began work on a new telegraph in 1873 out of his studies on how to visualize sound so his students could imitate and speak it. Thomas Sanders (Gene Lockhart) is much taken with the man who has done so much for his hearing-impaired boy that he introduces Bell to Gardner Hubbard (Charles Coburn) so that Bell might have a benefactor to help him develop the telegraph. Hubbard also wants him to help his deaf daughter, the beautiful Mabel (Loretta Young). There is instant chemistry between the young couple. As he falls in love with her, Bell quickly sets aside his telegraph in order to work with engineer Thomas Watson (Henry Fonda) on his new idea: the telephone. Through starvation, lack of funds and dismal living conditions, Bell finally makes the damn thing work. But selling the concept is another matter.

Americans are skeptical of its novelty, so Bell and new wife Mabel journey to England to demonstrate the box to Queen Victoria, who promptly gives the order to have the new wonder installed in Buckingham Palace. Unfortunately, while he is away, another U.S. company claims that they have invented the device first, and cancellations start pouring into Bell's new company. He fights them, and during a dramatic court case in which Bell energetically states his truth, he wins the battle out of court once Western Union (backing the rival company) finds out that they were basing their case on false information. They concede Bell invented the telephone, and offer a partnership.

For *Bell*'s filming the American Telephone & Telegraph Company furnished historic data and models of Bell's first instrument from 63 years previous. The machines didn't work, but lent authenticity. The film was budgeted at $1.5 million.

"In my latest picture, I get the gal!" Ameche told *Modern Screen* in a June article titled "Everybody's Pal." "There's no Tyrone Power in the cast this time!

Feverishly inventing the telephone.

I got quite a thrill when we went up to Boston recently for a publicity tie-up. You see, I play Alexander Bell and so, for the opening of the picture they thought it a good idea for me to talk over a phone from the place where Bell first spoke. Of course, the house that he used has since been torn down and an office building stands in its place. We got one of the offices and began. On the first hook-up, I talked with eight different people in just as many states throughout the middle and far West. Each of them asked questions which I answered in turn. On the next hook-up I think there were about seven throughout the Southern section. Y'know, darned if I didn't get a tingle up and down my spine to think that so many different places could be connected in at once and we could all hear one another."

Praise for Ameche's *Bell* was so enthusiastic, it's no wonder he was seriously thought of as the phone's inventor (even by a few schoolteachers who should've known better) for the rest of his life. One critic wrote, "Don Ameche has never accomplished anything so fine as his portrayal of Bell . . . Patient and persistent direction did away with one annoying mannerism and he gives a sympathetic, believable, and entirely sincere characterization. His enthusiasm is infectious—his despair—the saddest thing . . . ! And wistful little boy, determined man, and rapt genius are cunningly combined in his depiction." And "as for staging, direction, costumes, photography—the best, my friends, the BEST!" Another reviewer wrote, "For once Ameche drops his master-of-ceremonies flourish for a sincere effort at characterization, and he definitely succeeds in making the tireless inventor of the telephone a noble and even inspiring figure."

Variety reported on one of Zanuck's most ambitious film premieres: after 215 people arrived in San Francisco for *Bell* in late March 1939, Ameche was sworn in as mayor of Treasure Island for the duration of his stay by San Francisco Mayor Angelo Rossi. Most guests departed from Glendale on March 28 at 9:15 that night on a Southern Pacific train consisting of 16 cars. The overflow of guests was hauled in special attached Pullmans. Guests included Joseph M. Schenck, Mr. and Mrs. Darryl Zanuck, Tyrone Power & Annabella, George Hearst (son of publisher William Randolph Hearst), Lynn Bari, Constance Bennett, Mary Carlisle, Irving and Mrs. Cummings, Sally Eilers, Douglas and Mrs. Fairbanks, Sr., Norman Foster, William and Mrs. Goetz, Mr. and Mrs. Mack Gordon, Richard Greene, Sonja Henie, Al Jolson, Nancy Kelly, Mr. and Mrs. William Koenig, Anita Louise, Mr. and Mrs. Kenneth Macgowan, Fred Metzler, Mr. and Mrs. Gregory Ratoff, Harry Revel, Gilbert Roland, Cesar Romero, Mr. and Mrs. Lew Schrieber, Loretta Young, Mr. and Mrs. Sol Wurtzel, Lamar and Mrs. Trotti, and Mr. and Mrs. Sidney Toler. After the 12-hour trip, Elsa Maxwell was given the job of lining up entertainment to keep the star tourists busy: ceremonies at the Civic Center, a trek to Treasure Island, and an inspection of the exciting Expo thereon (also mined by Fox for *Charlie Chan at Treasure Island*).

Later, the luncheon at Treasure Island's Yerba Buena Club was a huge plush gathering of 300 people. Elsa Maxwell giggled when she introduced the Treasurer of Treasure Island, Don Ameche. "I must say that this Ameche handled himself with a modest dignity which was most impressive. Or perhaps he was just tired from our large evening on the train. He really is a swell gent to meet personally, regardless of what you may think of his screen personality. Perhaps you like his acting and perhaps you don't. Or, as I always say, one man's Ameche is another man's poison."

After lunch, everyone piled into the very slow moving "elephant train" at the exposition and donning motorcycle police escort again, headed for the building where the film was to be shown. On the way, one little girl tried frantically to focus her camera on Don, distressing Hymie Fink so much that he had to reach out, grab her camera, snap Don's picture, and hand it back. Another woman, in a mannish gray suit, skirt way above the knees, startling reddish-yellow hair and carrying a cane veered right across the closest cop and lunged for Ameche. "Oh boy! *There's* the man I've been waiting for! There's what I want!" She almost poked his eye out with the cane before Don managed to grab it. With a little persuasion from the law, the lady moved back and let the train proceed, but she was still "as gay as a cricket," waving her stick and repeating in a loud voice her firm conviction that Don was and always would be the man for her. Of course, Don wasn't the only one to endure such riotous action. A 20-year-old from the Northwest screamed to meet her idyllic Romeo, Cesar Romero, and sit in his lap—just for a moment. Romero acquiesced, and had his guest badge stolen. With it, she crashed the evening's dinner party and rode in one of the official cars for the rest of the two-day party.

On March 30, 1939, the *Los Angeles Evening Herald Express* carried a feature story on their front page of the impressive San Francisco event. The picture

The Story of Alexander Graham Bell, 1939.

showed a parade of cars, the likes of which are usually given to national heroes, streaming through a mile-long crowd of 25,000 people. Don, Loretta and Sonja were pictured in the first car. 200 policemen were forced to join hands to keep crowds back from the 225 Hollywood notables at Treasure Island. The event cost around $30,000. Even the red-eyed reporters, who had to cover the event and rush back through the night to file the story, agreed it was worth all the trouble. "As we write this," wrote the *Hollywood Citizen-News*, "we're hungry and we're tired. We've got a dark brown taste in our mouths, but we're glad we came."

Six hundred people attended the viewing of the film in the World's Fair Playhouse's picturesque Federal Theater in New York City. Don had flown in from New York for the San Francisco premiere. Meanwhile, in Washington, an audience of 4,000, including Bell's daughter Mrs. Gilbert Grosvenor, attended another triumphant premiere.

Los Angeles Evening Herald and Express called *Bell* the first picture to be previewed at a world's fair and with "rare insight they have given it the perfect cast. [Ameche] gives a splendid interpretation of the struggle in Bell's character."

Variety agreed that Bell was "a thrilling narrative. It ranks among the best pictures of any season. And of biographical drama there has certainly been no better example." *The Hollywood Reporter* repeated the applause, calling it "outstanding theatre-fare which copiously lives up to its 'must see' insinuation as history in the making." It continued, "Don Ameche rises to dominant heights . . ." and as usual praised the supporting players, right down to little Bobs Watson, the deaf mute son of Gene Lockhart. There wasn't a single bad review. Ed Sullivan wrote that Don was "finally handed a part into which he can sink his teeth," proving "that he is one of the best young actors in the profession." Louella Parsons stated that "Don Ameche is not only believable but magnificent as the intense young inventor. He looks and acts the part of the dreamer, the creator who almost starves to death so that he can complete his invention." Her praise was lavish over every aspect of the picture.

Another paper loftily proclaimed *Bell* "one of the greatest pictures ever produced in the history of the motion picture industry." *The Hollywood Citizen-News* loved the film and explained that "after one particularly moving scene, you couldn't hear the dialogue for a while because every other member of the audience furtively was blowing his nose."

It was no wonder that Don found himself typecast for a while in Hollywood as dreamer, inventor, historical figure, or all of the above.

One rousing Ameche and Fonda scene from the picture was used two years later in *Land of Liberty*, a history of the United States told using Hollywood film clips, which premiered at the New York World's Fair and the Golden Gate International Exposition in 1941.

Oddly enough, Jim Ameche also later played Bell in the star-studded fantasy, *The Story of Mankind* (1957), written and directed by the Master of Disaster, Irwin Allen.

The same papers that carried the *Bell* review and premiere stories also carried reviews of *The Three Musketeers* and *Midnight*, both also playing at that time. All three were raved about. Don Ameche was certainly at the peak of his career.

He scored one of his biggest aesthetic successes with *The Three Musketeers*, a delectable, though short (71 minutes), Fox musical. Originally under the working title One for All, it was a surprisingly faithful adaptation of the often-filmed Alexandre Dumas novel. It thankfully also gave Ritz Brothers fans a chance to see much more of their insanity.

Three tavern servants (the Ritz Brothers) find themselves inundated with three of the French King's Musketeers, all insulted on the road to Paris by a young upstart by the name of D'Artagnan (Ameche). The idiot servants can hold certainly their liquor better than the King's men, who soon pass out. Unable to resist the posh outfits, the servants put on the clothes and feathery hats just in time for D'Artagnan to enter for his duel with all three "Musketeers" at once. Luckily (in a way), Cardinal Richelieu's men arrive and the four join forces to defeat the Pope's men. The main plot of the piece involves D'Artagnan's sacred mission to retrieve the Queen's broach, given to France's enemy, Lord Buckingham (Lester Matthews),from the hands of Milady De Winter (Binnie Barnes) so that the Cardinal cannot prove the Queen's disloyalty to her public and King. The tavern servants join the quest, finally turning De Winter upside down and shaking the broach out of her bosom. The broach is raced back to a royal ball and slipped to the Queen just in time for her to reveal it to all.

Along the way some delightful Samuel Pokrass/Walter Bullock songs are sung, mostly by Ameche, with polished manic antics by the Ritz Brothers, most notably, their dance of tin pans near the film's end.

Don refused to grow his hair long for *The Three Musketeers* because he said it made him look silly during off-hours, so he wore a wig. Six different endings were shot for the Ritz Brothers. One, the comics fall into a river. Two, they walk across an ocean. Three, they kiss a pretty girl. Four, fight with Don. Five, walk on air. It was the sixth they used—simply marching off and singing.

Near the film's release, Don was best man at Tyrone Power's wedding to Ann Carpentier, better known on the screen as Annabella. The marriage took place at Ann's home in the Bel-Air district of Los Angeles on April 23, 1939. The Matron of Honor was Pat Patterson (Mrs. Charles Boyer).

Released on October 13, 1939, a mere five months before production began, *Hollywood Cavalcade* was a delightfully nostalgic journey back to the Hollywood crossroads when pictures first began to talk. Ameche plays Michael Linnett

Connors, the man smart enough to invent the pie fight in early silent comedies and dumb enough to reject Rin-Tin-Tin during his rise as studio chief. He discovers Molly Adair Alice Faye) while still a prop boy (at Globe Pictures), and through her, he rises to become one of the most influential directors/producers in pre-talkie days. But work is all that seems to matter. He loses Molly to leading man Nicky Hayden (Alan Curtis) and quickly begins a descent to the bottom of the heap because of it. Only when Nicky dies in a car crash that also put Molly in the hospital for months does Michael snap out of it. Seeing Al Jolson in the first talking picture, *The Jazz Singer*, clinches it. His determination is reborn: he re-shoots some of Molly's scenes when she comes out of the hospital and, with Molly by his side again, ascends right back to the top.

Though definitely a romantic story, much of the film's charm stemmed from its wise use of old timers from the Keystone Kop days (Hank Mann, Heinie Conklin, Eddie Collins), as well as master pie thrower Buster Keaton, who ably plants several custard creations on Faye's pretty puss. The standout scene is a screening of Connors' first work: a Keystone Kop race with all slapstick gags in place. It was the only part of the Technicolor film shot in black and white. Fox wisely retitled the movie from *Falling Stars* to *Hollywood Cavalcade*, since the Ameche's character was the only one to fall.

Critics cheered for *Hollywood Cavalcade*, most notably Buster Keaton smacking Alice Faye with the desserts. One paper wrote that "it's top entertainment. Love story and history have been nicely combined in the script." *Variety* praised it "as fascinating and stirring as any outside drama the screen has projected." It thought the "exhilarating, inspiring" film traced the rise of early pictures with "a grandiose and nostalgic reminiscence," with a compelling love story to boot. *The Hollywood Reporter* wrote: "The picture is entertainment, every foot of it, and as wide a variety of entertainment as you can imagine . . . Don Ameche was superb in his every scene, reaching the height of really fine acting with the bit in the hospital at the bedside of Alice Faye."

Based on a satirical novel about early Hollywood, Mack Sennett was the film's technical advisor, and even appears in one scene. Since Alice Faye was the bigger star at the time, she received top billing over Don (in the reviews as well as the films), though it was obviously his picture, with most of the scenes/lines going to him.

To hype the show, 15 members of the local (Hollywood) press were driven to a "secret destination" after dinner at Fox in touring cars. Zanuck drove a green roadster which the others followed to the Alexander Theater in Glendale where the film was screened. The picture was budgeted at a high $2 million, with all gross receipts from its premiere justly going to the Motion Picture Relief Fund.

Swanee River, released on May 1, 1940, brought the life of Stephen Foster alive in glorious color with an Oscar-nominated Louis Silvers score. After the credits, the preamble rolled: "This is the strange story of a Northern youth to whom the Southland brought immortal inspiration . . . Though his stormy life is long forgotten, his simple words and simple music live on in the hearts of the

Down and out in _Hollywood Cavalcade_, 1939.

whole American people."

The film begins on a theme that will become familiar: Stephen Foster (Ameche), engrossed in his pleasure of listening to the southern "darkies" sing, uses snatches of their "Here Come the Heavin' Line" to compose his own song. Luckily for him, his girl Jeanie/Jane McDowell Foster (Andrea Leeds) loves him enough to forgive him for making them miss the showboat they were to take for a picnic. Instead, the lovers settle under a tree as Foster tries to figure out the end to his latest creation, "Oh, Susannah." She whistles to him the way she thinks the Negroes would finish it and the delighted composer bounds her off to the local saloon in search of a piano to try out the new classic.

Called back to his father's waning coal company, Foster jumps from the family meeting in order to find E.P. Christy (Al Jolson), who is leading the noisy parade outside. In Christie's dressing room, the hungry song plugger sells the blacked-up Christie his "Oh, Susannah" for a mere $15. It soon becomes a smash hit, which drives Foster crazy. He is now forced to go back into the family business, on the side writing songs, such as "De Camptown Races," that continue not to sell to publishers. It gets so bad he must hock his watch to keep the landlady appeased, and Foster is forced to write Jeanie to admit that he'll never make enough to support a family. He trudges into a bar after mailing that letter where he finds the well-to-do Christie, and Foster gives the guy a good sock in the kisser. Christie bails the poor, talented man out of prison, rationalizing the volatile situation that he'd paid for an unknown song from an unknown writer. But he had been looking for Foster. They should team up. And do.

"De Camptown Races" and other songs are hits, but the composer has trouble with the singer over his "mushy" ballad, "My Old Kentucky Home," so Foster boldly hijacks the stage to sing it to the audience himself. Once Christie sees how transfixed the audience is, he joins in himself, backed up with a group of harmonizing black-faced performers who, in the best Hollywood musical tradition, instantly know the arrangement, key and words.

Proven himself with a fresh publisher's advance of $500, Foster races down south to marry Jeanie, but on his seafaring honeymoon he ignores his wife long enough to compose "Ring, Ring the Banjo." Jeanie is naturally upset, but once Foster plays her the start of "Jeanie with the Light Brown Hair" on his borrowed violin, she melts.

Life is good to the Fosters, but Stephen wants more. He has been working on his Suite for Small Orchestra for six months, but it fails miserably when premiered for the stuffed shirts of Broadway. Christie himself walks out on it, claiming, "I never attend my friend's funerals." Foster is told to stick to popular songs—and does. But not before drowning his sorrows all night and morning at a bar while Jeanie gives birth to their daughter. Foster's obsession with music and drink finally pushes Jeanie and his beloved daughter away, nearly ruining his life. Being alone, and falling out of favor with the coming Civil War (the Yanks object to all the Rebel tunes), breaks Foster into a desolate world playing piano for peanuts in a bar. Christie finds him there and pleads him to write songs again, but Foster knows that without his family, the muse has left him for good.

He finds salvation briefly when Jeanie comes back to him, eager for another chance. But as much as he needs her, he also needs to feel the music flowing through him. With one final effort, Foster writes "The Old Folks at Home" (the film's title song), but does not live to hear it. As he shaves to go to the premiere of his song that night, Foster suffers a fatal heart attack and dies with his love and Christie in attendance. At first the theater crowd boo Christie's show, but when Christie returns to honor the great American composer posthumously, the showman gives a touching introduction to the song, followed by the entire audience standing to join in.

It was one of Ameche's most lively and believable performances, as he again portrayed a brilliant man obsessed with finding "the answer," this time experimenting passionately, single-mindedly at the keyboard. He was the inventor again. While Nancy Kelly had once been in mind for the role of Jane, Ameche, Fox's resident "inventor" or "artist," was Zanuck's choice from the start. Don even learned to play the violin for one scene, and dance soft shoe. For the film's often majestic look, some scenes had been shot along the Sacramento River.

Don scored another critical hit with *Swanee River*. *The Los Angeles Examiner* called it "a tensely dramatic story" and that it "captured the true American folk song spirit and brought to the screen a vivid, nostalgic piece of celluloid entertainment." *Variety* called it a "production of striking beauty and charm," and wrote that "Don Ameche creates a sympathetic and admirable portrait of Foster, building the character with warmth but restraint, and singing his share of the songs most effectively with a musician's understanding." *The Hollywood Reporter* thought it was "about the best blending of story and song the sound screen has ever had . . . the picture should be a hit. It has hit ingredients in every reel." *The Los Angeles Evening Herald* thought it was "a sentimental masterpiece" and wrote "Don Ameche's portrayal of Foster is as sincere and as fine as Muni's Pasteur." Even British reviewers liked it, calling attention to the fact that while not many Europeans would know the name Foster, few people were immune to his music.

Way down upon the *Swanee River*, 1940.

If the October 12, 1939-edition of *Chicago Daily News* is to be believed, Ameche was up to his old practical jokes on the set of *Swanee River*. On location in Sacramento he had the hotel's operator rouse director Sidney Lanfield and first assistant director Aaron Rosenberg at 3:00 a.m. Next, he sawed on the legs of Lanfield's favorite stool, but the joke backfired when he forgot about it and sat down on it himself. Supposedly, Don laughed the hardest, though.

Two years later, Ameche had been up for the lead of a film originally bought by Fox for Alice Faye. But *My Gal Sal* (1942), based loosely on the life of songwriter Paul Dresser (brother of writer Theodore Dreiser), was considered too soon by the studio to put Don in another composing role, after *Swanee River*'s fame. The Technicolor musical gave Rita Hayworth ample opportunity to shake up the late 1800s, and Victor Mature took Ameche's place as Dresser.

Ameche was given only a handful of scenes in the tuneful *Lillian Russell*, starring glamorous Alice Faye in the title role. The film unrealistically combined modern (1940) songs with turn-of-the-century ditties, but provided a memorable showcase for Faye's sultry vocals and empowering magnetism.

Born Cynthia Leonard to an ambitious suffragette mother (who also ran for Mayor of New York City), Lillian's rise to imperial heights as a stage singer is, according to the movie, rather easy. She has extraordinary beauty and talent, but Tony Pastor (Leo Carrillo), the theater manager who discovers her, doesn't like her name. When Ms. Russell takes to the stage singing "After the Ball" (a song she was not famous for), she has admirers such as Diamond Jim Brady (Edward Arnold) who constantly litters her dressing room with fabulously bejeweled bracelets and necklaces. But she has already lost her heart to newspaperman Alexander Moore (Henry Fonda), the shy guy from Pittsburgh who saved her runaway horse, when the great singer was still merely Cynthia. Moore continues to be too reticent to make a move, and loses the girl of his dreams to composer Edward Soloman (Ameche) who has been writing her songs.

She marries the quick-tempered, surly Soloman and has a child with him, but the poor man works himself to death composing an operetta for her—something he knows will be so great, he provokes a fight with the easily upset Gilbert (Nigel Bruce) of Gilbert and Sullivan in order to get her thrown out of their London operetta. But Soloman drives himself at the piano too hard and has a heart attack, while Lillian is signing a contract with Moore in another room to give him her life story. Years later, after turning down Diamond Jim's wealthy marriage proposal, Moore and Russell finally lock into a lover's embrace at the end of the film.

Ameche is first seen backstage at the piano when Lillian is about to sing to President Grover Cleveland over "the Ameche." It was a role of bite and substance, but little chance for development, even though he was given second billing (which should have gone to Henry Fonda for his ample screen time). During a dinner scene, he sings one of the ill-fitting, modern songs, "Adored One," written by Alfred Newman and Mack Gordon. Part of the picture was shot in Santa Barbara, California, and, to lend authenticity, in Pasadena at T.J. Bradford's estate, which Russell herself had once leased in 1905.

Reviewers liked the nostalgic feeling, though some admitted the script was another Hollywood half-adaptation of the whole truth. Still, they liked the sets, costumes and everyone loved Faye as the deep-bosomed, big-hipped gorgeous queen of the music halls. It was commented often that Faye was too small to play the true Amazonian Russell, but it was rumored that the studio kept after her to eat and eat to build up.

It was also reported that on the set of *Lillian Russell* pranks between the stars still rumbled. Don stole Alice's hair rats and hung them from his dressing room ceiling with a large sign attached reading: "Faye, scalped by Ameche."

Alice Faye and Don Ameche in *Lillian Russell*, 1940.

Before filming his next picture, Don created a scandal by passing up a role in *The Night of January 16th* because he didn't like the story. Fox had loaned Don out to Paramount for the film, but when he held firm to not doing it, the result was Paramount suing him for $170,000. Paramount contended he would have to appear in *any* film, while loaned out, but Don thought differently. He was put back on salary when Fox needed him for retakes in *Lillian Russell*. The studio rewrote the *Night* script for Robert Preston, but the situation caused a bit of PR scandal at the time. Some reporters read more into it, claiming that such an action could upset the entire studio-star system, if an actor were allowed to turn down assigned roles. Since Don was being traded for Paramount's Fred MacMurray and Ray Milland, more than one picture was disrupted by the deal. It left bad blood in both studios.

It's difficult to see what Ameche objected to in this mystery/love story, based on the Ayn Rand book. A board member of the New York Faulkner Corporation, Steve Van Ruyle (Preston's/Ameche's role) takes it upon himself to clear up the murder of their President Bjorn Faulkner, and also find out if his secretary Kit Lane (Ellen Drew) really had been in on his $3 million embezzlement scheme. Naturally, the two fall in love and ultimately ferret out the truth in Havana, and then marry. The plot may have involved corporate greed, but it was kept light enough to prompt criticism that Rand's original plot only barely survived its film treatment.

Back on the home team, Ameche had another handful of scenes in 1940's *Four Sons*; it was Eugenie Leontovich's film all the way. As poor little Frau Freida Bern she was the mother of four boys in 1936 Czechoslovakia, in Kolna near the German border. Having lost her husband to the previous war, she is in no hurry to have her family divided for another slaughter, which is what happens. At the start of the picture, she gives her son Joseph (Robert Lowery) money to go to America (his father's dream) to be an artist. But fate is not kind to the rest of her family. Karl (Alan Curtis) is more than sympathetic to the Nazi cause, even leaving his wife on their wedding night when duty calls. Chris (Ameche) is just as violently opposed to "the cause," as he vehemently disagrees that, as Karl thinks, Germany is their homeland. As situations come to a head, and prominent town leaders are killed, Chris finds himself stalked by Nazis and is forced to kill one while hiding out in a swamp. It is, of course, Karl whom he shoots. Karl's widow blows the whistle on Chris who is now hiding in the family barn and is soon shot dead. As the Nazis begin recruiting boys to train and fight, Freida loses her youngest son, Fritz (George Ernest), to the Army. With nothing left for her here, Frau Bern takes her grandson and daughter-in-law on a train ride that will hopefully lead them to America.

Screenwriter John Howard Lawson wrote the script with Maria Ouspenskaya in mind for the starring role, though studio chief Zanuck favored Jane Darwell. It turned out to be the first screen credit for European stage actress and wife of Gregory Ratoff, Eugenie Leontovich. Fox had filmed I.A.R. Wylie's story before in 1928, directed by John Ford, with the same title. Ameche did not have much to do in this one. Richard Greene had been considered for his role.

The Los Angeles Times called *Four Sons* the "most powerful picture yet introduced concerning events in Middle Europe" and that "Ameche surpasses anything he has done, and reveals a new manner." Released in May of 1940, that paper thought *Four Sons* would be a good test to see how audiences would react to present war films. *The Los Angeles Examiner* named it "a timely, up-to-the-minute and deeply moving tale" and also praised the performances. *Variety* was harder on it, calling it "grim and gloomy," but admitted the performers were "uniformly effective."

That same *Variety* also carried an article about Don Ameche appearing in Washington, D.C. on May 27, 1940 to speak before the House Interstate Commerce against the Neely bill, which would require studios to furnish complete synopses and character information to theater owners and a government committee. Don appeared as one of many spokesmen for the Screen Actors Guild saying that a good deal of improvisation and changes go into every script, so it's impossible to furnish synopses of final movie plots. Directors George Stevens and Edward Sutherland also appeared against it, as did many contract players, urged on by their studios.

As *Four Sons* was winding up, Don gave away Ann Gura, the nurse in the Ameche home, at her Van Nuys wedding to Chuck Balzer. The Ameches paid for the wedding and trousseau as their gift to her. Honore was also expecting their fourth child, Larry (Lonny), during this happy time. Thomas Anthony,

A stylish press photo of Don in the early 1940s.

born July 20, 1939, and Laurence Michael, born July 20, 1940, shared a birthday a year apart.

Everything was going right. On April 20, 1940, *Box Office Digest* proclaimed Don Ameche a member of The One Hundred Percenters, "that exclusive association of those in the creative branches of the industry whose contributions to the screen during 1939 proved profitable both to employers and exhibitors." The recognition came in the form of a listing in their Annual and a certificate listing other top box office draws, including Bing Crosby, the Marx Brothers, Paul Muni, Tyrone Power, Spencer Tracy, Mickey Rooney and others in the Actor Group.

The Grapes of Wrath would have been a very different film with Don Ameche in the lead as Tom Joad, but though Fox had briefly considered him for John Ford's sweeping 1940 production, with Henry Fonda on the lot, the part was sewn up with heavy thread.

There may have been more story than songs in 1940's *Down Argentine Way*, but it was one of Ameche's most festive Technicolor love stories. The Mack Gordon & Harry Warren songs were augmented by several Carmen Miranda specialty numbers, with her band performing with her onstage in one of the leading nightclubs there. The film was originally entitled *The South American Way*, as Zanuck had wanted to make a "South American" *Kentucky* (a popular film for them two years' previous).

The plot involves young Ricardo Quintano (Ameche), who is instructed to sell off some of his father's prizewinning horses, but on no account are they to be sold to the interested Binnie Crawford (Charlotte Greenwood), since her brother Willis stole his girl when they were in school together, so father Don Diego (Henry Stephenson) now hates all Crawfords. Complications arise when Ricardo falls for Binnie's niece, Glenda Crawford (Betty Grable), and she for him. So she has to go under the name Miss Cunningham so that Don Diego isn't hostile to her. They also don't mention that they are secretly training his great show jumper, Furioso, to be what he should've been all along: a great racehorse. When he discovers this at the film's end, Diego is furious, but calms hugely about everything, including the Crawfords, when Furioso wins the big race.

Thin, ugly Leonid Kinskey (replacing Cesar Romero, then suffering from paratyphoid) was smartly cast as the professional guide who shows Grable around Argentina's nightclubs, but ends up with Charlotte Greenwood. Alice Faye had been set for Grable's part in *Down Argentine Way*, but was too exhausted by the treadmill of picture after picture, and her recent divorce from Tony Martin. Still, Grable gave the picture a lot more *movement*. Ameche's performance was suave, smiling and showed off his natural love for horses and racing.

November 4, 1941 saw the release of one of Ameche's finest films. *That Night in Rio* was the perfect starring, dual role to highlight his comic skills. Alice Faye received top billing, but it was Don's film from the start. Not even mega-hits from Carmen Miranda—"I, Yi, Yi, Yi, Yi (I Like You Very Much)" and "Chica, Chica, Boom, Chic"—could alter that fact. Perhaps it was the sheer number of scenes he had that helped.

The musical thumps open with Carman's spirited "Chica," helped out by Larry Martin (Ameche). When Baron Manual Duarte (also Ameche) leaves the country to salvage his ailing business, his advisors, Arthur Penna (S.Z. Sakall) and Felicio Salles (Curt Bois), employ Larry to impersonate the missing Baron so that the suspicious bank men wouldn't know any trouble's brewing. Larry makes the wrong gestures in the stock market room, buying up the wrong shares, but it's trying to pretend he's the Baron at home that gets Larry into hot water with wife Baroness Cecilia Duartel (Faye), and Larry's fiery girlfriend Carmen. When the Baron returns, failed and desperate, Cecilia is confused with who's who. Luckily for all concerned Larry makes another sloppy deal (pretending to know French) and unwittingly saves the day, and the Baron's hide, from ruin. Larry and Carmen reunite, as do the once estranged Baron and wife.

Not only was Don's singing superb, but he was given some pleasant, embarrassing moments and great comedy bits to chew on, such as the ambassador's reception when he makes use of a dressing screen to conceal his double from discovery. The lively Ameche was in nearly every scene, caught between the unfailing

Down Argentine Way, 1940.

temper of Carmen and the whimsical skullduggery of making love to his beautiful "wife."

The New York Times called it an average affair, but admitted that when Carmen appears on screen, "the film *sizzles* and *scorches* wickedly." Ameche and Faye had actually performed the famous "Chica, Chica, Boom Chic," but it was naturally cut in favor of Carmen's more excited version.

Along with *A Latin from Manhattan, Ringers on Her Fingers*, and *They Met in Rio*, Fox also considered the title of The Road to Rio for this picture, but finally bowed to a possible conflict with Paramount's recent *Road to Zanzibar*. Several "Baronesses" were considered, including Paulette Goddard and Rosalind Russell, but the most heated change for this remake of *Folies Bergere de Paris* (1935, United Artists) came about from an early draft of the script which the Breen Office did not care for. The convoluted objections concerned alterations, for example, of Cecilia kissing Larry when she knew it was Larry, to make her husband jealous, in a way that would not imply "the occurrence of an illicit affair." The final version was sent in November of 1940 to the Brazilian Ambassador in Washington, D.C., who gave its approval that it would be "the kind of picture that will be helpful to North and South American relations."

Since a legal problem between BMI and ASCAP resulted in studios not being able to pitch their pictures to radio audiences, a lavish "stage show" trailer (ad), featuring $10,000 worth of feather costumes alone, had been planned for this sixth and final teaming of Faye and Ameche. It was to have been presented before the film *Tobacco Road* at New York City's Roxy Theater, but was never put before the public.

The hilarious double scene from *That Night in Rio*, 1941.

Don's real-life love affair with everything equine was flourishing by this point in his bank account. Longtime friend Richard Frank recalled, "The Frank and Ameche families spent a lot of time together. We both had swimming pools; the Ameches had cows and chickens, and even a Victory Garden of fresh vegetables. Growing your own vegetables was a way to help with the war effort. This was about 1941 and the Second World War was upon us.

"The Ameche boys and Don and Honey, with my parents George and Barbara, were going around to all kinds of parties together, with the exception of the card games which Don kept to himself. We did get to go to the horse races together, though. We could not go to the betting windows! Dad had bought into the Hollywood Park Race Track in his name and the Santa Anita Race Track in Don Ameche's name. That meant that we had Turf Club seats and a box to ourselves in both racetracks. We kids sure had a wonderful time!

"To this day Donnie, Jr. says that the best thing that his father left him with when he died was a great love for horses. He inherited the passion to develop horses to the point that they loved to run and win races for him. I have a small place in Del Mar, California near the Del Mar Race Track, and Don Jr. will still visit me down there."

Tom Ameche agreed. "Dad was involved with horses in the '30s with Bing Crosby, who built Del Mar. Dad was there all the time. That was his love, what he really enjoyed. That's what I do now, too."

That Night in Rio, 1941.

Don's third lavish musical in a row, *Moon Over Miami* in 1941, starred Betty Grable as Kay Latimer, singer in a Texas hamburger stand, who is eager to find a millionaire husband in Miami, along with the help of her sister, Barbara (Carole Landis), and their aunt Susan (Charlotte Greenwood). Posing as a wealthy woman vacationing with her secretary (Landis) and maid (Greenwood), Kay sets her sights on wealthy young Jeffrey Bolton (Robert Cummings). She hooks him easily, but along the way is chased by Don Ameche as Phil McNeil (wrongly credited as Phil O'Neil in the closing credits), Jeff's old and, it seems, equally rich friend. The trouble is, Kay ends up falling for Phil, who is actually penniless; he, too, was after a rich mate. But all's well in the end when Barbara and Jeff find they are more than compatible. Even Susan lands herself a boyfriend, the morally rigid bartender Jack O'Hara (Jack Haley), keeping comic relief and love constantly spinning the picture forward.

The New York Times called it "gaily packaged and pretty as a Fourth of July skyrocket display," which "once again shows what Technicolor can do for an otherwise very average musical comedy." Apparently, everyone *looked* better than they acted, with Ameche making "a suitably sluggish lounge-lizard."

Variety wrote on June 16, 1941 that "for the average picture patron this piece of elegant filmusical will hit close to 100% entertainment satisfaction and will prosper accordingly." It praised the cast, Florida background, lush Technicolor, and Alfred Newman's musical direction. *The Los Angeles Times* agreed that "this film really presents a bouquet of beauties, and is replete with good music, the spell of frivolity and romance, and some excellent comedy," going on to hurrah the supporting talent and Grable's dancing.

Originally called *Miami* (which would match its title song), director Walter Lang's glitzy musical, shot throughout March and April 1941, was based on Stephen Powys' play, *Three Blind Mice*, which had opened in London three years earlier. (A Fox film of the same name had been produced also three years previously, starring Loretta Young and Joel McCrea.) The breezy musical premiered in Miami on June 18, and featured a stellar score by Leo Robin and Ralph Rainger, most notably "Miami" ("Me Oh Mi-ami!" sang the harmonizers over the opening moments) and the convivial ballad, "You Started Something." Some of its scenes were shot in Florida (Ocala, Silver Springs and Cypress Gardens), but plans to shoot the majority of the film in the Sunshine State had to be scrapped due to continued bad weather.

The film was significant in its firsts: it was the screen debut of Jack Cole and his dancing company, as well as famed Fred Astaire choreographer Hermes Pan's first credited screen appearance. John Payne and Dana Andrews had been considered for male leading roles, though whether in place of Ameche or Cummings is unclear; its three leading female roles had been originally conceived for Betty Grable, Virginia Gilmore and Gene Tierney.

Ameche's name was mentioned in talks for *Cadet Girl* (1941), which could have starred Walter Huston, Jack Oakie and Alice Faye as well, but ended up as a vehicle for Carole Landis and George Montgomery. Don was also up for Paul Muni's part in *Hudson's Bay* (1941), a 17th-century biography of the French-Canadian trapper Pierre Esprit Radisson, but Zanuck decided against it. It was Muni's first freelance picture after leaving Warner Brothers.

Zane Grey's masterly action novel *Western Union*, published just three days before his death in 1939, was made into a topnotch Fox film two years later. Ameche had been set to play the lead role, Richard Blake, based loosely on Edward Creighton, a Western Union engineer who helped survey and extend the telegraph line from Omaha, Nebraska to Salt Lake City, Utah, amidst much Indian trouble. Ameche was replaced by a borrowed Robert Young (MGM). It

Grable and Ameche in *Moon Over Miami*, 1941.

would've been a handsome picture for him, supported by Randolph Scott, and quite different, being his first Western.

He had also been briefly considered for the 1939 role of Gilbert Martin in John Ford's *Drums Along the Mohawk*, a part which more aptly went to Henry Fonda.

Back to musicals, *Kiss the Boys Goodbye* was a bold comedy vehicle for spirited Mary Martin, as southern girl Cindy Lou Bethany who had come to New York City a year ago from Georgia in order to set Broadway on fire. There wasn't even a whiff of smoke yet. So when she hears about director Lloyd Lloyd's (Ameche) new show about the south, and that they are seeking a real southern belle for the lead, insidious Cindy travels down to her ol'

Southern plantation to have her relations Shanghai Lloyd and his pianist/composer friend Dick Rayburn (Oscar Levant) off the train. Staying the night in the land of Dixie, Cindy sets to singing for them, backed by a Negro chorus, who have seemed to step right out of the cotton fields. Lloyd easily sees through the devious setup and resents her strong-arming and thick magnolia accent all through the picture. Only the kind heart of Rayburn keeps her in the running for the lead. They rehearse a great striptease number, which Cindy performs on a diving board for all the New York press producer Bert Fisher (Jerome Cowan) could assemble. But, as is always the case, boy loses girl and Cindy runs crying home to Georgia. Lloyd, realizing he's falling for the girl who's shown herself a fake, follows her back home and rigs an apology with his own moving arrangement (with Negro chorus, of course), and all ends in kisses and music.

Released in 1941, *Kiss the Boys Goodbye* was based on a play by Clare Boothe Luce. The catchy songs came from director Victor Schertzinger and Frank Loesser (later, famous songwriter of *Guys and Dolls*). Don was given a single song to sing, the ballad "I'll Never Let a Day Pass By," which he also croons at the end to win the girl. He seemed to have fun in the role of put-upon director and straight man to the bad actor, but highly witty Oscar Levant, who was given manifold opportunities to dig into the piano and roll off stinging quips.

Shot during the first 29 days of July 1941, *The Feminine Touch* was easily one of Don's funniest films, placing him in the role of Digby College professor John Hathaway who is disgusted at having to compromise his principals in order to pass the dumbest (Gordon Jones) of the idiot football players in his class. At last the psychology professor snaps, quits and spirits the wife, Julie Hathaway (Rosalind Russell), off to New York City where he's determined to sell his heady text on how to beat jealousy to big-time publisher Elliott Morgan (Van Heflin). His assistant, Nellie Woods (Kay Francis), really the brains behind the outfit, loves the book, while Elliott simply loves Julie. What irks Julie most is that John practices what he preaches—he's never, *ever* jealous of his wife, so it doesn't seem to matter to him the constant, nearly stalking attention that Elliott lies on her. Julie is a simple woman, but deeply in love with John; still, she wants him to prove *his* love with a fight now and then. Meantime, John is working a lot of hours with Nellie to get the book ready; she wants the marriage chapter beefed up more, and disagrees with the concept that jealousy isn't necessary. John is surprised. "After all," he says, "the very symbol of liberty is a woman." "Yeah, but did you notice," Nellie dissents, "she's carrying a torch."

At the same time Elliott is fed up chasing Julie, whom he finally admits is "a good girl," Julie herself is fed up with John's confounded complacency. She sets the scene to make John jealous before taking an overnight bag to Elliott's secluded cabin. Nellie, finally happy that Elliott has consented to be hers (now that he thinks Julie is a cold fish), is at once disillusioned with Julie's clues leading to the cabin and forces John to take her to there. It's not until Elliott shaves his goatee (Julie hates beards) that John becomes enraged. "Why did you shave your beard

Mary Martin does not *Kiss the Boys Goodbye* in 1941.

off?!" he keeps asking, trying to knock his publisher's block off. After the men conk each other out, the women start a row, but it all finishes with smiles as Elliott and Nellie are finally married. Coming out of the Justice of the Peace, a man whistles at Julie, and John rushes up to answer the call. When he comes back with a black eye, everyone, even John, smiles brighter.

Elliott's character had originally been written with John Carroll in mind. Working titles of the film included *Female of the Species* (the title Nellie suggests for John's book), *Heartburn* and *All Woman.*

The World War II drama-romance, *Confirm or Deny*, placed Ameche as take-charge managing editor "Mitch" Mitchell of the Consolidated Press of America. It was one of his most forceful starring roles—it was *his* movie, and a welcome change from comedic parts.

It's London, 1940, and Mitchell is waiting for the greatest story of his career: the invasion of England. But on his way to work, during a blackout, he meets the girl of his dreams, cute Jennifer Carson (Joan Bennett), who is walking back from her job as teletypist for the Ministry of Information. They and everyone else nearby are forced into an Underground (subway) station where they get acquainted and finally sleep together (along with fifty other strangers). The next morning: chaos. Consolidated Press' building has been bombed to rubble, but Mitchell's confident, go-getting personality spurs everyone on to drag everything salvageable to a new location: the wine cellar of the Regency Hotel, run by Mr. Hobbs (Eric Blore). Mitchell has secured the help of Ms. Carson, who becomes increasingly taken with this Yank's bold demeanor. But when their building is also demolished, trapping the would-be lovers in alone with only a working teletype machine and invasion news that Mitchell needs to broadcast, which he hasn't been cleared by the government to broadcast, they wrestle until Mitchell locks Jennifer away among the wine. It takes the death of little Albert Perkins (Roddy McDowall), still at his post on top of the old Consolidated building, looking out for pigeons that bring news of the invasion, to bring Mitchell to his senses not to broadcast information that could tip off the Germans as to just how much the British know. Instead, he types up a stirring tribute to the lad who gave his life for his country, and wins back Jennifer's confidence, as the couple are dug out with jackhammers.

The end of *The Feminine Touch*, 1941.

It's apparent that Ameche thoroughly enjoyed carrying this film, shouting out orders to everyone, but with enough sprinkled romance to make him likeably human. Tyrone Power had been originally set to star as Mitch, but was soon replaced. Fritz Lang had also been scheduled to direct the picture, but after six days of shooting, suffered gall bladder problems and was replaced by Archie Mayo. A special trailer was to have been produced with Ameche, Gene Tierney from *Belle Starr* and Anne Baxter of *Swamp Water* discussing their upcoming roles, but it was never made. *Confirm or Deny* was shot during August and September of 1941 and released on the 12th of December.

It's a shame that *Song of the Islands*, 1942, had been rewritten and recast to star Betty Grable, Victor Mature and Jack Oakie, when it could have starred Alice Faye, Don Ameche and the Ritz Brothers. Originally, Joan Davis had been set to star, but the Hawaiian musical was rewritten for the *You Can't Have Everything* team. Then rewritten again without them all.

Publicity at the time indicated that Ameche was to have had the Cesar Romero (Monte Blanca) role in *Week-end in Havana*, starring Alice Faye, Carmen Miranda and John Payne, but was again recast. Early screenplay drafts of *A Gentleman at Heart* were also written for Ameche in the lead (to co-star with Simone Simon or Annabella), but the role of the New York City bookie finally went to Cesar Romero in 1942.

For Thanksgiving, Don and Honore took some time off to visit Dubuque again, staying with her parents at 1206 West 14th Street, just after attending the Notre Dame-Illinois University football game at Champaign on Saturday.

Confirm or Deny, 1941.

Confirm or Deny, 1941.

They were supposed to make a two-week vacation out of it, but ended up only staying four days, as Don had an urgent summons to fly back to Hollywood for a new picture. While in Dubuque, Don visited his old stomping ground, Loras College, guest of the President, the Very Reverend M.J. Martin. If his schedule could be arranged, Don promised to come back for the dedication of the new stadium.

The new picture:

Henry Fonda's lovable, lazy hick charm carried *The Magnificent Dope* (1942) into a Frank Capra-like satire of Everyman vs. The Establishment, proving the popular moral: even if you're outnumbered, you can still be right. Go-getter Dwight Dawson (Ameche) finds that his motivational system of turning ordinary people into high-powered successes is going down the tubes. Bills are stacking up and the bank wants to foreclose. Luckily, Claire Harris (Lynn Bari), his sweetheart and secretary, comes up with a million bucks worth of free advertising in the form of a contest to find the perfect Dawson subject (actually, the laziest man on earth). Thaddeus Windship Page (Fonda) is found and gratefully accepts the $500 prize-money which he'll use to buy his small town a fire engine; but he has no interest in the Dawson course. He's happy the way he is—lazy and very content. Dawson and Horace Hunter (Edward Everett Horton), Dawson's main instructor, find out that Thaddeus (Tad for short) is in love with Claire, and convinces Tad that she'd only fall for a success. Tad takes the course, but has better luck teaching his relaxation techniques to the many stressed city folks he comes in contact with. To become a success, he takes a long, meaningless title at a company selling insurance. No one wants insurance, so Dawson tricks him into selling a fat policy to a man who has been turned down *many* times for high blood pressure. After buying the fire engine outright with his commission, Tad finds out the truth

E.E. Horton, Henry Fonda and Ameche in *The Magnificent Dope*, 1942.

and has to cure his client of high blood pressure before the examining doctor comes. The policy is approved. Tad gets the fire engine, and the girl, and Dawson gets a new, lucrative lease on life and work: teaching Tad's roll-your-head-around relaxation bit to full classrooms.

Edward Everett Horton may have been vastly underused in this one, but Don Ameche had something to shout about, almost continuously, barking out orders and taking charge in a comic counterpart to his dominating presence in *Confirm or Deny*. Perhaps his best scene came at his birthday party, when Tad unexpectedly shows up, and so Dawson has to keep everyone from mentioning the fact that Claire and he are an item. The look on Lynn Bari's face when Don sings "Shortenin' Bread" for the fifth time, just to keep ladies from talking about their impending marriage, is priceless.

Working titles for the film included *Lazy Galahad* and *Strictly Dynamite*. The Hays Office objected to the final title, wanting it renamed to *The Magnificent Stupe*, but the studio won the argument. The film once had to be shut down for three days due to dope Fonda breaking his finger while working on a tractor at home. He and Ameche both appeared in the *Lux Radio Theatre* broadcast of the story on September 28, 1942.

Director Harold Schuster scored a jocose hit with the not-wisely-titled *Girl Trouble* (1942), starring Don as Pedro Sullivan, a reforming playboy from Brazil who must secure a loan with American banks in order to keep his father's faith in him and keep the family company in business. Joan Bennett as June Delaney gives the farce a deadpan class, and flighty Billie Burke as Celeste Rowland supports the romantic comedy with her usual light-headed zeal.

June has lost most of her money due to foreign investments which the war destroys. She's forced to rent out her New York apartment to handsome Pedro, and stays on as his maid when he assumes she is Ms. Delaney's personal maid. It brings in a few bucks more, though she still has her pride and keeps her identity a secret, causing much confusion and comedy along the way among her friends and rival socialite Helene Reynolds (Helen Martin). Naturally, Pedro and June fall in love as time goes on, with June saving Pedro's business by blackmailing a gun-collecting banker (Frank Craven) into trading a loan for an old blunderbuss she found in her father's trunk.

The romantic comedy would have been more aptly named if they had kept one of their alternate titles—*Man from Brazil*, or *Between You and Me*—but *Girl Trouble* was yet another light-hearted Fox lark for Ameche to showcase his peeved fire and comic timing.

Gregory Ratoff produced and directed the crowd-pleasing *Something to Shout About* in 1943, with Ameche loaned out to Columbia for this Cole Porter movie musical. The film contained one of Porter's most beautiful wartime ballads, the Oscar-nominated "You'd Be So Nice to Come Home To," introduced by Janet Blair (Ameche sings a little of it too, near the end of the picture). Mary Martin had been considered for her role, and the film marked the screen debut of Lily Norwood (later and better known as Cyd Charisse) as "Lily."

The story begins with poor, drunk, has-been Broadway producer Willard Samson (William Gaxton) being shanghaied off a train and sobered up to meet one-time chorus girl Donna Davis (Cobina Wright, Jr.) who, after a two-million dollar divorce settlement, wants to produce a musical so she can become New York's greatest star. "You'll be the sculptor, I'll be the clay," she says. Samson thoughtfully replies, "I hope I don't mold you into a bust." Clutching at the opportunity like a full bottle of rye, Samson agrees but soon rues the situation: Donna is pushy and has *no* talent.

One unforgivable act she commits is hiring his old New York City PR man, Ken Douglas (Ameche) to build her up. Ken has just fallen for beautiful songwriter/music teacher Jeanie Maxwell (Blair) and tries to get her songs into the show. But egotist Donna Davis has eyes for Ken too, and never likes to be upstaged by true talent.

When Ken suggests an outdoor photo shoot for Donna in the country, Samson has the pair arrested so he can sneak in Jeanie as the lead to the show, *Something to Shout About*. Donna turns up at the wrong moment and inserts herself back into the show. It flops. Jeanie returns to Altoona, PA, but after a talk with old friend Larry Martin (Jack Oakie), who runs a boarding house for fantastic but out of work actors, Ken gets the idea to use the rest of the two weeks' theater rental to put on an old-fashioned vaudeville show, filled with the best acts in the house. Ken races to bring Jeanie back, but she doesn't return immediately, only at the end of opening night, singing "I Always Knew," with Ken joining in. The show is a smash.

Thematically, like *You Can't Have Everything*, it was a vigorous musical and one of Ameche's best (if it could have had the Ritz Brothers, it might've been perfect). Don was on form all the way, with good material (including another in-joke about inventing the phone, this time delivered by Don personally), though most of the songs went to Janet Blair.

To be a film star requires the hours of a company CEO and an understanding family. The incredible stress of making three and four pictures a year, coupled with the tenacious promotion required for the films *and* himself, kept Don away from home more than he, and Honey, would have liked. Her feelings of neglect and distance from his glittery world only increased as his roles attracted more stature and recognition. So, she tried filling her life with her children and their house with guests. And, too often, reporters, furnished by the studio.

The Ameches would sometimes have guests in from their Chicago radio days, seeking a door into the film world. There was always someone foraging in the icebox or helping wash the dishes. People would come, go, dress and do as they please. Honore wore slacks, a jersey and her hair in its usual braids for what seemed like constant interviews. Naturally, the one truth she could never tell was her disillusionment with Hollywood, even though she herself was a celebrity by

Cobina Wright, Jr., Don Ameche, Janet Blair, Jack Oakie and Veda Ann Borg in
***Something to Shout About*, 1943. Courtesy of Laura Wagner.**

association. (In a March 15, 1943 *Life* mustard ad, she was quoted as saying, "We use Coleman's in our cooking. The extra flavor it gives always makes a hit!")

"I was afraid," she told one reporter, "for a little while, when we first came here from Chicago. I was afraid then, but the house we have here made me understand I had nothing to fear.

"You see, in Chicago we had always lived in a little place. And when we came out here, we took a little place too, because the rentals were terrific! Don wanted a bigger place, but I said no, and stuck to it. But it was damp there, and finally we had to leave because of my sinus trouble. So we had to move here. And it costs three times what we paid in Chicago! That was when I was afraid.

"But it hasn't made a particle of difference in the way we live—or in Don. That's why I'm so sure that no matter how much money Don makes in the movies or how famous he becomes he'll always—we'll always—be the same.

"If we didn't lay his clothes out, he would go out wearing one red sock and one blue, the coat of one suit, the trousers of another. And yet he is as careless and casual as a six-year-old about what he considers 'unimportant matters.' And he considers himself unimportant. Not that he is falsely modest. It just wouldn't even occur to him that there is anything to be modest about. He thinks of himself as a business man with a job to do. He tells people that his ambition is to be 'a good provider for my family.' And he is. Vanity just *isn't*, where Don is concerned.

"He never buys himself anything. Yes, he did, too, I take that back. He bought himself his car. And he's mad about the races. And he has a passion for barber-pole striped ties. Otherwise, he has no extravagances. I have to do his shopping or there just wouldn't be any done. I even bought his suits, few as there were, before we came to Hollywood. Now that he is here, he realizes that he must dress well, so he goes to a tailor. The other day, he wanted a pair of shorts to play tennis in. He didn't have any. He was wearing a pair of long white ducks. He got a pair of scissors and then and there, cut them off to his knees. The effect was sort of scalloped, to say the least.

"No, Don won't change. We won't change. I'll tell you why. It's because the babies are our whole lives. We're interested in them and each other. He isn't one bit different from the boy I used to go with, meet Saturday afternoons for the movies or to visit an ice-cream parlor. Seldom both. Because we never had more than fifty cents to spend. It never mattered. It doesn't now. Don would tell me what a fine lawyer he was going to be and I believed in him. I knew he would make good then, as now.

"We've never had any money to spare. We're saving, putting everything we can into trust funds and annuities and educational funds for the children, so that, in a few years, we'll be able to travel and see the world and have some fun. There have been the heavy expenses of the babies' births. Don has bought a small ranch for Grandma and Grandpa Ameche. Then there are his younger sisters and brothers, most of them still in school. They come out here in the summer. This ring (star sapphire with small diamonds), Don gave me this last Christmas. I was supposed to have had it Christmas before last. But we had the baby instead.

"Then, after we married and Don's work increased and the babies came and I was so ill and Don was doing two jobs, his and mine, Gabriel came to help us out. I don't know now what we could do without him. He cooks like a streak. He takes care of the babies as efficiently as I do. He takes care of Don's clothes and is with him at the studio most of the time lately. Don, by the way, is no businessman at all. He knows nothing whatsoever about insurance and income taxes and things like that. I take care of all that sort of thing."

Troutman agreed. "Well, he has no realization of the value of money in a business sense, if you care to consider that a fault. Money to him is something to be made easily, then circulated as quickly as possible. To Honore Ameche it is something to be saved, too. There is still much of it to be put away after everybody has been taken care of. Don has a great dislike for routine and frets under it. He lives by impulse. There are times when he has need of a more practical nature.

"Volatile, mercurial, he lives from one extreme to the other. There is no halfway point. The most constant thing about him is gay recklessness about life, his laughter, his optimism, but there are brief times when he is steeped in melancholy, morose, silent, shut off from the world."

Don and Honey on the town.

It was that at-times aloof Ameche nature that kept Honore such a necessary part of his Hollywood home life. She continued in her interview: "Anne and I tackle his fan mail. Anne came to us while we were in Chicago. And she and I divide up the work of the house and the babies. If Anne is busy cooking or something, I bathe and dress the babies. If Anne is with them, I do the washing and ironing. They are in no sense of the word servants. They are members of our family. They all, Don, Gabe, Anne, the babies, call me Honey. We all call Don 'Daddy.'

"Anne and Gabriel have their friends in, as we do ours, together or not as the case may be. They dance and play games and use the radio in the living room. Sometimes we get someone to stay with the children and all four of us go to the movies. Saturday nights we often pile into the car and drive to Venice and go on the merry-go-rounds and to the fortune tellers and everywhere. We have a lot of fun. We just all pitch in together and get the chores done. Don does his share, too, if he has to. Of course, he doesn't have much time now, what with the studio and the radio work. But he's just as handy around the house and with the babies, as any one of us. And he's the most marvelous disciplinarian. I give him credit for the good behavior of our first child. I was so ill after his birth that the full care of the baby fell to Don. He did everything for him. And I must say he did a masterly job.

"There is never an unkind word in our home. It is the one thing that Don and I demand of our home—that it be perfectly harmonious. We wouldn't have regular servants now, not even if we needed them, not while Gabe and Anne are with us. It might place them in sort of equivocal positions. If and when Don and I do have company and want to be sort of 'elegant,' Anne and Gabe don uniforms. Gabe cooks, and they serve a marvelous dinner with all the finesse of accomplished retainers. They understand that this is part of the set-up, and they love it and enjoy the masquerade and never for one instant step out of character. It's simply a case of our being one for all and all for one, and there's never been one uncomfortable moment for any of us. Don dislikes the idea of servants. There is something in his sensitiveness which rebels against giving orders, drawing that sharp distinction between himself and his fellow man or woman. He just can't be the overlord. The autocrat isn't in him.

"There's one more thing that will show you. Don could give up his radio work now, if he wanted. He could get along very nicely without the money because he is making more than enough in pictures. And most men would give up radio, too, because that work is a great deal harder than picture work. It takes a fearful nervous toll which Don doesn't feel in his picture work. Yet, he doesn't give it up. He won't give it up. He never will."

He would come to lean on it heavily as his film career began to slip away—temporarily.

Chapter Five

Heaven Can Wait

Don Ameche thought that he reached the peak of his career in 1943 with one film. No awards were lined up for him in *Heaven Can Wait*, but it was by far his favorite role of his career (and, he said, his last prime part at Fox), partly because of the sharp mind of its director, Ernst Lubitsch (responsible for *To Be or Not To Be, Ninotchka* and other earlier classics). Nominated for Best Picture, Best Director and Best Color Cinematography, Ameche was strangely again passed over for any Oscar honors.

The flashback movie begins with 70-year-old Henry Van Cleve (Ameche) meeting with Satan (Laird Cregar) to talk his way into a deserved place in Hell. He describes his life to the well-dressed devil: born in 1872, he discovers girls at an early age, which includes his French tutor who doesn't mind romancing a fourteen-year-old. When he is 26, he falls heavily and immediately for Martha Strabel (Gene Tierney), the fiancée of his smug cousin Albert (Allyn Joslyn). When he met her at a bookstore, he didn't realize she was betrothed to Albert, but Henry doesn't let that stop him. When he finds that she returns his love, they elope. But he doesn't know how to treat a woman; he's the neglecting, charming kind who sees nothing wrong with paying other women attention. On his 36th birthday, she leaves him. He follows her to her parents' house and lays on the charm again—which is certainly mixed with real love and a sense of self-loathing. The couple again elope, and the years pass. Their son, Jack (Michael Ames), takes after his father, though as more years pass, the roles reverse: after Martha passes away, Henry returns to his philandering ways at age 60, while Jack is now a respected businessman. Henry can't help himself, and dies 10 years later. Satan is unmoved by "his class of people" and urges him to apply elsewhere. Henry is surprised and disappointed that he should not pay for a life of cheating and excess. But the horned executive assures him that there is a special someone waiting for him in another place. Henry nervously, happily realizes who it is, and takes the long elevator UP to meet her.

The movie's working title was *Birthday*, based on an English version of a Lazlo Bus-Feketes Broadway play of the same name which had opened in 1934. Ginger Rogers had been considered for the female lead, but who was to star as Henry was much more uncertain. Some sources state that the part had been written for

Fredric March or Rex Harrison, while Lubitsch himself had been very interested in Joseph Cotten. Though Reginald Gardiner had once been announced in the role, Zanuck requested that Ameche test for Lubitsch. The director (his first Fox and first color film) was impressed, and asked Don to shave his mustache so that he might portray a man of 23. He was required to age 70 years, turning the film into what director Lubitsch called "a three-haircut picture." To achieve the oldest look at age 70, the medical science department was asked to help. One thing Don had to endure besides the grayed, thinning hair and padding was drops of dionin in each eye, which contracted and washed out the irises, as elder people have. The effect did no harm and wore off in a few hours.

Heaven Can Wait, 1943.

Don Ameche joined Maureen O'Hara for the *Lux Radio Theatre* production of the film, broadcast on October 10, 1943. With it came the end of an era in Ameche's life.

In a promo piece in June of that year, Don told *Movie Show* magazine: "Two months ago when I was doing make-up tests for *Heaven Can Wait* (in which I age from fifteen to seventy, and no cracks, please) I announced with sincere fervor that I was giving up smoking until after Lent.

"'Ha,' sneered one of the technicians on the picture, and a good pal of mine, 'I'll believe it when I see it, Don.'

"'All right, bud,' I said. 'This time I mean it. I'll bet you ten bucks.' And believe me, I was really convinced that it was the safest bet I've made since I bet on *Whirlaway* to win.

"The picture started, and I actually had to look at a cigar for two whole weeks. What I went through! Those boys took special delight in lighting up right under my nose. At long last, I thought, I'm getting character. I was as pleased as punch with myself. 'Look at me,' I said to everyone I could corner, 'I don't smoke anymore. Just made up my mind to give it up for Lent. Don't miss it at all.' They tell me I was thoroughly obnoxious.

"Well, there is a scene in *Heaven Can Wait* where I am supposed to smoke a cigar. Wait till I get my hands on that author. The day we were ready to shoot the scene I saw my pal, the technician, watching me with an evil gleam in his eyes, and an itching palm. But I fooled him. I held the cigar in my hand. I even put it in my mouth when the script called for it, but I absolutely did not smoke it. Never have I felt so much like an early Christian martyr. I could even feel my wings sprouting. At the end of the take director Lubitsch glared at me indignantly. 'What ees dees, Mestaire Ameche?' he demanded. 'You don't smoke de ceegar? You fake somethink in a Lubitsch peecture? Nevaire, Mestaire Ameche. Next take you smoke de ceegar. I inseest on realism.'

"'But Mr. Lubitsch,' I argued. 'I've sworn off smoking for Lent. If I smoke this cigar now I'll take up smoking again as sure as God made little apples.'

"'So?' countered Lubitsch.

"So, I'm smoking again.

"Well, I decided, if I can't give up smoking, at least I can give up those 'corny jokes' my friends are always kidding me about. I love to play jokes on my co-workers. I always have. Sort of a hangover from boyhood I guess. I've never understood why the minute an actor comes on a set he feels that he has to be pompous, dignified, and as stuffy as an old mattress. I think a sense of humor is just as necessary in your work as it is in your home. But picture-making is extremely difficult these days under wartime conditions, so I decided that I would be, if not a pompous actor, at least a serious one.

"That lasted all of one day. The second day on the set I had a scene to do where I step inside a telephone booth in Wanamaker's and try to make a phone call. When I picked up the receiver, whose voice should come out of it but Gene Tierney's, flippantly inquiring, 'Is this the Don Ameche who invented the telephone?' I'll never live down the telephone gag I guess. I've resigned myself to that. But if Gene Tierney can play jokes, well—

"Gene, like a lot of other Hollywood people, bought herself some chickens not long ago, so she could at least count on having eggs during the meat shortage. She bought some beautiful white leghorns, and they promptly started laying six eggs a day, and I've never seen anyone as proud as Gene. Then the California rains started, and when it rains in California, brother, it rains. Gene became so nervous she could hardly keep her mind on her lines. Between takes she'd run to the stage door to look out mournfully at the downpour. 'My poor little chickens,' she'd groan, 'they'll drown. I know they'll drown. Won't this rain ever stop?

My poor wet babies. They'll have pneumonia.'

"Several days I went through this with Gene. Imagine having a beautiful star in your arms who is far more interested in her leghorns than she is in your embraces. One day I learned that Gene had a nine o'clock call, but that I wasn't needed on the set until two. It was still raining. On my way to the studio that day I stopped by Gene's house, gathered up her precious chickens, and put them in a coop I had had specially made on my ranch. I delivered the coop filled with squawking wet feathers to Gene's fluffy dressing room on the set. I attached a card which read, 'You've worried so much about these darned birds I thought you'd like to have them with you, Don.'

"At present—give me some wood to knock on, quick—I have no butter or milk or egg problems. My wife and I, and our four boys, Donny, Ronny, Tommy and Lonny, live on a ranch near Encino, in the ranch house Al Jolson and Ruby Keeler built. My servants left, of course, for defense jobs months ago, all except the nurse for the baby, and the hired man who looks after the ranch and milks my two cows. We have closed the downstairs of the house, all except the kitchen, for the duration. Recently, my four boys came down with chicken pox all at the same time, and poor Mrs. Ameche, what with cooking and nursing, had her hands full.

"I stayed at the studio during the contagious period. The first Sunday I was allowed to come home I certainly expected my beloved family to fall into my open arms. But instead, the boys sort of stood back and stared at me as if they had never seen me before. Has chicken pox brought on amnesia, I thought? Don't they recognize their adoring father? Then I understood. I had shaved off my mustache. My children had never seen me without my mustache.

"I think you will like **Heaven Can Wait** very much. It's the best picture I've had in ages. I've had quite a few stinkers, as you well know, this past year. Nobody's fault. Actors go through cycles. I've had my bad luck, so now I'm going to have good luck again.

"One scene in the picture is very dear to me. It's the scene where I follow Gene into Brentano's bookstore in New York and pretend to be a book salesman so I can get acquainted with her. I was once a book salesman in real life. While I was studying at the University of Wisconsin, I got a part-time job as a salesman in a bookstore near the University. The first day I was terribly enthused. I had always liked to read, and I felt very important surrounded by so many books. I decided then and there that I would make selling the right books to the right people my life's work. Very conscientiously I took home all the best sellers and read them carefully so I could discuss them intelligently with my prospective customers. I hadn't been there a week when one day a nice-looking, well-dressed woman picked up a book that was receiving much publicity at the time and asked me, 'Young man, would you recommend this book?'

"'No, I wouldn't,' I said frankly. 'It is badly written. It is mawkish and sentimental. You wouldn't like it at all. Now let me see, I think I have something here that would interest you a great deal more.'

"All right, you know the rest. The woman was the author, checking up on sales. And not only was she one of the most popular fiction writers of the day, but she just happened to be a personal friend of my boss's. So ended my literary life."

Once *Heaven* could *Wait*, Ameche considered his glory days as an actor finished. He would receive a few more starring roles at Fox, but was becoming increasingly dissatisfied with what was chosen for him; it had been bugging him for some time. He admitted that he was happier to work than to demand roles of more importance, but as early as 1940, he told *Picture Play* magazine, "The struggle for survival runs strong in every human being. And the fight for self-preservation is one of the instincts. This pertains to the actor as well as anyone else. It becomes a vital necessity once one has gotten a start in his work. If he doesn't fight for this cause, he might as well quit the game because no one will take up the battle for him.

"An actor is often accused of lacking judgement in determining what roles are good for him and which ones are bad. It is said that he is too close to his own work to have perspective. This may be true. None of us is infallible in making decisions. However, there is one point of which an actor should be certain, and that is his sympathy for a character, his feeling that he is suited to the part. If he isn't interested in the man he's supposed to play, if he does not believe in the story or the part itself, then how can he give a sincere performance?

"In pictures, the player can't afford to have many strikeouts. There is an old saying that 'You're as good as your last film,' and while this may be exaggerated, it is worth remembering.

"I honestly appreciate the trust of the people who have been nice enough to like my work, and they are the ones who influence my decisions. And when I say that I don't intend to break faith with them—insofar as this is possible—I mean it. An acting career to me means just one thing—entertaining people, and keeping their confidence by doing the sort of parts they want me to play. I felt *The Night of January 16th* did not fill these requirements."

Don had also been under consideration, along with Franchot Tone, for the lead role of architect David Naughton in the domestic drama *Claudia* (1943). Dorothy McGuire and Robert Young ended up playing the young couple in Fox's film, an adaptation of Rose Franken's play based on the popular short stories published in *Redbook* magazine.

His studio also planned to use Don in a film entitled *Diplomatic Courier*, to be directed by Harold Schuster or Louis de Rochement sometime between 1942 and 1945, but the only film of that name to show up was in 1952, with Tyrone Power and Patricia Neal in Fox's espionage flick.

Whether he felt it or not, Ameche's versatility *was* often exercised in these gloomy days. Some consider Fox's *Wing and a Prayer* to be Ameche's last truly great film of his golden era. Indeed, the World War II drama starring Dana Andrews, William Eythe and an aircraft carrier full of actors was a peerless presentation of flyers' anxious lives and the dangerous missions they faced. Though Don Ameche had top billing, the war was the movie's true protagonist.

The mission: to engage but not combat the enemy by air and water, to lure the Japanese into a false sense of security. Taking place three months after the attack on Pearl Harbor, their planes are merely to fly back and report, so that the enemy will think the United States' fleet is scattered and their moral shattered. But it is a secret mission, to prevent leaks. Not even the men who are risking their lives are allowed to know why they can't attack, which causes extreme resentment and anxiety among Torpedo Squadron 5. The ensemble film was led by Ameche as hardened Air Officer, Commander "Bingo" Harper, in charge of the squadron and its morale through these uncertain times. His best scene comes at the end when he has to bark out his philosophy of command: he is tough on his boys because he is *responsible* for them. When the men find out their true purpose, nerves relax, simply because now they *know* what they're doing.

Wing and a Prayer, 1944.

Wing and a Prayer, 1944.

As Harper walks away from the briefing room, having cheered up the pilots by telling them that two of their thought-lost comrades were picked up by a destroyer, a rousing "Anchors Aweigh" begins as Harper marches through the rain-swept deck to get to the radio room to request "orders for tomorrow." The war never ends, but the score and Ameche's forceful nature make the film's end, and 1944, a time from which to gather hope.

It isn't a melodrama filled with dialogue of the men and the lives they've left behind, but the mechanics of fighting a war, day by day. "For the purposes of military security," states the prologue which follows the opening credits, "the names of men and some of the ships in this motion picture are fictitious, but the important incidents and the heroism are history." The film was subtitled *The Story of Carrier X*, and earlier had working titles of *Queen of the Flat Tops* and *Torpedo Squadron 8*. Originally Fox wanted the story to follow a more historical account of the Battle of Midway (the 1976 movie *Midway* held the same tone of "war as the star" that *Wing and a Prayer* enjoyed), but as all fliers in that squadron except Ensign George Gay were killed, "a certain high Government official" thought that such a picture, during wartime, would have a defeatist attitude. However, the film did have the distinction of containing the first-ever War Department-approved footage "of any action on one of the new post-Pearl Harbor fleet plane carriers." Some sequences had been shot on location in San Diego, California, but much of the carrier scenes were shot aboard the USS Yorktown II. That realism, combined with a lot of well-filmed stock shots, made *Wing and a Prayer* one of Hollywood's best wartime propaganda films, achieving an Oscar nomination for Best Original Screenplay for Jerome Cady (coauthor of *Call Northside 777*).

Don told *Movie Show* magazine, "It's the most comfortable role I've ever had. In other pictures I've had to wear high collars, starched collars, and celluloid collars, while I went around inventing things, or playing the lives of practically everyone except Don Ameche. I've had to wear skin-tight britches, snug-fitting jackets, and shoes sixteen inches high. But in this picture I play a Navy air officer in the Southwest Pacific, and I go through the entire picture in khaki work clothes, with sleeves rolled up and no tie. I play a kind of a heavy too, which I like for a change.

"A lot of the actual shots of the fighting at Midway are used in the picture. So we spend a lot of time sitting around on the set between shots. The other day a bunch of us got to talking about the jobs we used to have, and how we certainly never expected that they would lead to movie contracts. Dana Andrews said he worked as a grease monkey in a gas station to pay for singing and acting lessons. Charles Bickford said he was a discharged lieutenant in the Engineers after the last war and got into acting because it was the easiest thing to do. Bill Eythe said, 'I was a guide in Radio City. I developed my voice telling the folks about the murals and the architecture.'

"'I'm willing to bet I had the softest job of all,' I boasted. 'I was a real, honest-to-goodness mattress tester. While I was at the University of Wisconsin, I had to take jobs during the summer to help pay my tuition. One summer I got a job as a mattress tester. I got paid so much an hour for sleeping on various kinds of mattresses while scientific people took readings from wires attached to my neck and ankles. It was nice work, but I lost it because I did my job too well. After I tested a mattress, I would fall asleep on it. After one too many of these naps I got fired. It was the nicest job I ever had.'"

Ameche next stepped quickly into another shade of wartime drama, *Happy Land*, shot over June and July 1944. Based on the novel of the same name by MacKinlay Kantor, this fantasy tearjerker examined an increasingly common tragedy: losing your son to the war.

The film opens with pharmacist Lew Marsh (Ameche) receiving word that his only child, Rusty (Richard Crane), has been killed in action. As grief overwhelms him, Lew draws into himself, not even talking to his wife Agnes (Frances Dee). Only when the ghost of his grandfather, Edward Marsh (Harry Carey), comes does Lew revisit his and Rusty's past lives and find strength in knowing he raised a good boy. His closure is complete when Rusty's friend Tony Cavrek (Harry Morgan) arrives at Marsh's drugstore to talk about Rusty. Tony has no family of his own, but Lew is happy to offer Tony some wine and a nice meal at his house; it's the start of an imminent, loving friendship.

Not such a *Happy Land*, 1944.

Don also starred in its *Lux Radio Theatre* adaptation, broadcast on April 10, 1944.

Natalie Wood was discovered during the filming of *Happy Land*. According to newspapers of the day, as the townsfolk of Santa Rosa, California gathered around to watch a scene between Don and Harry Carey, four-year-old Natalie Wood (Natasha Gurdin) broke away from her mother and ran up to director Irving Pichel, who thought she was so cute he gave her a bit part in what became her first film. In the scene, Natalie drops her ice cream cone and Don brings her another.

Nineteen-forty-four also brought Fox the splashy, though dull Technicolor musical *Greenwich Village*, stocked with bright songs by Nacio Herb Brown and Leo Robin. It's 1922. Stepping off the tour bus into New York City's Greenwich Village, Kenneth Harvey (Ameche) ambles into Danny's Den, a nightclub run by Danny O'Mara (William Bendix) during the days of Prohibition. Ken inadvertently flashes a roll of hundreds at singer Princess Querida (Carmen

Miranda), which immediately procures him a seat at Danny's table. Thinking the suave stranger is loaded, Danny puts in his pitch about the new musical he's hoping to open soon to combat Ziegfeld's current theatrical reign. But the spell is broken when Bonnie Watson (Vivian Blaine) takes the stage to sing. Bonnie and Ken begin to fall for each other once he tells her of his dreams of being a classical composer. He has come from Wichita, Kansas, where he taught music at a small college, to interest music publishers in his new concerto. Alas, concerto is a dirty word among publishers—they want popular songs, as does Danny for his show. Ken pens a few new ditties, at the same time trying to interest the great conductor Kavosky (Emil Rameau) in his classical piece. Danny knows he will lose Ken's music in the show if Kavosky wants him, so he pushes the rehearsals quicker to premier quicker. He needn't have worried. Hofer (Felix Bressart) was lying when he told Ken that Kavosky would produce the concerto at Carnegie Hall; all Hofer wanted was a fee for orchestrating, after which he quickly skipped out with Ken's $3,500 check.

Happier here than he seemed in *Greenwich Village*, 1944.

At rehearsal, featuring a hot black jazz number, Bonnie admits her feelings for Ken to Danny. It softens Danny, and he has one of his strong-arm boys find Hofer and return the dough. After a few more incidents, including Princess Querida having Ken arrested so he can't run back to his hometown (thinking that Bonnie had been part of Hofer's shakedown plot), Ken sees the show, which begins with a glitzy opening of his concerto featuring three grand pianos on stage. A rousing "Gimme a Bandana Bandana" later, the ballad, now titled "Whispering," from Ken's concerto, is sung by Bonnie. She runs into the wings and kisses Ken into THE END.

The film was a pleasing bit of fun, but Don did not seem terribly joyful or energetic in his non-singing role (he did sing a little at the piano early on). The script and pace lacked the punch of *That Night in Rio* and his and the studio's earlier efforts, but contained some good business, ably supplied by Bendix, such as throwing Ziegfeld's talent scout (all dolled up in drag at the costume ball thrown to raise money for the show) out the door.

Ameche and Linda Darnell had been set for the leads in *Pin-Up Girl*, under the working title of *Imagine Us*, when it was still wholly based on Libbie Block's short story. But the studio decided to cash in on Grable's popular WWII pin-up status, and a new script was begun.

With that, Don Ameche's tenure at 20th Century-Fox came to a close.

It was also around this time that the Ameche family unit finally split up. Donnie, Ronny (and later Tommy and Lonnie), along with friend Richard Frank, had been sent off to boarding school: St. John's Military Academy. The young Ameches did not enjoy their time there.

Don, Jr. recalled, "We went to boarding school all our lives. From the time I was a freshman in high school, I went to school in Iowa and I was gone all year. I did spend two or three of the summers at home, but once I was a senior in high school, I had been gone all the time. So the only part of the entertainment side that we were exposed to with any great extent was very early in his movie career, the late '30s and early '40s. We went home for Christmas and things like that."

Richard Frank also enlisted in the Sisters of Mercy at St. John's Military Academy, in 1941, and graduated as a First Lieutenant in 1950. "My father had connections with Father Cassasa, through Don Ameche, so what better way to get a guy to focus then under the patient guidance of the good Fathers at a Catholic University."

According to Frank, "The place did not seem to be hard on the Ameche boys. There was no fuss made about any of the kids. The newspaper bunch was not very active at the time, I guess. We all lived there and came home only on the month-ends, that is if we were not on detention for getting too many demerits for misbehaving. All the kids were friends and the teachers who were 'Sisters of Mercy' in the Catholic church and the staff treated everyone as children of God. All equal.

"Phil Harris's son was there, as well as the Crosby boys, Gary, Philip, Dennis and Lindsay, all there with me. Dennis DeConciene and Louie Caratan had famous fathers as well as Ted Fio Rito, Jr."

Tom Ameche recalled, "I went with Larry to St. John's Military Academy in Los Angeles and from there we were sent to Dubuque, Iowa. Meech [Don, Jr.] was there also, he was in high school, we were in grade school. I stayed with my grandparents there. I got asthma and they sent me to Brofeet Preparatory College in Phoenix, Arizona, so I spent five or six or seven years there before I went in the Navy."

Richard Frank stated that "when we came home for the holidays the Ameches and the Franks went back to New York to visit Monty Proser at his Copacabana restaurant. We also hung out with Benny Bennit and visited the main theaters around town. (I remember that the priest at Saint John's Military Academy used to only allow us to go see only the films that had the highest 'decency' ratings that were approved by the church.)"

Don, Jr. has no regrets and loves his father, but believes that balancing a roomful of boys and a film career was just too hard on both his parents. In an obvious morality piece written for *Photoplay* in July 1944, Don Ameche, or someone under his guidance, penned "My Commandments for My Children," which capsulated his individualistic feelings on child rearing.

"When I use the word 'commandments' in the title of this article, I do so for want of a better one to describe the means of pointing out a pattern of life and character which I hope my children will follow. For I do not believe any human being has the right to give commandments to another under normal times and circumstances. Parents can only plan for their children, hope for them, pray for them, counsel and guide them. This, rather than an arbitrary laying down of commandments, is what Honore and I try to do for our sons when we say:

"*They must laugh.* This may seem a trivial thing to put first in the raising of children. But it isn't. For the spirit of joyousness, the quality of being merry about things is the most important one we can wish for those we love. The very sound of laughter is a heartening, healthy thing in your house, or mine—or in the house of life. After all, what distinguishes a happy from an unhappy person, an extrovert from an introvert, is the ability to laugh—at himself as well as it, or with, others.

"*They must move often.* By this I mean that I hope they will not live all through their childhoods in this one farmhouse we call home, in this one town or even in this one state or country. Basically, I am all for the 'old homestead' idea. There is something rooted and substantial about the ancestral home in which you were born, and your children after you and their children after them. Children need a base, a sense of permanence, a sense of security.

"But it can be carried too far—and too long. I believe that roots struck too deeply in one soil bleed when they must come up. I believe that one environment, without variation, from infancy to maturity, makes it difficult, painful and sometimes downright impossible for people to adjust to change when it comes, as come it must, especially in our world today.

"It is not possible for Honore and myself, or for most families, to gypsy about from place to place in order to make it easy for our youngsters to adjust. But we are sending the two older boys, Donnie, aged ten, and Ronnie, aged seven, away to boarding school. Military school. Later, we hope to send them to Eastern or mid-Western colleges and for as many visits and trips, far from home, as possible. Our hope is that if they move about often enough they will be at home, not only in their immediate neighborhood, but in the world.

"*They must make up their minds.* Shortly before Donnie's last birthday, his mother and I asked him what he wanted to do to celebrate the occasion, and what he wanted for a gift. He said he wanted to go to my broadcast and to Lucey's for dinner, afterwards. That was fine. That was definite. But when it came to specifying a gift, he didn't know, thought of something he wanted, changed his mind, was wishy-washy about the whole thing. Well, he went to the broadcast and we took him to Lucey's for dinner. But he didn't get a birthday present. 'Awfully sorry, Meche,' I said, 'but you couldn't make up your mind.'

"I can't think of anything more devitalizing or more downright demoralizing than an inability to decide what you want to do or to have or to be. We insist that the two older boys do their own shopping, choose their suits and hats and ties, make their own selections from a menu when we eat out, decide what they want to do with their Saturdays and other holidays. When they ask us, as they sometimes do, 'Which shall I buy, Daddy?' or 'Do you think this baseball is better than that?' My answer is always the same: 'Make up your own mind. It's something no one can do for you.' Perhaps this will make it simpler for them, in later life, to decide on jobs and friends and sweethearts.

"*They must have secrets from us.* Yes, I mean it. I mean that I hope they have, and will continue to have, a few secrets from their mother and me. For every individual, of every age, should have his inner self, his little and strictly private world into which he can retreat; the still places in his heart and mind which no one, neither wife nor husband, nor mother nor father has the right to enter. People without reserves remind me of minnows swimming on the surface of a shallow pool.

"*They must not have too many possessions.* For surfeit dulls the bright edge of delight in material things. Each one of the children has what he really wants and really uses. But their nursery is not an overcrowded shop window for toys. And they must be serious about what they want. When, recently, Ronnie asked me to buy him a trumpet to take to school, I said, 'Do you intend to learn to play it, as well? If so, you may have it. Otherwise . . . ' And when Donnie lost a new baseball glove in the pool, forgot it until the next day and then retrieved it, sodden and useless, I said, 'Sorry, I paid a lot of money for that. If you want a new glove, you'll have to do extra work to earn enough money to get one.'

"Once or twice a year, Honore insists that the boys go through their cupboards and pick out some toys to give away. Nor does she allow them to take only the things of which they have tired. They must each take something that hurts a little to part with. Then she piles boys and toys into the station wagon and drives them to the nearest orphanage.

"*There must be no commotion.* The boys know that, where their routine is concerned, they must be punctual and *quiet*. Their meals are served at certain hours and without ado they must be washed and brushed and ready for them. And they must eat what is set before them. There are no arguments. There is no choice. They know when it is time to take their naps and their baths and their vitamins and are expected to take them, without protest. They know the hour of bedtime and must go to bed, without lally-gagging. Between whiles, they may be as noisy, as wild and whoopish as they please. But where their schedules are concerned, there must be order.

"They must not have money they do not earn. We have told the two older boys, and will continue to impress upon all four of them, that we intend to give them the best schooling we possibly can but that when their educations are completed, they must go to work. We tell them that no man should have money he does not earn. The sooner the youngsters learn this, the better for their integrity and self-respect as adults. Our youngsters are learning it. They are not given

gratuitous allowances. The older boys shine their own shoes, keep their dresser drawers in order, pick up after themselves. All four boys help their mother skim milk, churn butter, garden. For these overall chores, Donnie and Ronnie are paid fifty cents a month; Tommy and Lonnie, twenty-five cents. In addition, Donnie keeps the service yard clean and Ronnie has charge of the front patio. If they slack or skimp on their jobs, their wages are 'docked.' If they put in extra time, they get 'overtime.' And if they are enterprising enough to think of extra chores to do, they are paid accordingly. The point being, they do not get something for nothing; and, at the same time, they are realizing the value of the laborer's being worthy of his hire.

"*They must face reality*. Pain is reality. It is something every individual faces, in greater or lesser degree, at one time or another. When the children are badly hurt and scream or cry, that is justifiable. For the Spartan boy belongs, I think, to literature rather than to life. But if they whimper or whine over some superficial scratch or bruise, they are quickly shamed out of it. Or if they have some unpleasant ordeal to face—an apology, perhaps, to a teacher at school for a misdemeanor—they know they must do it themselves, that we will not act as buffers or go-betweens.

"When they are old enough, I intend to take them through hospital wards, jails, juvenile courts, tenements, county workhouses. I want them to see with their own eyes and hear with their own ears the lot of the underprivileged and the maimed and the weak. So that they may have in their hearts compassion for those less fortunate and gratitude for their own kinder fortune.

"*They must be tender toward women*. As little boys, they must be courteous and gentle with little girls. This is in the hope that, as men, they will make good husbands and fathers, gentle and wise and strong. To give them this sense of tenderness and protection for girls was one of the many reasons for our deciding to adopt two little sisters for the four brothers. The boys named them, by the way, after many a family counsel. Barbara Blandina will be called Bonnie and Cornelia Roberta will be called Connie.

"*They must study music, dancing, art*. Whether they are interested in the arts, or not; whether they have any special aptitude for any one of them, or not, they must be at least familiar with them. An appreciation of music, dancing, painting and sculpture puts color into the life of any man, and a song, and a dream . . .

"So we think, and hope, and pray that if they laugh, these children of ours, and move about the earth, make up their own minds, do not whimper over nothings, have tenderness for the weak and tolerance for the crippled of mind as well as body, they will be fit to be called men. Good men, and strong."

When the boys would return from the Academy, it was an event. One such weekend Don related, in a July 1944 article in **Movie Show**: "Last Easter Sunday we had thirty-five people sitting around our festive board—all of them relatives. And not a servant in the house. This would send many a poor housewife these ration-point days into a mild state of hysterics, at least. But not Mrs. Ameche. After twelve years of being married to me, Mrs. A. is not easily floored.

"After sitting up half the night coloring Easter eggs for the children's Easter egg hunt, Honey was up bright and early Sunday morning making ice cream, simply because the two oldest boys, Donny and Ronny, home from St. John's for the holidays, had made a special request. And what did I do to help? Well, played baseball with Donny and Ronny (my back still aches) until I came within a hairline of breaking a window on the sun porch. And then after dinner I went to sleep. And almost missed my broadcast. 'I do wish you'd spend one holiday at home, without a broadcast,' said Honey wistfully as I tore out the front door on the way to my car. Which I thought very flattering. Especially when you consider that I am not much of a handy man around the house. I can't even fix the telephone.

"Next to my wife I am very proud of my sons. Donny and Ronny look very handsome indeed in their military uniforms. The two small boys, Tommy and Lonny, stay at home with us, of course. Honey does not believe in kindergartens as she thinks they give the kids a wrong idea about school—makes them think it's a place to play. In the summer, and on vacations, they all have their jobs and chores to do around the ranch, and in this way they earn their spending money. Donny is even learning to milk. They are allowed an hour to swim in the pool in the morning, and two hours in the afternoon. All four of them are excellent swimmers. I should be as good.

"All four boys also take piano lessons. Honey insists upon that. Donny had his birthday dinner at Lucey's, and casually announced over the spumoni that he would like a trumpet. We think the two older boys are big enough now to know what they want. His mother said he might have a trumpet provided he kept up his piano lessons, too—don't look now, but I think we are going to have a Harry James in our family. And by the way, if you are planning to spend your nervous breakdown with us, don't do it. If the piano doesn't drive you nuts, the horn will.

"Barbara and George Frank, who live across from us, have a wonderful vegetable garden, with more tomatoes, corn, peas, beans and beets than they can ever expect to eat themselves. The Ameches have a dairy, no less, with more milk and butter than they can possibly need. So we exchange. We have seventy-five chickens, too, and if they keep on laying as enthusiastically as they have lately, I shall probably call up Bing Crosby or Chet Lauck (Lum of Lum and Abner) and suggest bartering some eggs for some horse meat for my police dog, King Solomon, who, I am pleased to say, does not hold out for tender filet mignons. Chet and I used to own a racehorse together, named Alice Faye. I sincerely hope that Solly never gets his teeth into a joint of Alice Faye. I was very fond of that nag.

"We have three cows now, one of them a fractious cow, and a problem character if I ever saw one. Her name is Bambi, of all things. Bambi evidently had her feelings deeply hurt by the female of the species when she was young and impressionable. As she had not had the benefits of modern psychiatry, the poor dear still had a terrific hate for women. Especially Mrs. Ameche. Once Bambi knocked over a separator trying to contact with Honey. Another time she rudely managed to jump over a wire fence that separated her from Honey, who was calmly feeding the chickens. I think she stays awake nights trying to figure out ways she can annoy my wife. Fortunately, she suffers from myopia, and if Honey is wearing blue jeans she can walk around the dairy in peace—until she gets directly in Bambi's line of vision. Then all hell breaks loose. Need I add that Bambi is extremely fond of me.

"We have installed an ice plant in the small playroom by the swimming pool, and here we keep frozen chickens that have been killed and dressed, and also a steer which we fattened by forced feeding, and killed according to government regulations.

"Johnny and Mack, cousins, help us with the ranch work, and operate the milking machine for us. But I've noticed that when the power goes off it's the women who have to do the milking. All the men just suddenly disappear. Myself included. Honey has an aunt staying with us who is a great help, and also a young cousin named Hilda. Hilda had only been married to a young soldier for a few weeks when he was sent to Alaska, so she is spending the duration with us. 'This is such a mad house,' says Honey, 'that no matter what Hilda gets into from now on it will be mild.'

"I was very pleased the other day when I overheard Honey telling Betty Young (Robert's wife, and among our best friends), 'You know, Betty, we are having more fun now than we ever did have with a house full of servants. We don't have to worry about eating at certain times just to please the cook. Don isn't at all fussy about meals, and doesn't care in the least if dinner isn't ready until midnight. He loves steaks and spaghetti, and always insisted upon cooking them himself, even when we had cooks and maids. I suppose I shouldn't admit it, but I really don't mind housework.'

Don and Honey.

"Honey says it's rather nice, too, not to find yourself suddenly in Rio de Janeiro, Paris, Churchill Downs, or Las Vegas these days. And I think she's got something there. I used to be a very impulsive, restless, sort of a guy—the horrible type who right in the midst of a good dinner says, 'Let's take the plane to San Francisco and have fresh lobster at Fisherman's Wharf.' I'd never go any place without Honey, and she, being the swell sport she is, would never let me down. Though there is one time in particular that I am sure she would have murdered me if she had had anything handy.

"It was several years ago, and I had gone to Palm Springs with the family, to have the desert sun bake out a cold. One Saturday afternoon I was listening to a football broadcast at the Racquet Club, and it sounded so exciting I called Honey and told her that I was getting reservations (in those days you could get them) on the Chief the next day so we could be in Chicago for the big Notre Dame game the following weekend. 'We'll only be gone two weeks,' I said assuringly, 'don't pack much.' Of course, Honey only had a few summer sports dresses with her at Palm Springs, but she went to Desmond's on the main street there and hastily bought two suits and a velvet dress. We drove to San Bernardino the next day and caught the Chief there.

"Well, we'd been in Chicago only a week when one afternoon I was sort of pacing around our suite at the hotel. 'For heaven's sake, Don,' said Honey, 'stop acting like a caged lion and take a walk down Michigan Boulevard while I do a little light laundry.' And that's where she made her big mistake. I was sauntering down Michigan Boulevard when suddenly my eyes lit upon some gay posters in a travel bureau window. Carnival time in South America. Well, to make a long story short, when I got back to the hotel an hour later I breathlessly informed my long-suffering wife that she and I were taking the plane to New York that night, and were sailing for South America at ten o'clock the next morning. Honey claims that the most embarrassing moment of her life occurred on the promenade deck of our Southbound boat the following day. 'Mrs. Ameche,' shouted one of the photographers from a New York newspaper, 'would you mind gathering your luggage together? I'd like to take a picture of you sitting on top of it, with your legs crossed.'

"'My luggage,' said Honey scornfully, 'consists of a suitcase and a hat box. My entire wardrobe, if you're interested, consists of two suits, one I have on, and a velvet dress. I thought I was spending two weeks in Chicago.'

"Well, the war quickly put an end to all that nonsense, and no one's happier about it than my wife. But just to keep Honey from getting too set in her home life, I give her a jolt every now and then by calling her on a Friday afternoon from the studio and saying, 'We're going to San Diego tomorrow for a camp show. Run out and buy yourself a hat.'"

Chapter Six

Hollywon't

"Why don't you kiss me goodnight?"
"Because I'm not facing that way."

In 1944 Don Ameche made what he considered to be the greatest mistake of his life. In a 1991 TV interview, *Reflections on the Silver Screen*, he told Professor Richard Brown that he had been the first person MCA ever asked to represent; they offered him $75,000, but he had let his current agent and close friend George Frank continue handling him because Frank had just bought a huge home and was in drastic debt. Between the two of them Ameche and Frank thought they could pick scripts better than Zanuck. Don was becoming increasingly dissatisfied with the quality of his pictures and roles (*Greenwich Village* being a particular stinker). Zanuck offered Ameche no raise from his current salary, but had a three-year contract prepared. He'd been told at the time that he was the second highest paid actor on the lot, and believed it. Frank and Ameche discussed it, and turned it down. Richard Frank remembered it

George Frank and Ameche.

differently: "There was a studio change that was on the table and Don decided he wanted out. My father tried to talk him into staying and was not successful in keeping him either as a client or at the studio." Mistake made, Don began his short film career as a free agent, hitting and missing.

Filmed from November 1944 to January 1945, and released by United Artists in July of that year, *Guest Wife*, starring Don, Claudette Colbert and Dick Foran, proved the old maxim that you should never loan out your wife, not even to your best friend. But Chris Price (Foran) had always been in such awe of his best friend, foreign correspondent Joe Parker (Ameche), that he could never say no to the man. Not even in college when Chris ran interference while Joe took the football and the glory to the end zone. So when Joe asks to borrow Chris' wife Mary (Colbert) to show off to his rich boss, who thinks he's married, of course Chris agrees with a smile and a light heart and complete confidence in his hero.

Guest Wife, 1945.

Mary does not and never did share the idolization Chris heaps upon the man she considers less than perfection for not letting Chris "carry the ball." When she sees a chance to get back at Joe for ruining what was going to be Chris and her second honeymoon in New York, she makes Joe believe she's falling for him. Joe, for all his faults, is just as faithful to his friend as Chris is, and is shocked that Mary could have such feelings. Alone in a room in the boss' stately Long Island mansion (while Chris smiles yet half-wonders upstairs), Mary makes Joe think that if he doesn't love her, life's not worth living. After she writes what seems like a suicide note (really an explanation for the dope to read at the end of the movie), Joe sits vigil in the rain on the patio so she can't jump off. Chris sees the two of them briefly on the patio after the rain stops, and the friendly scene fuels his jealousy. He's had enough and storms downstairs to punch Joe in the jaw and take his wife away. Mary loves it; he's finally running with the ball. She tells him the truth in the car, and Joe resigns himself to losing his wife, telling his boss she's run away with Chris; the heel becomes a martyr-hero.

Don gave an energetic, magnetic performance in this romantic farce. He also had a real stake in the film, under contract to profit-share (along with Colbert—her first film after leaving Paramount) in this Greentree Production, which was made at a cost of $1,750,000. Its working title of *What Every Woman Wants* didn't seem to fit the situation, but the movie itself captured much of the pace and charm that had worked so well in *Midnight*. Don and Dick reprised their roles on the *Lux Radio Theatre* broadcast on December 10, 1945, though Claudette was replaced by the very able Olivia de Havilland.

So Goes My Love, literally a family comedy, kept Don busy at Universal from the end of October to late December of 1945. Part romantic comedy, part historical fare, based loosely on the biography of Hiram Percy Maxim, the film had a charm to it from the superb chemistry between Don and Myrna Loy.

In 1867 Jane Budden (Loy), a pig farmer's daughter with class, is determined to land herself a rich husband. Instead, she ends up with a charming, eccentric inventor, Hiram Stevens Maxim (Ameche), who doesn't supply much in the line of financial security, but she's sure that he will be a great man someday. He continues to come up with inventions that are eventually hailed as fantastic (the real Hiram having invented, among other things, a mousetrap, and a steam-powered water pump). Once the House of Science formally recognizes his great work, they want a professionally painted portrait of him, but it's the last thing in the world Hiram wants to waste his time with. Only after Jane is taken gravely ill and recovers at the end of the picture does Hiram gladly sit for a family portrait with the wife and children.

It was Myrna Loy's first starring role after she'd left MGM to freelance, and Bobby Driscoll was borrowed from Disney to play the eldest son, Percy. Ameche was, of course, Universal's first choice for such an inventive role, based on the Maxim book, *Genius in the Family*. Critics were kind to it. One paper wrote, "Ameche again proves that he can play practically anything thrown in his lap." Don and Myrna also appeared in the radio version of *So Goes My Love* on *This Is Hollywood*, heard at 7:15 p.m. on December 14, 1946.

Why Don appeared in a singing cameo for Fred Allen's *It's in the Bag* is difficult to say. Perhaps, as his brief scene regrouped him with old radio friends Rudy Vallee and Fred Allen, he did it as a favor. Some sources claim that it was his first picture as a freelance actor after leaving Fox. The slight plot involved Allen's hunting for money hidden inside one of the five chairs his millionaire great-uncle Frederick Trumble left him in his will. He doesn't realize this until he sells off the chairs, so the hunt is on. One chair has been sold to Jack Benny, providing one of the funniest scenes in the picture. Two more chairs are found in Phil's Naughty Nineties Café, where, disguised as a singing waiter, Fred sings with Don, Rudy Vallee and Victor Moore. After a comic murder mystery is solved, the cash is found, enough to pay off all of Fred's debts, get him out of the flea circus business and buy his daughter the biggest wedding in town.

Over the opening screen credits, Allen announces, "Who needs Jack Benny, a little radio actor, in a picture like this when we have Don Ameche, an outstanding personality, William Bendix, a three-fisted he-man, Victor Moore, grandma's

Fred, Rudy, Victor and Don in *It's in the Bag*, 1945.

glamour boy, and Rudy Vallee, fresh from Yale." The original title of the 1945 United Artists film was *Fickle Fortune*.

Another cameo had been lined up that year, but never materialized. Released in 1945, but filmed over August to November 1944, *Where Do We Go from Here?* starred Fred MacMurray as a man who wants to get into the Navy but can't because he's 4-F. When he finds a genie in an old lamp in a scrap metal yard, he speaks his request and finds himself in different American wars in different time periods. The original script for the film was to have had Don Ameche in a cameo for a gag in which Fred meets Don aboard the Santa Maria. "I'm inventing the telescope," says Don. "I don't know if it's 1492 or 1942," exclaims Fred. The screenplay was rewritten and the gag was not filmed.

Since the freelance film biz wasn't satisfying Don as much financially or artistically as he'd hoped, the versatile actor turned to other pursuits.

He'd kept up with horseracing during his Hollywood glory years, and would lean on it heavily in his later life, investing in and breeding horses. He got very close to the Kentucky Derby's winner's circle in 1945, so the 1944 press advised. His pair of 2-year-old colts, Sir Bim and Son of Chance, were kept at Col. E.R. Bradley's Idle Hour Farm in Kentucky. They had impressed the experts enough to secure good press, plus the rumor that Don would indeed enter them in the Derby next year. He bought them in 1943, raced them the following two years and sold them in the spring of 1946, after which he said he felt "a little lost without them."

Thanks to Honore, the Ameches had saved up enough to be now in the position of investing in non-film notions. And on October 23, 1945, Don announced his most ambitious, original venture yet: the forming of a corporation to operate a Los Angeles football team in the new All-American Football Conference, to begin playing next fall.

Richard Frank recalled, "In 1945 Don tried to put a football team together to be called The L.A. Dons. I remember being over at the Ameche house with my parents as they all worked on the idea of putting together the All-American Football Conference. It was fun listening to all the talking and ideas! Arch Ward was the famous sportswriter for *The Chicago Tribune* and he got the idea to start the Conference. I remember being in the Encino house of Don Ameche with my brother Steve, and all of the Ameche boys. We were busy throwing around the football and thinking to ourselves that we had a chance to grow up and be on a football team!"

Don functioned as president of the club, with other stockholders being Louis B. Mayer (head of MGM), Bing Crosby, Pat O'Brien, Benjamin F. Lindheimer (executive director of the Arlington Park and Washington Park Jockey clubs), Daniel F. Rice (investment banker in Chicago), Leo Spitz (chairman of the board of International Pictures, and former Chicago attorney), and Norman W. Church (retired and once principal owner of the Elgin Clock company). At the time, the All-American Conference consisted of

THE BALTIMORE COLTS, 1947–1949
THE BROOKLYN DODGERS, 1946–1948
THE BUFFALO BISONS, 1946 (RENAMED THE BUFFALO BILLS, 1947–1949)
THE CHICAGO ROCKETS, 1946–1948 (RENAMED CHICAGO HORNETS, 1949)
THE CLEVELAND BROWNS, 1946–1949
THE LOS ANGELES DONS, 1946–1949
THE MIAMI SEAHAWKS, 1946 (THEN RELOCATED TO BALTIMORE)
THE NEW YORK YANKEES, 1946–1949
THE SAN FRANCISCO 49ERS, 1946–1949

The regular schedule consisted of each team playing every other team twice on their home ground. At the season's close, the leading club of the Northern division would meet the top-ranking team of the South for the championship playoff.

Edward P. "Slip" Madigan was signed on as general manager of Don's still unnamed Los Angeles (The Dons) team on December 18, 1945. His job was to pick a coach from the half-dozen applicants. The Dons were to play their home games in Gilmore Stadium until the Coliseum was made available to professional football.

Bob Hope wrote in his 1946 newspaper column "It Says Here": "Professional football got off to a flying start here in Hollywood when Don Ameche's Los Angeles Dons played the New York Yankees at the Gilmore Stadium. Professional football . . . that's 'Murder Incorporated with noseguards.' I won't say the 'pros' are rough, but every time Fullback John Kimbrough hit that line, the California Institute of Technology reported an earthquake.

"The opening game was a grand success, with all the movie stars present to cheer Ameche's boys. Betty Grable sat on the fifty-yard line and had the backfield making passes all day.

"That Don Ameche certainly uses unusual methods. In the second quarter his boys ran onto the field all carrying a ball. The coach of the Yankees took one look and screamed, 'Ye gads . . . what's he invented now?' It was very exciting, especially when Don started giving signals from the bench by telephone and his quarterback kept yelling, 'Wrong number!' . . . yessir, that line sure was busy.

"Naturally, the game was conducted a little differently from that in the East. Out here in sunny California the players don't have to warm up before going in . . . they have smudgepots under their benches."

Four-star Admiral Jonas Ingram, commander of Allied forces in the South Atlantic during World War II, took the helm of the All-American Football Conference on February 26, 1947. The 61-year-old was signed up at a whopping $50,000 a year, which matched the salary of Bert Bell, then commissioner of the National League. Ingram hoped for friendly relations with the other league, and was against gambling. "We will not condone any sort of gambling in the All-American Conference."

On January 6, 1948, Don announced that St. Mary's all-American halfback, Herman Wedemyer, had just signed a two-year contract with the Los Angeles Dons. Unofficial reports put the amount at $25,000-$30,000 for the two years.

The press hyped the fact that there was a "war" on between the National League and the All-American Conference for the best players. Football executive Alexis Thompson thought that was foolish, claiming that it would take six leagues to keep all the good players in work. Los Angeles, Chicago and New York were the only problem spots in which the Conference was taking good players away from the NFL. It was the money that was the problem. The Conference didn't have the necessary capital to fight the old established firm. Some named Ameche himself with starting all the fuss. Don had been friends with Arch Ward, sports editor of *The Chicago Tribune*, and Elmer Layden, once head coach and athletic director at Notre Dame. Ward had been credited by some with pushing professional football into the limelight, and was revered by many of its NFL members. Don had wanted an L.A. franchise and Ward put the proposition before the league, confident the owners would say "Yes" in a hurry. But two other men heard about it and expressed interest in a franchise if one was granted to Don. This slowed down the discussion and though Ward put up a check (probably Don's) for $50,000, he was asked to wait outside while the deal was discussed. That got him hot, so when the NFL turned him down, that got him mad. The vote had been 8 to 3 in favor, but it required a 9 to 2 majority to go through; the Bears, Cardinals and Eagles were against it. Ward lobbied the three abstainers, but couldn't move them. He was now determined to get Ameche a football franchise even if he had to form a league himself. Ward was secretive as he enlisted owners and named Jim Crowley as the Conference's commissioner.

One thing reporters admitted as being on the Conference's side was that it was a new thing, with definite box office appeal because it was creating history. Also, they were selling new faces: a chance to pick out new heroes. But though attendance proved good, there were just too many start-up costs involved. An extensive article in *The Quarterback* claimed that it would take over $350,000 to operate a football league in 1946: $185,000 for players' salaries, $40,000 for coaches and trainers, the same for traveling expenses, $10,000 for the stadium (ushers, etc.), $17,000 for training expenses, $9,000 for legal and doctor fees, $7,000 for taxes, and on and on. It looked as though with bonuses, to attract new players hesitant about the reliability of the new league, the Conference's budget would come in at least $50,000 over that as well. The NFL insisted that the Conference wasn't at war with the NFL, but with the almighty dollar. The NFL claimed that they only netted a profit of $1,600 in 1946, and they were well established. "The All-American Conference is licked before it starts," the NFL said at the time.

While the Dons were at their height, *Star-News* asked Don to MC their third annual Sports Jamboree on May 26, 1948 at the Pasadena Civic Auditorium. Sixty trophies were given out to champion teams of schools, who were also furnished with free football tickets. The event was populated by royalty of stage, screen and sports.

Don appeared as a speaker at an event, which also included Jim Phelan, coach of the L.A. Dons. Phelan had coached for 29 years at Missouri, Purdue, Washington and St. Mary's. The year before he joined the Dons he was President of College Football Coaches of America.

Don attended as many of his team's games as he could during his picture and more prolific radio work. The Dons trained in luscious, beachfront Ventura, California, so he wasn't able to get to training sessions as often as he would have liked.

On July 7, 1948, Don was pictured handing out the first tickets to the upcoming game between the Dons and the San Francisco 49ers. It was a benefit game for the Pasadena Boys' Club (for their new clubhouse) scheduled for August 18 to be played at the Rose Bowl. Tickets went for $3.60, $2.50 and general admission tickets of $1.50.

On October 15, 1949, the *Los Angeles News'* sports headline read MARKS TUMBLE AS DONS MASSACRED. Ben Person reported that the Los Angeles Dons "got the biggest licking in their history" from the Cleveland Browns. In front of 27,437 fans at the L.A. Coliseum the Dons lost 61 to 14. This was the year the Dons finally folded. Even though they'd won their opening game against Baltimore that year, only 20,000 fans came to see it. Large write-ups against the team in *The Los Angeles Times* didn't help. Though they had a good manager in Jimmy Phelan and competent playing by fullback Josea Rodgers and wingback Dixie Howell, the All-American Conference Dons had to go.

The Conference lasted just three years, from 1946 to 1949, but accomplished a lot in so short a time before the Browns, Colts and 49s were gobbled up by the NFL as part of their franchise. The Browns had actually been the first professional team to remain undefeated in all its (1948) games.

To augment his investments and keep busy in the public eye, Don turned back to radio with a passion and continued with it until television murdered sound. Sponsored by Elgin, the two-hour *Victory Salute*, broadcast over CBS on November 22, 1945, was a big deal that garnered a lot of press. Don was master of ceremonies, with Ken Carpenter as announcer, joined by a stellar radio cast: Fibber McGee and Molly, Frances Langford, Edgar Bergen and Charlie McCarthy, Jimmy Durante and Garry Moore, Cass Daley, and others, and as special guest, the wife of General Vicente Lim, missing Philippine war hero. Don also appeared in the poignant dramatic spot with Maureen O'Hara about an English widow of a GI buried in Normandy coming to America to visit his mother's home.

It was broadcast from the Vine Street Theater in Hollywood via short-wave around the world to celebrate the victory of the Allies and the end of World War II.

It was the fourth year that CBS had broadcast its Thanksgiving Day parade of stars, and the third year that Ameche hosted. It cost the watch-making sponsor an incredible $120,000 to produce. *Variety* thought they went overboard on the commercials, "lest not be forgotten amidst all the talent," but thought that Don "wrapped the whole thing up—but neatly," and "it all added up to a boff holiday program." *Citizen-News* called Ameche "smooth, genial and well-spoken."

As an emcee, Don was always held in high regard by listeners and sponsors alike. He played host to the *Elgin Christmas Greeting* a month later, joining Bob Hope, Red Skelton, Jack Benny, Allan Jones, Bob Crosby and his Bobcats, Larry Storch, Vera Vague, Ginny Simms, Allan Reed, Artur Rubenstein, Ella Logan, The Charioteers, Mel Blanc, Arthur Q. Bryan, and others. *Variety* wrote that with a cast like that the show couldn't, and didn't, fail. It was "a finely beveled, skillful presentation, so on this report card the bearer rates a new scooter." Benny spoofed Agnes Moorehead's *Sorry Wrong Number*, Skelton did his mean widdle kid bit with Verna Felton, and Ameche "impressed" *Variety* with a moving drama with Frances Robertson and Billy Brow.

The Milwaukee Journal reported on September 20, 1946 that Don was set to star in a new radio series which would ultimately give Don Ameche another slice of immortality.

Drene Time originally included singer Joanell James, comedian Pinky Lee and the instrumental music of Joe Lilley leading a 28-piece orchestra. The deal with Ameche to emcee it was finalized in March and the papers were signed at the Kentucky Derby in Louisville on May 4.

Reviews were lukewarm to its pilot. *The New York World-Telegram* thought there was a bit too much Ameche in the proceedings (singing, trading jokes with everyone, even helping out with commercials), but admitted that "the dramatic portion of Mr. Ameche's festival was nicely done. It was, in fact, very touching." Ida Lupino played opposite Don in some scenes from *Goodbye, Mr. Chips*. The death scene was most effective, though followed a bit too closely by yet another commercial. Pinky Lee was also hailed as great fun.

A review from John Crosby's September 30, 1946 column of the new Don Ameche show (7:00 p.m. on Sunday) also thought that there was just an overstocking of Ameche: he "sang, clowned and acted. Next week I expect he'll invent something." Old, bearded jokes were another thing he objected to when it came to the exchanges between Pinky Lee and Merle Oberon:

"I was coming out of a butcher shop with some sirloin steak sticking out of my pocket and I backed into an electric fan."
"What happened?"
"Look in my pocket—hamburger."

And later:

"Come take my hand and let us flee, flee, flee."

"I'm already married."

"Every time I meet a married woman she has a husband."

That episode also featured Don doing dramatic scenes from *Dark Victory* with Miss Oberon. Crosby stated: "That's the trouble with the Ameche show. It's a little too much of everything and not very much of anything. About all that was lacking was a quiz contest." A format change that would make history was in the works.

Meantime, Don and Jim Ameche starred together in the opening show of *Love Story Theater* in "Concerto in C Minor" on October 25, 1946. The idea was to present original love stories selected by a board of fiction writers. The brothers had rarely played together before, such as on a *First Nighter*—but the next day hundreds of letters had piled into the studio asking what was the idea of having Don play two different parts without even trying to change his voice. As of October 7, 1946, Jim had just completed 13 weeks as the star of NBC's *Grand Marquee*. He was to begin another series in the next few weeks.

Don returned to Elgin for their Thanksgiving Day, 1946, special, hosted by Don, and again included a *wealth* of stars: Jack Benny, Jimmy Durante & Garry Moore, Red Skelton, Vera Vague, Peter Lind Hayes, Mel Blanc (doing the voices of Bugs Bunny, Porky Pig and Jack Benny's parrot for the station breaks), Desi Arnaz, Burl Ives, Margaret Whiting and others. Ken Carpenter again announced.

His next job would give Don Ameche almost 30 years of work.

The format for Don's *Drene Time* changed drastically in December of 1946. Don wanted a dramatic formula for the new series, possibly swayed by the continued good reviews of his dramatic spots, but was overruled by Procter & Gamble, owners of the sponsoring Drene shampoo. They were concerned about its being opposite another drama, *Theater Guild on the Air*. The show changed to Sunday night at 10:00 p.m. on WNBC and dropped singer Joanell James, comic Pinky Lee, and writer Hal Kantor, the latter replaced by Bickersons-creator Phil Rapp. Danny Thomas was brought in as comedian (and John Bickerson's infuriating brother-in-law, Amos), whose set always included a comic song written for him by Jerry Seelen, his usual writer. Frances Langford became the singer, with Carmen Dragon still retained as musical director. The first half of the show now included a Langford song, comic banter between Carmen, Don, Frances and Danny, merging into fanciful patter for Danny which showcased him as an inventor, explorer or satirical character. The second half of the new formula was *much* more influential.

When Philip Rapp's "humorous creation" the Bickersons debuted on *Drene Time* in 1946, it was a truly original piece of business, even for its stars Don Ameche and Frances Langford, who had never played *this* type of comedy before. No one had. Ameche had been cast in many film roles as the hot-headed editor and take-charge film director, so he knew how to yell with the best of them. But for singer Frances Langford, who had until then only helped with some Bob Hope gags while touring with the comic, the Bickersons was a total departure from her on- and off-screen persona.

"Phil always said, 'Just play it like a nagging wife,'" recalled Frances years later. "And I would do it, and he would say, 'Nastier.' Actually, it wasn't hard to do at all. Phil's scripts were so well written that the laughs got themselves. And I got all that bad temper out of my system."

Don, Frances and Frank Morgan arguing on *Drene Time.*

THEME:	(*Soft And Plaintive*) "PLEASE GO AWAY AND LET ME SLEEP"
ANNOUNCER:	(*Over Music*) The Bickersons have retired. Three o'clock in the morning finds Blanche tense and restless as poor husband John suffers another attack of intermittent insomnia or Woodchopper's Syndrome. Listen.
DON:	SNORE LUSTILY . . . SNORES AND WHINES . . . A BROKEN RHYTHM SNORE FOLLOWED BY A PITIFUL WHINE
LANG:	Any minute he'll go into orbit!
DON:	SNORES AND GIGGLES.
LANG:	Oh, dear.
DON:	SNORES AND GIGGLES MERRILY.
LANG:	John!
DON:	Mmm.

LANG: Turn over on your side! Go on!

DON: (*A Protesting Whine*)

LANG: Stop it, stop it, stop it!

DON: Stop it, Blanche. Whassamatter? Wassamatter, Blanche?

LANG: That whining and giggling and grunting and snarling! It's driving me *crazy*.

DON: Me too, Blanche. Who's doing it?

LANG: You're doing it. It amazes me you can sleep at all with your guilty conscience!

DON: Not guilty. Put out the lights.

LANG: I will not! This is one night you're not getting away with it!

DON: Blanche, what's the matter with you? It's three o'clock in the morning. You had a good time tonight, now why don't you let me sleep?

LANG: I had a miserable time. It was the unhappiest anniversary I ever spent. Why didn't you show up for the party, John?

DON: I told you. I got stuck at the office.

LANG: Sure. That's always your first excuse. If I don't fall for that, you have a second excuse, then a third and a fourth. What were you working on?

DON: A fifth.

LANG: You'd better not be so bold, John Bickerson. For your information I got a call from Louise Shaw.

DON: What about it?

LANG: She saw you coming out of a saloon at midnight. She saw you—now don't you deny it!

DON: I'm not denying it.

LANG: Why were you coming out of a saloon at midnight?

DON: Because I had to come out *some*time.

LANG: I'm warning you, John. You'd better give up that habit. Every time you go into a saloon the devil goes with you.

DON: Well, if he does he pays for his own drinks. Goodnight.

LANG: Oh no! What time did you leave the office?

DON: I left the office at eleven o'clock. I caught the bus at eleven five. I got off at eleven fifty-four. I stopped at the cocktail bar and bought a corkscrew and waited an hour.

LANG: Why?

DON: Because it was pouring outside.

LANG: And what were you doing?

DON: Pouring inside! Are you satisfied? Is that what you wanted me to say?

LANG: No, I just want the truth.

DON: The truth is I was working. Blanche, I've had a rough day. I went to work at seven this morning—no breakfast, no lunch, no dinner ——

LANG: Who told you not to eat dinner? I left a whole roast chicken for you in the kitchen. Why didn't you eat it?

DON: I didn't like the stuffing. What'd you stuff it with?

LANG: I didn't stuff it with anything. It wasn't hollow.

DON: Put out the lights.

The characters of John and Blanche Bickersons were the sole creation of Philip Rapp, one-time writer for Eddie Cantor and Fanny Brice, and currently employed writing films for Danny Kaye. Rapp often said that he based the Bickersons on his own marital strife, sometimes gleaning a few situations (such as the bagged garbage mistaken for lunch) from activities or notions his wife

Mary might initiate. Phil and Mary, who met in their early vaudeville careers, remained married for over 60 years, however, never divorcing.

Columnist John Crosby didn't care for the original *Drene Time*, but gave the reformatted version another try and thought it vastly improved. Especially the new husband and wife sketch. "It's news to me that Miss Langford is a comedian . . . Though I scarcely believe the evidence of my own ears, it was character comedy with teeth in it; that is, it revealed a very unpleasant relationship between husband and wife and still was very funny. In the theater, it would be dismissed as a rather mild example of its kind but to find this sort of comedy on the air at all is a very heartening sign."

It *was* biting and original radio fare that gave a new dimension to the usual "clean" comedy overrunning the airwaves then. If only for its novelty value, it made the Bickersons a hit—and also prompted an incredible amount of hate mail by those unready for its sharpness. Two movie studios were bidding for the film rights (though nothing came of it) to "The Honeymoon Is Over," during which time writer Phil Rapp was seriously considering writing a stage version of the Bickersons for Broadway, though it would not happen until years later in California, without Ameche or Langford.

The Bickersons also influenced a generation of television. Rapp later sued Jackie Gleason for ripping off the idea/characters for his *Honeymooners*; even Fox Television came to Rapp in the '80s, wanting to put the Bickersons in a series. When Rapp would not relent total control and copyright to the network, they passed, and went on to initiate *Married . . . with Children*.

Elgin's all-star Christmas special of 1946 had Don emceeing again and had him joining Frances Robinson in a dramatic vignette based on Handel's *Messiah*. The show cost $55,000 to put together, and gave Bob Hope, Cass Daley, Metropolitan Opera tenor Set Svanholm, Roy Rogers, Victor Borge and others a chance to spread some postwar cheer.

During the Christmas Day broadcast, Don parked his car in an autopark near Hollywood and Vine at a broadcasting station in Hollywood, and a few hours later it was gone. The enterprising thief, 18-year-old sailor Robert Goodapple, drove the vehicle 1,900 miles, then rented the car to a man and his girlfriend for four dollars. They rode around for a while, and rented it again a few days later. When they finally looked at the registration, they drove the shinny new Chrysler sedan straight to the police. Ameche had to appear the next month in Los Angeles Municipal Court to testify. Goodapple had claimed Don was his uncle when he was first picked up.

At the end of January 1947 Don was signed as one of many stars to lend his voice to a Back to Church campaign sponsored by the Religions of America. They wanted to use modern advertising methods, including radio, to induce citizens back to worship. It was something Don was wholly in favor of.

Don, Loretta Young and James Stewart starred in the premier presentation of *The Family Theatre* radio series on Thursday, February 13, 1947 at 9:00 p.m. The half-hour program began with "Flight from Home," written by True

Boardman, and concerned a husband who loses everything to drink. The series was conceived by Father Patrick Peyton, known as the Apostle of the Family Rosary. No wonder Don Ameche agreed to take part in its inception. Every star who appeared on the program signed a contract with Father Peyton, which agreed: "To offer to American families the most necessary and fundamental protection against the dangers of our age, and for the purpose of bringing down upon our country the special blessings of Almighty God, I am willing to help realize the proposed radio plan of popularizing the practice of daily Family Prayer."

It was popular enough for Armed Forces Radio to snap up the program to rebroadcast to the services over its sixteen short-wave stations that transmitted over the Atlantic and Pacific oceans, and even into Germany and Russia.

After the broadcast Father Peyton sent Don this telegram: "DON GOD AND OUR LADY ARE PROUD OF YOU AND AS LONG AS I LIVE I WILL ALWAYS BE YOUR FRIEND FOR WHAT YOU DID TODAY FOR OUR LADY TO MAKE HER PROGRAM THE BEST THAT EVER WAS THANKS A MILLION."

Variety did not think there was much original or praiseworthy in the show's debut. "Here is another instance of networks relying on film names to carry a program, instead of concentrating on a strong script, and suitable actors." The reviewer felt that either Young and Ameche were grossly miscast or didn't apply themselves to the uninspired, sentimental plot. Regardless, the series was embraced warmly enough to run until July 4, 1956.

Also around 1947 Don signed up with Jack Benny, Burns and Allen, Eddie Cantor, Fibber McGee and Molly and other big radio acts to start a thirteen-week *Here's to Veterans* series that would be distributed to 900 stations. One component of the 15-minute series would stress that veterans should hold onto their National Service Life Insurance or reinstate their lapsed policies.

On January 29, 1947, the new Hooper listening poll statistics (ratings) were out. At 8.2% Don prospered well considering the pinnacle was 33.2% for Bob Hope, though he was down from 9.4% from January 13. After the close of *Drene Time*, the Bickersons would snore loudly again to bring him back up.

By the beginning of June 1947 Don, Frances Langford and Frank Morgan were all set to star in *The Old Gold Show*, which first lit up on September 24, 1947. Budgeted at $17,000 a week, the *Drene Time* formula had basically become *The Old Gold Show*, replacing Danny Thomas with the boastful Frank Morgan, tall-taling his one-upmanship on whatever expert was a guest that week. Frank never appeared in the Bickerson sketches in the second half of the show, so poor husband John had some relief that way. Brother Amos was never to complicate the Bickersons' lives again. The cigarette company's show puffed on until June 25, 1948.

"A Rosary of Stars" gathered together for a Mother's Day broadcast in 1947 to dramatize and recite The Rosary. The Sunday afternoon broadcast went out to 10 million people on the Mutual Broadcasting Network. Under the direction of

Father Patrick Peyton, the half-hour program starred Ethel Barrymore, Loretta Young, Ruth Hussey, Irene Dunne, Margaret O'Brien, Rosalind Russell, Charles Boyer, Pat O'Brien, George Murphy and of course, Don Ameche.

Don frankly needed the push back to stardom that radio afforded him. He wasn't finding it in films these days.

Early titles for Republic Pictures' *That's My Man* included *Gallant Man, That Man of Mine, King of the Racetrack* and *Turf Café*. The 1947 equine drama, directed by Frank Borzage, starred Ameche as accountant Joe Grange, whose life is turned around one day when he quits his job, buys a horse (a dream he's had since he was eight years old), and meets his future wife Ronnie (Catherine McLeod), a soda clerk in a drugstore, all on Christmas Eve in

That's My Man, 1947.

Hollywood. The ambitious Joe almost seems to will his horse, Gallant Man, to win and win, but as his horse-racing empire grows, so does his thirst for gambling. Eventually, his wife and small son are neglected in favor of his dice and they leave him; he's broken too many promises. When the racing circuit gives Joe trouble, he decides to retire Gallant Man undefeated, though it breaks his heart. Joe takes an accounting job in Florida, only to be called back to California when he reads that Gallant Man has come out of retirement to race again. Joe is very concerned for his old friend and rushes back just in time to see his horse win the exciting Hollywood Gold Cup Race and its $100,000 purse. Ronnie, legal co-owner of the horse and missing Joe badly, only wanted Gallant Man to run again to bring her husband back home. And now Joe is ready to come home—for good.

The film was shot from mid-November to mid-December, 1946. Borzage originally considered Henry Fonda for the role, but Ameche was made for the part. Horses; winning a house in a card game; a touch of family neglect—it sadly echoed his real life a bit too closely. His portrayal as the dreamer was a bit wooden, but it was a solid star vehicle for him as self-loathing father and apologetic husband. His scene at the card table, in which he loses every cent he has in the world, is especially gripping. When the film was reissued in 1953, it was given the title *King of the Racetrack*.

The *Washington Daily News* liked nothing about *That's My Man* except some of the scenic gags. "Don Ameche tries desperately to be dashing as a horse and card lover, but gets nowhere at all." It ended on the rather cruel, foreboding thought of "what's holding up the Ameche-For-Oblivion movement?" *The Hollywood Reporter* thought it was one of Don's best portrayals, adding the fact that he had to stretch himself "to supply substance to the inexperienced inadequacies of Catherine McLeod in the assignment of his wife."

The happy ending for *That's My Man*, 1947.

After *That's My Man*, newspapers announced that Don had been signed by Skirball-Manning to play in the film *Sunny River*, at the generous sum of $100,000, but nothing came of it. As of mid-July 1947, Ameche was also publicly announced to star with Richard Hart in *Luxury Liner*, but for whatever reason, the musical went ahead without the radio star.

Between pictures and the airwaves, Don filled in the odd gaps with another venue dear to his heart: charity work. With Frances Langford, they performed their Bickersons in mid-October 1947 in the Civic Auditorium for the Pasadena Lions Club's gigantic benefit for the Boys' Club building fund. And in the first week of November 1947 he played host at the Thousand Club dinner party in the Topaz Room to benefit the Santa Rosa Memorial Hospital. The dinner was given for all those who contributed $1,000 to the fund. The event raised almost $169,000 for the 91-bed hospital.

He also participated in the 4th Annual Frank Borzage Motion Picture Golf Tournament at the California Country Club on May 23, 1948. He was pictured in the *Los Angeles Herald-Express* playing straight man to his bumbling caddy, Oliver Hardy.

Whether or not he *truly* enjoyed the schmoozing half of Hollywood society, he knew it was part of the game. Singer Martha Stewart recalled, "I remember Don at Toots Shor's. He was so cute, standing at the bar sipping his vodka. He loved to watch everybody and what they were doing. He wasn't a very expressive man, but he loved to watch quietly. He was a gentleman, always dressed to the nine's. Though you couldn't get into Toots' without a tie on—it was old school. Don was divine, always pulled your chair in for you. He could also out-drink everyone in the world, and there were some heavy drinkers there. I saw him put Jackie Gleason to sleep one time!"

Don emceed another Elgin Christmas show in December of 1947 starring Edgar Bergen, Bob Hope, Amos 'n' Andy and others. *Variety* loved the show, and wrote at length on Don Ameche's plaudits. "To this corner he is the closest approximation to The Indispensable Man as is to be found in radio. Several tradesmen fell to discussing Ameche's emceeing job after the Christmas show and there was not a single dissent to the prevailing opinion that he is the big difference between excellence and mediocrity, and that across the breadth of the industry there's not one who could give the assignment his superb touch. Whether it's high drama or low comedy, he bridges the span with effortless artistry. His emceeing is flawless and a fluffed line or missed cue rarely mars his work. His value to the show is of such high order that were he to be unavailable it is doubtful if the present format would be continued. He's the straw in the brick that keeps the show together and rolling smoothly. All this and a nice guy, too."

Such radio popularity often helped him acquire sponsorship deals. "I lived in Milwaukee," said Don in a full-page ad in 1948, "and I ought to know . . . Blatz is Milwaukee's finest beer!" Kenosha was close enough to Milwaukee . . .

Like his *Gallant Man* role, the real Don Ameche was still gambling: a New York newspaper reported that Don won a bundle from Eddie Arcaro, a very famous jockey, at the Saratoga dice tables. And he was still investing most of his winnings. At the top of 1948 he speculated in the grain market. When a Senate committee was looking into some four thousand wheat speculators, who were in the Chicago wheat future market on September 17-20, 1947, Ameche was listed as holding some 90,000 bushels of wheat futures in September. He bought many thousand more that same month.

By this point Don and family had moved out of the big house, with 11.5 bathrooms in the San Fernando Valley, into Arline Judge's former home in Bel Air. The Swiss chalet at 989 Bel Air Road had fewer bedrooms, just enough for the family, and cost $85,000.

It was also reported that Don sold his racing stables in January of 1947. He frequented the Turf Club and his grandstand box at the Santa Anita racetrack, with or without Honore. He wasn't hurting for money, but he was finding decent film roles hard to come by.

When United Artists re-teamed Don Ameche and Claudette Colbert in 1948 for the gaslighting *noir* thriller ***Sleep, My Love***, Don found himself as the heavy for a change. The fact that most reviews of the day gave away the fact that Richard Courtland (Ameche) is trying to drive his wife Alison (Colbert) insane so he can take over her fortune must have proved, in critics' minds at least, that this is a psychological mystery and not a whodunit. Still, it is a mystery to Bruce Elcott (Robert Cummings), who slowly finds out that Richard is employing Charles Vernay (George Coulouris), a photographer, to pretend to be psychiatrist Dr. Rhinehart (Ralph Morgan) and play mind tricks on her. Richard hopes to have Alison committed so that he will be free to marry the rather distant vamp Barby (Rita Johnson). He also tries to induce his wife, by drugs and hypnosis, to jump from her bedroom balcony, but again Bruce, now in love with her, stands between her and death. The villains fall out at the end, Vernay shooting Richard to make it look as if Alison were the culprit, and Vernay falling to his death when chased by the ever-active Bruce.

Based on the novel of the same name by Leonard Q. Ross (Leo Rosten's pen name), the story first saw print serialized in *Collier's* in the summer of 1946. It was an average post-Fox film for Ameche, with his other two co-stars receiving more screen time and certainly better roles. *Sleep, My Love* was the first film produced by Mary Pickford (Triangle Productions) in ten years. She and husband Buddy Rogers collaborated on the theme song. Claudette Colbert's husband, Dr. Joel Pressman, coached Claudette on her scenes involving hypnosis.

Being vamped by Rita Johnson in *Sleep, My Love*, 1948.

It was a change for the Ameche smile. Louella Parsons commented on this villainous reversal of roles: "I couldn't be more surprised if Shirley Temple did a striptease." Seattle, Washington's *Post-Intelligencer* raved, "If you like real unashamed melodrama, all dressed up with mystery and thrill stuff, you'll find it in *Sleep, My Love.*"

In 1948 the *Chicago Sunday Tribune* ran an article about the Ameche home life. In their Swiss chalet-type house they would always have a full house of relatives, friends, stray children, etc. When the reporter was there, the home contained an ailing priest upstairs, an odd-job young man (Gabriel), whom Don was sending to college, and various Ameche & etc. kids frolicking in the swimming pool. At one point Don's oldest sister Betty was living there with her four daughters. There were usually others on the ranch, too, since Don took in several families during the Southern California housing shortage.

Honore's Auntie Mary Bourne also lived with them for a spell. She told Jim Carling in *Movie Show* magazine, "I first met Don in Chicago, when he began courting Honey. He was doing radio work then. But Honey lived in Dubuque, so every time Don wanted to see her he had to drive almost two hundred miles from Chicago. He did it at least twice a week—the money that boy spent for gasoline! And almost always he'd take me with him.

"At night, after a broadcast, he'd call up and say, 'Auntie, I've got to see Honey. Let's go!' We'd arrive in Dubuque at three or four in the morning. Honey would be waiting up, for Don always telephoned to say he was coming. Then they'd go into the kitchen. They did all their courting in the kitchen, because Don was so hungry after the drive." With thousands of miles of road to talk through, Auntie and Don became quite close.

Auntie had joined the household in 1943 after a serious operation in Chicago. Don insisted she come out West to recuperate. "Naturally, the rest did wonders. But eventually I felt I should be getting back to work again. When Don learned that, he sent for me, very formally. I remember going into his den, wondering what he wanted. He sat me down in front of him and asked why I thought I should go back. 'Well,' I said, 'a person must eat.' 'You're eating now, aren't you?' he teased. 'I'm asking you to stay, not because you're Honey's aunt, or a relative, but because I want you here with us. Please remember that.'"

The Ameche clan had also been increased recently, by adoption: twin baby girls, Bonnie and Connie Ameche. In a later interview, Don stated, "After Lonny's birth, Honore was told there could be no more babies, and she was bitterly disappointed. She so badly wanted a little girl. So, when Lonny was five, we adopted two little girls of almost the same age, just two-and-a-half weeks' difference. We named them Barbara Blandina and Cornelia Robert, and without Bonnie and Connie, as they came to be called, I doubt that I could ever lay claim to being one hundred percent happy."

Connie: "I was born on April 1, 1945 in Salt Lake City, Utah. My Aunt Betty (my father's older sister) flew with me from Utah to Los Angeles when I was three days old. My sister and I were officially considered foster children until we were about two years old, when the adoptions became official. According to my father, because of his job and the fact they already had four children, it took awhile to convince the courts or child services that they would be good parents.

"I always felt special because, as my father had explained it, we were *chosen* by being adopted. And, because he had wanted girls so much, it really was obvious that we were treated differently. The boys went to boarding school from the time they were very young, some as young as five years old, while Bonnie and I stayed with our parents until we went to boarding school for high school. My father really encouraged me to always do my best and live up to my potential, which meant to me that he saw me as special. My sister was the gentle, caring little girl and I was considered intelligent, capable, and sensitive.

"I didn't really care about my biological parents until: 1) my sister became very earnest about it, and 2) I had children of my own and I wanted to know about my medical history for their sake. My father used to tell my sister and me that we came from very healthy parents with no known predilections to disease or illness, physically or mentally. Whether this is true or not, I don't know. I never searched very hard, though. My father was aware of my sister's longing to find out, but he didn't discourage or encourage her. He seemed just to accept it as a matter of nature.

"We only celebrated our birthdays. Since it wasn't a big deal to us or our parents or brothers that we were adopted, we didn't celebrate our adoption day. We received dolls and toys, clothes, and hair accessories when we were young; clothes and little things like stockings, a special dinner at a nice restaurant, when we were older. Our parents did not give us extravagant gifts and I, for one, am very grateful. I learned to appreciate the thought of the gift rather than the cost.

"Bonnie and I did not spend much time with my brothers. They came home for Christmas and sometimes for summers. We didn't have sibling rivalry for a few reasons: 1) Bonnie and I were like dolls to the boys until we were pre-teens, 2) we didn't see that much of them, so it was a holiday and always fun when we got together, and 3) they are a bit older than we are—Meech (Don, Jr.) is 12 years older, Ron was 10 years older, Tom was 6 years older, and Larry was 5 years older.

"I never felt close to my mother. My father was the one who wanted daughters and pushed for our adoption. My mother had very difficult pregnancies and deliveries. She delivered the four boys by caesarian and lost one baby—a boy, I believe—between the second and third. I really feel that she was more than

The Ameche family.

willing to quit after two children were born, but her faith and my father prevented that. My father said that it was a good thing that two girls were available at the same time or he would have walked around holding one little girl all of the time and would have spoiled her something awful.

"Mother was not maternal in the usual sense of the word. She was a good mother, but sort of distant, which I think was caused by her deep down unhappiness. Her dream was to have the little house with the white picket fence. She was always uncomfortable in any kind of spotlight. She and I discussed this shortly before she died. She loved my father and in some ways needed him, but couldn't conform to his lifestyle. He was gone a lot of the time, especially when the children were young and, I think, she felt abandoned. One of her happiest memories was having a Victory garden in Los Angeles during WWII, where she was able to do something productive, even churning butter by hand. She was well educated, with a quick wit, who could be very funny. Her drinking was her way of avoiding pain. I know it is a disease, but I think loneliness, fear of being in the public eye, and not living up to some kind of expectation or standard opened the door to it."

During further lean times that would follow in the 1970s, Don philosophized on himself as a dad. "I was a very stern father. Maybe too much so. But you can't look back. You just have to feel that you did the best you could.

"We wouldn't let our children go into situations, for example, where parents were spending thousands of dollars on a birthday party. They were false values, and we just decided to pull them out of that kind of situation.

"But my wife and I are deeply grateful that we have six very, very good children, so we must have done the right thing. I have asked them if I had been too strict, and they say, 'Look at us, Dad. Look at what we are like. Think how much you did for us.'"

It was a time of transitions. On May 9, 1948, Don said goodbye to Charlie McCarthy and Edgar Bergen, as guest on their final show from Hollywood. Bergen and dummy were then to leave for New York to do three shows before heading for Sweden. Though according to an article in *The Chicago Sun*, Ameche was still part of the team, then being written out of the script for a few weeks while recovering from laryngitis. Yet it was clear that Ameche, like most everyone else, was giving up radio in favor of television. But first, one more Hollywood picture.

Certainly one of his better freelance entries came in 1949, when he supported Dorothy Lamour pretending to be *Slightly French* in order to land herself a Hollywood film career. Like *Hollywood Cavalcade*, Ameche, in the role of the tunnel-visioned John Gayle, carried this picture with his sheer domineering attitude and his quest to construct the supreme motion picture. When he is fired off his last picture, for just such perfectionism, he realizes his only way back onto the set is to secure a replacement for Yvonne La Tour (Adele Jergens), who quit because of his tirade. At a local carnival, he finds Mary O'Leary (Lamour), who makes a living dancing, singing and spouting foreign accents in its various shows.

Slightly French, 1949.

John takes her under his wing and passes her off as Rochelle Olivier, his friend from France. During the training process, she falls for him, but quickly learns that John is only interested in his career. The studio loves her but not having to deal with Gayle as part of the package. When the Hollywood brass learn that she's not French, John is fired for fraud, but she's kept on to finish the picture. The new director cannot do anything with a lovesick star, however, and once John realizes he's got it bad too, the couple reunite for a happy ending.

It was to be Don's last feature picture until 1961.

Because of his sports blood, Don was signed to narrate *The Best in Football*, a 30-minute Technicolor picture from May of 1949. It was shown by Dale Gentry for the men of St. Michael and All Angels Church.

In the late '40s Don appeared on a few radio episodes of *The Jimmy Durante Show* with Vera Vague and Candy Candido. *The Philadelphia Bulletin* claimed that "Don Ameche is the best stooge Durante has had since Garry Moore left but he too is pretty badly handicapped by his material."

He was making the gradual, necessary move to television. On October 5, 1949, he was seen on *The Hot Stove League*. It was an odd one. Don, Harry Kerry, Frank Mestrely, and George Wagner talked about the World Series while playing golf, with Bernie Milligan moderating.

At the top of November it was announced that Don would guest in a dramatic role on *The Lassie Show*, in the episode titled "His Master's Eye." Based on real events, he would play John L. Sinykin, the pioneer who first trained guide dogs for the blind. Lassie would portray "Chekko," the German Shepherd who became the first guide dog. It was a fitting role for Don who was by then acting as a director of the Masters Eye Foundation, a nonprofit organization which furnished guide dogs for the blind.

His charitable exploits continued to be written up by the press. *Motion Picture Magazine* announced Don's "pet charity" then as the Nazareth Home for Boys in Van Nuys, where, during wartime, he delivered a carload of meat to the 120 boys every Saturday. He told friends, "Don't ask me where I'm getting this meat. I'm getting it—period."

On December 8 he served as altar boy in the San Jose Church (oldest church under the American flag) in San Juan, Puerto Rico for Father Ciriaco Berasategui, who claimed "Ameche was the best altar boy I have ever had." Having stepped off the plane from New York for the opening of Conrad Hilton's new Caribe Hilton Hotel, Ameche asked a reporter where he could go to mass, and was introduced to the Father. Neither spoke the other's language, but when the Father said, through an interpreter, that he was short-handed for the feast of the Immaculate Conception, Don gladly offered to help.

Back to TV, on December 12, 1949, *The San Francisco Chronicle* rightly or wrongly reported that Don would make his *first* television appearance that night over KRON-TV at 8:00 p.m. in "The Door." Written by Associated Press reporter Jeb Stuart for *Chevrolet Tele-Theater*, the story told of a young combat veteran (Dennis Harrison) and his psychiatrist's (Ameche) efforts to relieve him of his war neurosis.

Around the end of 1949 Don and Phil Silvers were both pinch-hitting as emcees on Milton Berle's show when Mr. Television left on a two-week vacation. But first, Don and whole family flew back to Dubuque for a hometown Christmas.

He appeared around March 7, 1950 on *The Jack Carter Hour* as an inventor (playing "himself"), in which he has rigged up a device that allows him to see through the television and watch the people watching TV. Ameche had grown tired of the inventor gag, but it was a gig.

The fact that Ameche was *not* mechanically inclined never seemed to matter. A few times, at a host's house, if a water pipe burst, the hostess would hand Don a wrench, certain he knew all about it. And every inventor in the country sent invention ideas to Don, sometimes suggesting they split 50-50. He was also sometimes sent the inventions themselves, such as an automatic page turner for books, which tore 50 pages of a 18th-century (borrowed) book on Egypt history Don was reading one night. And when he used a gadget to make a fireplace flue open, the guests at his home at the time found themselves covered in soot. Don paid the cleaning bill—though a $450 Adrian gown refused to clean.

"Anyone who looks like an inventor frightens me," Don said. "After several painful lessons I now never open any inventions that are forwarded to me. I always return them unopened."

Luckily, television, for a few years, would be good to him, and light on the inventions.

Chapter Seven
TV MC

Once film work dried up, Don Ameche changed coasts to put his full-time efforts into that new medium with the hungry appetite: television. New York City was both throneroom and kitchen to its constant, often cheesy-looking assembly line. The local Dubuque newspaper reported that the Ameches had rented a house at 1855 Wood Street, near Nativity School where Tommy and Lawrence were then enrolled. Honore wanted to be with her father, J. David Predergast, who recently underwent surgery. Don was supposed to commute between Dubuque and New York during his television jobs. That continued for a year until the family moved into a Colonial country home in Shawnee, Pennsylvania, from which Don commuted to a Manhattan apartment. It afforded him the opportunity of, as he did in his Hollywood glory days, putting in 115% of his time and attention. Because of this, Don was often absent from home life, leaving Bonnie and Connie in Honore's lonely charge.

Connie recalled, "Talking about my mother is difficult since I didn't get along with her very well and when we did talk it was usually strained. We didn't argue, but we didn't talk or talk openly. She was intelligent, unhappy, and doing the best she could. I spent the most intense time with her when she was so ill at the end, and she was very lucid. Even then, though, I didn't learn a whole lot about her, except about her wish to have a 'normal' family.

"The little things I do remember are like pictures/vignettes. I remember brushing her hair, something she really liked. She had incredibly beautiful hair. I remember walking down Fifth Avenue with her when I was really young, holding her hand and feeling her mink coat sleeve on my wrist. I didn't remember California, since Bonnie and I were only 4 when we left, so New York was more my home and where I grew up."

Don was set to participate in *The Triumphant Hour* over NBC and Mutual at the end of March 1950. Sponsored by *The Family Theatre* and the Catholic Church, the hour-long television show was produced by the Reverend Patrick Peyton, and starred Rosalind Russell, Pat O'Brien, Don, Ann Blyth and others. Even the Dionne Quintuplets filmed a bit to be inserted. All cast and crew donated their services.

Ameche did, however, take some time off that year to witness the graduation ceremony for the Ameche and Frank boys from St. John's. And always made time for his daughters.

"In 1950 we were in New York," recalls Bonnie Ameche. "We were very cut off from knowing anyone or doing anything. We lived in a penthouse from the time Connie and I were in the sixth grade, and we never even knew the two other people on our floor. Daddy would work so we weren't out and about that much.

Don and his Honey.

We would go out to dinner at Toot Shoor's, The 21 Club, places like that, but there wasn't a lot of doing things with other people. Mom would take care of us while he was at work. We had to be in bed by eight, because we had to get up at six o'clock since we went to Mass and Communion every day before we went to school, a private Catholic school called St. Lawrence Academy. Things were pretty regulated. There were always tons of homework. In high school we went to the same nuns, the Sisters of Charity of Mount St. Vincent, and went to a boarding school in Tuxedo Park, New York, which was *wonderful* because you got to be away Monday through Friday and then you were home on the weekends. Then we went to college, when Connie spent a year out in Hawaii and I went to Georgetown University's school of nursing. I'd wanted to be a nurse since I was about eight years old and Daddy always encouraged that. So I had a real specific goal which really helped me.

"He was really opposed to us being involved with showbiz at all. A solid financial future was important to him. He didn't seem to keep hold of money, though he did have a lot of investments, including the horses. When I used to go to the track, I would go from barn to barn visiting the animals, and when Daddy finished watching the horses train, we would go to a wonderful restaurant where the trainers and jockeys ate. We'd have a nice breakfast there and then drive back. This was when I was in the 6th, 7th and 8th grades before I left for high school."

He may not have been the best balancer in the world, juggling a family and career both, but to Don's mind, securing jobs meant all balls were kept in the air. He was determined to make television work for him. In February of 1950 he sat with Jack Carson, Dennis Morgan, Oliver Hardy and others on the Hollywood Committee for Television Research.

From October 1, 1950 through December 24 of that same year, Don was emcee for the television game show, *Take a Chance*. Sponsored by Sweetheart soap, this NBC series chose contestants from the audience and gave them $5 to start with. Don asked four questions of the players, with each correct answer winning a prize of varying amounts. Whenever they wanted to not Take a Chance they could quit, but answering all four questions correctly gave the contestant a shot at the $1,000 question and 1,000 cakes of Sweetheart soap. If the answer was wrong, the player forfeited his last prize. The show was broadcast live on Sundays in the 10:30 to 11:00 daytime spot.

Ameche spent the early summer of 1951 emceeing *The Breakfast Club* program in Chicago, and in July he took over as manager of the *Holiday Hotel* from Edward Everett Horton, himself running things for the unseen owner "Mr. Holiday." The big-budget ABC series, sponsored by Packard Motors, received poor reviews since its beginning on March 23, 1950. The musical revue show involved the Manager trying to keep all his wacky guests happy and under control. Packard Motors had a showroom on the hotel's ground floor, for easy access to commercials, and after the regular comedy sketch by the usual cast, the scene shifted to the ballroom where the week's guest star would perform. Musical production numbers were also staged there by composer Gordon Jenkins.

Don was brought in at the end of the first season, but response was still lukewarm. In a last effort to save the show, it went through a complete overhaul in its last months of life. It now became *Don Ameche's Musical Playhouse*, with the same format, but with Don as manager of a playhouse rather than a hotel. The cast—Betty Brewer, Florence Halop, Joshua Shelley, etc.—was the same, but the show could not be saved. *The Playhouse* closed its doors to audiences on October 4, 1951.

Variety's September 20, 1950 review of the show "indicates that it has a good potential which may be realized once a few shows are under the belt. One of the major improvements lies in the fact that Don Ameche is now in the tophost role and he endows this spot with a warm personality and name value." It went on to praise Don's voice and flair for comedy in his "first regular series," and also liked the sets and musical direction. But the camera work of early television and smoothness of continuity had a lot to learn. On this reviewed episode, Betty

Brewer sang, as did the Don Craig Glee Club, doing "Ol' Man River." Of course, the sponsor's new model Packard was emphasized, and Don played the inventor yet again to straight man Joseph Buloff.

Don was having talks with CBS around this time. They thought he would make a good comic star of his own half-hour series. It eventually led to something:

In October of 1951 it was announced that Don and Frances Langford would star in a new ABC variety show, five days a week, from noon to 1:00 p.m. It was budgeted at $40,000 a week. Don at that time stated, "Daytime audiences are vastly more loyal than nighttime audiences. They will watch you every day for years, and they usually watch more intently. Maybe it's just that there aren't so many people around to distract their attention." He also knew that housewives wanted more variety than just cooking and shopping programs, that their tastes did not automatically change at 7:00 p.m. A few articles gave the daily *Kate Smith Show* credit for making the Ameche-Langford show a foolproof enterprise, and why the show had such a high budget—producers thought the public would eat up another daily variety show with big names.

With not much time for rehearsal, *The Frances Langford-Don Ameche Show* relied heavily on a Teleprompter. It was broadcast from the Little Theater at 240 W. 44th St. in New York. There were to be no huge sets or complicated lighting or many sets, just an intimate setting that producers hoped would get the audience closer to the performers. Ameche and Langford would act as a sort of "Greek chorus" between acts, such as a regular newlywed sketch. Don was also doing *Musical Playhouse* for ABC at this time.

"If you get set with a good show," he told reporters, "with a good format, you can go on for a long time. Unlike a big stage hit, you never grow tired of your role. Unlike movie making you keep pretty regular hours. In this new day-time series I'll be able to live the life of the average business man—roughly 9 to 5."

The Frances Langford-Don Ameche Show was one of many embarrassing early live television shows that played much better in its day than today. A popular vehicle for the stars, it was a daytime variety show which actually had a spin-off series, *Heaven for Betsy*, starring the two players of their regular "Couple Next Door" sketch (a newlywed version of The Bickersons) starring Jack Lemmon and his then-wife Cynthia Stone. Music was provided by Frances' old friend from their Bob Hope days, Tony Romano. The series ran from September 10, 1951 to March 14, 1952.

It has been rumored that Don was part of the more famous variety series, *Star Time* (September 5, 1950–February 27, 1951), which featured The Bickersons significantly in its hour format, but he never appeared on the series. The role of John Bickerson was ably, somewhat differently portrayed on this and the 1951 radio series, *The Bickersons*, by Lew Parker, best known as Marlo Thomas' father in *That Girl*.

Don Ameche, Jr. recalled, "They tried to do the Bickersons on television a couple of times, and Dad felt it wouldn't go, because he felt so much would be lost, you needed the imagination."

Yet there were few opportunities he would not embrace when pickings were slim. Around 1952 jobs were so scarce, Don took a job in Chicago announcing over the radio races from Arlington Park, for $150 a week. He'd sold his townhouse and beach mansion and rented a small beachhouse in California, since he was not sucking up much west coast sun these days.

In the last week of February 1952 he gave a speech before the Guild of St. Luke, Boston's distinguished society of Catholic doctors. His faith in God was significant in the Ameche perseverance never to give up in his chosen profession. He told a Boston newspaper: "Do I find it strenuous getting out to Mass and Communion practically every day? Gosh, no, I find it glorious! TV and other commitments keep me pretty much on the hop these days, but nothing phases me after I receive Communion. You come out of church saying, 'Glory be to the Father,' and you look up at the broad expanse of God's sky, and then you know that everything is okay. You're ready to start the day's work with a happy smile.

"To me, faith is a gift, and God is always ready to give a person grace if only he will cooperate with God. When I was a student back at St. Berchman's, we had to go to Mass every morning, and I used to go to Communion every day. When you're that age, you wonder what it's all about. But think of all the graces I was storing up! I've often wondered how many times in my life since then I've fallen back on that reservoir of graces. That's why I'm so keen on Catholic education. It prepares the child for later life in more ways than one!"

And it kept him in the game during the hard times. Already Don was looking at expanding his workload with stage projects. Richard Frank explains, "When I was in Van Nuys High School in 1953 Daddy George was once again assisting Don Ameche with finding him more stage and screen projects. A new nightclub act for Don was on my father's mind, so he wrote the act to include some song and dance to intermingle with the Ameche charm. When the format was complete, Don and Honey and George and my mother Barbara traveled down to San Diego in the new Chrysler car that my father had just purchased. Don did not get anywhere with that act, so he did his own things from that time on."

From April 29 through October 23, 1953 Don Ameche was the host of the popular 15-minute musical program, *Coke Time with Eddie Fisher*. This television series featured Fisher at the height of his popularity, where he sang most of his hit records, including "I'm Walking Behind You," which went to number one on the charts afterwards. Fisher would begin each show singing his "May I Sing to You" theme song, with guest singers appearing regularly. When Don left after only several months, announcer Freddy Robbins took on the extra duty of hosting the series.

Jim Ameche made a surprising resurgence in the public eye when the *Chicago Daily Tribune* ran a story about his cooking abilities, complete with recipe for Chicken Rosemary and Calves Liver Ameche (which sounds more like a Blanche Bickerson creation). At the time he was employed as a disc jockey at a Chicago radio station, spinning records every day but Sunday.

But it was Don Ameche who was to set the media on fire again, in one longshot of a career comeback that would put an Ameche horserace to shame.

Chapter Eight

The Comeback Kid

Either disillusioned with the politics or roles of television, or the fact that not enough work was coming his way, Don began traveling the country doing stage work. Mostly musicals. He played in at least three light operas: *Show Boat* on the East Coast, *Hazel Flagg* in Dallas, Texas, and *The Three Musketeers* in Louisville, Kentucky.

In November 1953, a year and a half before it opened on Broadway, Don was chosen by producers Cy Feuer and Ernie Martin for Cole Porter's last stage show (his *last* musical would be his next, the made-for-TV *Aladdin*), *Silk Stockings*. Before auditioning for the role, Don took singing lessons five times a week for two weeks. Once the lead was his, for the next fourteen months he took singing lessons with Herb Greene, who later became the conductor of the show. "I had never had a singing lesson before," Ameche told the press. "All I did in front of a microphone was croon. First thing Greene did was tear all that down. I don't know how he did it. I don't ask too many questions. But it sure must have been right."

Silk Stockings was Porter's second musical for Feuer and Martin. It went into rehearsal on October 18, 1954, six months later than planned, and began out-of-town tryouts on November 26. Based on the film *Ninotchka*, about a stern Russian agent who must save her comrades from Western decadence while trying not to fall in love, the musical ran at the Imperial Theater for 478 performances, from to February 24, 1955 to April 14, 1956 and cost $370,000 to produce, one of Broadway's most expensive musicals at the time. It made more than its money back.

It's not known whether Don and Cole spent any real time together reminiscing on their 1943 days from *Something to Shout About*, but it was literally a torturous time for the legendary composer. The poor man had been in pain every day of his life since 1937 when he suffered a horse-riding accident which crippled his legs. The theatre was losing its magic for him. To *Silk Stockings* rehearsals he brought a slew of pills, suppositories and six bottles of witch hazel for dabbing around his eyes every morning, plus a portable urinal and other necessities like a pepper mill, two cocktail shakers, music manuscript paper, a writing board, pencils, cooking utensils, and the New York telephone directory.

George S. Kaufman, his wife Leueen MacGarth and Abe Burrows (author of *Guys and Dolls*), shared co-credit on the show's book, while Porter wrote music & lyrics and Kaufman directed. Though Philadelphia critics were enamored of the show, producers Feuer and Martin felt the direction and book were weak. They hounded Kaufman for more and more gags, wanting a much more snappier package to take to Broadway. Finally, Kaufman and his wife had enough and bowed out of the production. Abe Burrows was brought in to revise the book and Feuer himself took over the direction.

Living in Manhattan on East 66th Street Don Ameche hoped for a comeback with *Silk Stockings*. He got it, and even got to introduce the show's only real hit and standard, "All of You." Photos, articles and praise poured in for his role as Steve Canfield opposite German-born Hildegarde Neff as Ninotchka. Unused to opening nights, the only one he'd attended was the previous year's *The Boy Friend*, but at the *Silk Stockings* premiere, he claimed "it was the biggest kick I ever got out of show business."

Brooks Atkinson of *The New York Times* certified that "we can all afford to relax now. Everything about *Silk Stockings* which opened at the Imperial Theater Thursday evening represents the best goods in the American musical comedy emporium." He called it witty and on the same level as *Guys and Dolls*, and assured readers that Don was "the perfect musical comedy hero, crackling in style, deadpan, assured, sardonic."

Atkinson's lengthy March 27, 1955 review admitted that the "score is tonic and the lyrics witty," and he loved the performers. "In the garish splendor of a Paris hotel Don Ameche is the ideal leading man. He sings loud—an excellent habit. He is cocky, suave, masculine and good-naturedly cynical. He gives a gratifying impression of being thoroughly at home in the midst of bedlam." The February 25, 1955 review in *The New York Journal-American* wrote that "Don Ameche is a big new star all over again; at long last here is a leading man who can sing without posing and flinging his arms about, who can read a line in an entirely natural manner, whose performance is unostentatious and charming." Reviewer John McClain was grateful the performances were so good since "this is by no means a great Cole Porter score."

But everyone loved *Silk Stockings*. "You'd better rush to the Imperial box-office right away if you want to relish it in the near future," wrote *The Daily Mirror*. "*Stockings* is wonderful subversive propaganda—on our side," wrote *The Daily News*. Walter Kerr of the *New York Herald Tribune* affirmed that "Mr. Ameche is a decided find—if he can be called that at this juncture—for the musical comedy stage. Possessed of a penetrating show-baritone that plugs a song handsomely, and of an easy-going authority that is never smug, he leers, scowls, smirks, and furrows those pyramiding eyebrows with great humor. He can look as though he's listening to someone else sing, too—no mean achievement." Yet, it was Gretchen Wyler who was the showstopper.

"At that time," recalled Wyler, "it was the longest tryout ever. At that time, shows were always tried out on the road, they never opened cold. Philadelphia, New Haven, wherever. *Stockings* had fourteen weeks on the road, with many

changes, many new endings, many new songs. Yvonne Adair, playing Peggy Dainton in our show, had been Carol Channing's sidekick in *Gentlemen Prefer Blondes*, and there was great publicity on her and Don and Hildegarde, but Yvonne had become ill in Philadelphia soon after the show opened to less than good reviews, so her understudy had gone on. The producers knew me and asked me if I would come to understudy the understudy. It was an amazing downer for me because the understudy was *terrible*. But Yvonne came back and was wonderful, but ten days before the show came to Broadway, which would be February 14, 1955, the understudy had taken a train to go to an audition in New York; she had been really annoyed that they had not given her Peggy's part. I watched the end of Act 1, and saw Yvonne collapse on stage. It was one of the great Gypsy stories of all times. I went tearing back to the chorus girl dressing room because I was the only one who knew I had to go on. Cole Porter, Abe Burrows, the producers, everyone was out in the audience that night. I went on that night, and they all came to my dressing room to say 'You will open in 10 days on Broadway' because Yvonne Adair was very ill, and they did not like the current understudy.

"Don Ameche was terribly charming, had that wonderful wry kind of humor.

He was a big movie star ten years earlier, but this was a great break for him. Obviously his songs were low-key, very nice songs, but no showstopper among them. But he was not a showstopper kind of guy. He was wonderful, likeable, good humor, attractive, but he was no Bob Goulet, the kind of guy Broadway was clamoring for. And Hildegarde Neff was a big German movie star, but she was scared to death. One of the musicians knew hypnosis and he would hypnotize her nearly every night before the show just to get her through it. So between the two of them, we really didn't have the kind of excitement that one expects with a Broadway show.

"On opening night, I know that Don had reportedly fainted; Hildegarde was throwing up. It was a big opening at the Imperial with all the critics and everyone in the audience. I was 22 years old and I could not *wait* to get out there! I stopped the show two times. Broadway stars do not like to be upstaged. There was nothing they could do about me, so they chose to ignore me. I've often said that it was the most exciting thing that ever happened to me before or since. I would stop the show nearly every night. When I went out for my applause, the audience screamed, because the numbers were showstopping numbers. 'Stereophonic Sound' was a brand-new technique in film, done downstage, lots of flash; this brazen movie star character is surrounded by a lot of reporters. Then in the second act there was 'Josephine' with cartwheels and splits and bumps and grinds—it was just *huge*. When I came out, the applause went up to the roof; when the stars came out, the applause went down. It was awful. They never spoke to me, neither one of them.

"Everyone knew that Don was a majorly religious man, and everyone knew that he was madly in love with Hildegarde Neff. He adored her, he was at her feet. And she had to suffer such humiliation from this brassy blonde showstopper called Gretchen Wyler. It was just too much for him, and it was sad for her. We would go to events together. I'll never forget going to the Plaza Hotel. The three of us were invited. The two of them sat together and they requested that I not be seated with them. They couldn't even get themselves to be civil or theatrically pleasant. It was the greatest thing that ever happened to me, but it was also one of the saddest years because the two stars of the show, who were billed over the title, did not like me. I understood it, but it didn't make it any less painful for me to be around that."

Don said at the time: "I don't think there was any doubt that it was an established fact as to how cold I was prior to this show. Of course, I had kept active enough during the past few years but I was never fortunate enough to get a successful TV series and I still think that TV was the right move for me to make. Consciously, I don't know that it bothered me a great deal falling out of things the way I did, but I suppose that subconsciously it did. It never really depressed or threw me. Fortunately all along I managed to make good money. I know when the show came out a hit all the good friends I've made were so elated for me that I guess they were more concerned about the drip than I was. I had never looked upon show business as a guaranteed permanent thing. I knew it would all end some day."

But Broadway's revival was more than a career boost, it was a much needed ego jumpstart. *New York News'* April 10, 1955 article, entitled "He's Wearing Well," pictured Don and Honore on the cover and read like a barely updated press release from the good ol' days. He called himself a New Yorker at heart since he doesn't go to bed before two or three in the morning and seldom rises before noon. Honore must set the alarm for 6:30, though, to get the kids off to school.

Apparently, they were as happy as ever and certainly weren't going without in their new life. Honore boasted, "With the butler's pantry and the huge kitchen we have here, I feel as though I'm sitting in the lap of luxury. We even have a maid's room, but no maid. I use it for our office and I use the maid's bathroom for a laundry." But Mrs. Ameche wasn't entirely happy. The location, not the situation, was the only thing that had changed.

Catching rays from the limelight again was especially helping Don. "Funny thing about it all, I'm down to 156 pounds. Being a performer, I have to keep myself in shape, so I exercise a little more, eat a little less-never eat lunch—do calisthenics every morning, and whenever possible, walk to wherever I am going. Of course, I've been on the go ever since we opened with the show in Philly. This was last November 26 and since then, we've played Boston and Detroit before we opened here in New York.

"It's real good being back, too. I'm a sports fan and where do you get more sports than right here? When we lived out on the Coast, I couldn't wait to get my hands on a New York paper to find out what was going on at the ballparks or at Madison Square Garden. Now, I'm here and maybe I won't be catching many night games but you'll be seeing a lot of me out there in the afternoons."

The 1957 MGM film version of *Silk Stockings* starred Fred Astaire and Cyd Charisse. Don later said that he thought Sinatra, not Astaire, should have played his role on screen; naturally, no one from Broadway was asked to reprise their characters in Hollywood, not even showstopping Gretchen.

Broadway's high profile meant that TV offers were now coming to *him*. On November 24, 1956 at 9:00 p.m. Don appeared on NBC's Saturday Spectacular version of *High Button Shoes* with Hal March and Nanette Fabray. In December of 1956 the Ameches were visited by *Person to Person,* Edward R. Murrow's television interview show. Only Don, Jr. couldn't make it as he was in the Navy, stationed in Hawaii. The family spent that Christmas in New York, where Don was rehearsing his new play, *Holiday for Lovers,* and missed their usual Iowa holiday.

After Broadway's *Silk Stockings* Don talked with Ronald Alexander about starring in his straight comedy, *Bon Voyage* (once called *Bon Voyage, Darling*). The role had been slated for Robert Preston, but opened on Valentine's Day, 1957, as Holiday for Lovers with Ameche in the lead. It played at the Longacre Theater for 100 performances, closing on May 11. It starred Carmen Mathews as Mary Dean, Don as husband Robert Dean, with Sandra Church as Betsy Dean and Audrey Christie as Connie McDougal.

The plot involved Robert Dean (Ameche), an insurance salesman from Minneapolis, taking his family (wife and two unattached daughters) on a

European trip (from France to Spain). It was yet another good vehicle for Don's shouting side.

Opening night was a success, with a responsive audience in tow, though the *Daily Mirror* found the plot tedious and couldn't figure out why everyone was laughing. *The New York Journal-American* was far more charitable toward it and Ameche: "he is at his ingratiating and attractive best." *The New York Post* title of "The Pleasant Tour of Don Ameche" gave most of the play's credit of charm to its star. "Wasn't there a belief in his movie days that Don Ameche was rather a stuffy actor? If there was, it must have been Hollywood's fault, because on the stage he is the very picture of easy geniality, relaxation and warm-heartedness, and a model of pleasant unpretentiousness."

Don did his best not to let work get in the way of what he thought was important, though he didn't always achieve it. During early *Silk Stockings'* rehearsals he was asked to give the major addresses at his old college, Loras, where he had completed his pre-law studies in 1928, for the May 30, 1954 commencement services. And while visiting Honore's ailing mother in Dubuque, Don stopped over at Cornell College to serve as Master of Ceremonies at which 96 colleges and universities took part in an impressive procession into King Memorial Chapel. He also gave the commencement address. Don, Jr. and Ronald also went to Loras College, where Ronald received the American Legion Silver Perfection medal for being the top drill cadet of the year.

When the hit Broadway musical *Junior Miss* was made into a 90-minute Christmastime comedy for CBS on *The DuPont Show of the Month*, Don starred as the father of Junior Miss, played by Carol Lynley. It was broadcast on Friday, December 20, 1957.

The experienced cast featured old friend Joan Bennett as Harry Graves' (Ameche) wife, and Paul Ford as his boss, J.B. Curtis. The music was by Burton Lane, with lyrics by Dorothy Fields. The farcical plot takes place in New York City, where Judy Graves (Lynley) gets her father into trouble by misconstruing a simple kiss on the cheek of his boss' daughter, as well as a few other innocent mix-ups.

As of March 1958 Don was taping *Don Ameche's Real Life Stories* for broadcast every morning, Monday through Friday, from 10:30 to 11:00 a.m. Prerecording gave him time for more theatrical excursions.

Goldilocks, written by Walter and Jean Kerr, opened on October 11, 1958. The two-act musical comedy contained a delightful score by LeRoy Anderson and lyrics by Joan Ford. It starred Elaine Stritch as Maggie Harris and Don Ameche as George Randolph Brown and ran for 161 performances, closing on February 28, 1959. It was nominated for five Tony Awards, winning for Best Actress (Pat Stanley) and Best Actor (Russell Nype).

It is New York City, 1913, and musical comedy star Maggie Harris (Stritch) is giving her farewell performance in *Lazy Moon* before running off to marry young socialite George Randolph Brown (Nype). When director Max Grady (Ameche) steps in and threatens to sue if she doesn't stay to finish the picture

Original cast album of *Goldilocks*, 1958.

she's contracted for, her would-be hubby understands, little knowing that the shooting schedule will be stretched because the great director is determined to make Maggie fall in love with him. She soon realizes she's fallen out of love with George, since she and Max truly have film in their blood.

The role was perfect for Don, its plot so reminiscent of *Hollywood Cavalcade* and *Slightly French.* Alas, Walter Kerr, being theatre critic for the *New York Herald Tribune* (and Jean as the popular author of *Please Don't Eat the Daisies*), did not save the show from failed notices.

John McClain's review of *Goldilocks* was disappointed. "Probably like everyone else, I expected too much." He called it occasionally extremely funny, but lavish and pretentious. It was the "slight" plot he found most grating and the Walter and Jean Kerr book "conspicuously meager." As to the cast, "I'm not sure that Don Ameche was ideally cast as the movie director. Again he established his professional competence both as an actor and song dispenser." But he did praise "There Never Was a Woman," calling it "an excellent ballad."

Brooks Atkinson of *The New York Times* wrote that "*Goldilocks* is a beautiful, handsome musical comedy with an uninteresting book." In fact, he claimed that the book ruined everything the actors accomplished, "for you could hardly ask for a more winning pair of actors than Don Ameche and Elaine Stritch." But without doubt it was Miss Stritch's show. She "can destroy life throughout the country with the twist she gives to the dialogue." Don had his fair share of praise, though: "A cocky, dapper guy with a good voice and quick intelligence, Mr. Ameche undermines civilizations with equal dexterity." But for all its qualities, reviewers commonly found the show lacking in a story swallowed up by overproduction. It was deemed an unexciting musical with lots of glitz and little substance.

But Robert Coleman of the *New York Mirror* wrote that "Don Ameche . . . puts the right bite in the role of corner-cutting megaphoner," and generally liked its old-fashioned gloss. His favorite component of the evening was the usual favorite: the take-off on the shooting of an Egyptian film epic in a freezing cornfield.

Don had replaced Barry Sullivan in its Boston try-outs. Sullivan reportedly withdrew because he felt "uncomfortable" in his first musical stage assignment. Don had originally been considered for the starring role, but "final agreements failed to materialize." Walter Winchell's column stated that Don hadn't been hired because the producers wouldn't meet his price; when Sullivan didn't work out, they had to pay Ameche almost twice what he was originally asking. When Sullivan left, the *Boston Pilot* welcomed the change of someone who obviously enjoyed the role. "Ameche has a good baritone, professional polish, and diction as perfect as anyone in the business." The reviewer considered him the perfect hustler and the ideal "fathead through and through." According to *The New York Herald Tribune* Don had been thrust in the role just nine days before paid previews began in New York, requiring him to learn an entire Broadway lead role almost instantly. And just twelve days before opening night.

The media was then lamenting the fact that in March of 1959 Don had to bow out of a season of a new TV show entitled *Too Young to Go Steady*. He was to have played Brigid Bazien's father, a role that ultimately went to Donald Cook. *Chicago American* wrote, "It had been my hope that *Too Young to Go Steady* might start a long period of TV going steady with Don Ameche." The series, starring Brigid Bazien and Joan Bennett, only lasted a single season anyway.

When one medium slowed up, Ameche was one of the lucky ones to have a second cushion to fall back on. He returned to Broadway on March 2, 1961 in *13 Daughters*. The show rehearsed for about three months in New York, and opened in Philadelphia. The music, lyrics and semi-autobiographical script came from Honolulu-born Eaton Magoon, Jr., with some additional material written by Leon Tokatyan. It was directed by Billy Matthews, stage manager on hits like *Bells Are Ringing* and *Dial "M" for Murder*. Even though it was nominated for two Tony Awards (George Jenkins for Best Scenic Design and Pembroke Davenport for Best Conductor and Musical Director), *13 Daughters* still could not get past 28 performances before closing on March 25.

The story followed Ameche as the wise Chinaman Chun, who marries a beautiful Princess in Hawaii in spite of the curse that promises nothing but daughters from the marriage, and that none of the daughters shall marry. Thirteen daughters later, Chun still isn't deterred to marrying off his daughters, which takes up most of the plot.

Its humor was quite alternative and refreshing to Broadway audiences of the time, as illustrated from this quote of the title song, sung by Ameche:

THIRTEEN DAUGHTERS
THIRTEEN DAUGHTERS
THIRTEEN BLOSSOMS FRESH AND FAIR
MY BEGUILING FLOWER GARDEN
BROUGHT TO BLOOM WITH LOVE AND CARE . . .
AND I MUST ADMIT
A LITTLE BIT
OF CHINESE "SAVOIR FAIRE"

THIRTEEN DAUGHTERS
THIRTEEN DAUGHTERS
SWEET AS ROSES ON THE VINE
EVERY PETAL PURE AND PERFECT
NO BOUQUET COULD BE MORE FINE . . .
AND I DOUBT THERE IS
A GARDENER WITH
A GREENER THUMB THAN MINE!

Don spent ten days with Mr. Magoon in the fall before the musical opened, to gather up the realism of what Magoon's grandfather was really like. It was the 1890s, a time when, according to Magoon, the island of Oahu was under the influence of the Chinese who had come over seeking paradise; the British, seeking to expand their worldwide empire further; and American missionaries, who wanted to convert everyone they considered pagan. If nothing else, *13 Daughters* was teeming with local color and island history.

The Philadelphia Inquirer launched its review with the imposing statement: "It is altogether possible that the musical comedy the season has been waiting for is *13 Daughters*, a charming low-pressure show." It singled out Don's voice as lifting "an easy baritone in several story-building songs, many of which begin with a quaint recitative." More than once Don's role had been compared to a Charlie Chan caricature. The *Philadelphia Daily News* wrote on January 31, 1961: "Don Ameche's customary air of the cat-that-ate-the canary stands him in good stead as the wily Honolulu business man." It also thought the show was overlong by 20 minutes and more of a period piece than anything else.

Unfortunately, New York reviews were also mixed. Though the production looked good, mixing Hawaiian sights and sounds, it was that inconsistency of style that rankled some reviewers. *Daily News* gave it the best benefit of the doubt, calling it "charming, unusual and beautifully mounted." The story was "pleasant," the lyrics "graceful," and the dances "are the best we have had in the musical theatre this season." *New York Mirror* admitted, "Magoon's score falls pleasantly on the ears, his lyrics are serviceable, but the book is pedestrian. Don Ameche is well-cast as the clever merchant, more given to the observations of

13 Daughters, 1961.

Benjamin Franklin than Lae-tse. Don is a good actor, and knows what to do with a song."

New York Herald Tribune's Walter Kerr, author of Don's previous Broadway outing, took exception to all the "it is written" sage sayings and admired Ameche's nerve for doing them. But the important paper, *The New York Times*, was mostly positive, calling *13 Daughters* ingenuous, "oddly and partly disarming . . . The prevailing atmosphere is naivete."

Nona Beamer, choreographer assistant and Hawaiian consultant, recalled, "Mr. Ameche always wore a bowler hat and would hang it up in the morning. We would come bursting in the door and look for that hat, and if it was hanging there, we would calmly, quietly walk into the theatre, but if it wasn't there, we would burst in like a bunch of Indians. He was a good influence on us, made us a little more professional.

"We thought the show was a success. The achievement of melding the cultures was a big factor in our hearts. I think we got that across. It was during the Easter season, and I think a lot of people had given up Broadway for Lent. The crowds were thin. But we were well received when we opened in Philadelphia. We found that encouraging.

13 Daughters, 1961.

"There was one amusing thing: in New York, the union said we had to have panties for each dancer. But with long dresses on, it seemed unnecessary so we didn't budget on that. We did end up putting them in pantaloons. We didn't know a lot about the various rules and regulations of the unions there, but we learned."

Funnily enough, later on, during a guest spot on TV's *To Tell the Truth*, Don failed to recognize one of three women claiming to be a woman's fencing champion (the idea of the show was for three contestants to pretend to be the same person, with celebrities trying to pick out the *real* person) as an actress (Gloria Gabriel) who had played one of his daughters in *13 Daughters*. Don was as floored as the audience.

Two seasons after his rebirth in *Silk Stockings*, he was a healthy 160 pounds and enjoying the life an actor again. It was showtime!

Chapter Nine

It's Showtime

It wasn't until 1961 that Don had his first hit TV series. *International Showtime* was an ambitious departure from the normal variety programs of the day. Where other series would have acts come in to plain-looking studio settings, *International Showtime* went on location to find the acts. For the adventurous spirit of Ameche, who admittedly was not a particular fan of circuses, it was a chance to stay busy, with little chance for boredom and a great deal of constant travel which he thoroughly enjoyed. Every week from September 15, 1961 to September 10, 1965 at 7:30 p.m. on NBC Don would introduce ice shows, magic shows and mostly circuses, give a bit of history or circus lore before each act commenced, then sit back among the audience to enjoy the show. Its flamboyant, larger-than-life, larger-than-studio European spectaculars was a novelty few series would ever match (though the idea was revamped briefly in the late 1980s), and as its host warmed to the show, Don's happiness grew. "I'm attracted to anything that's good. And when circuses are good, they're very good."

Originally, executive producers Larry White and Joe Cates had not conceived *Showtime* having an on-camera emcee, but at the suggestion of a sponsor, Don Ameche was signed. The plan was to tape each circus in its entirety and edit the show down to 45+ minutes for an hour's worth of television. But no one considered the script. Don's perfectionist attitude did not like those first few weeks when cue cards were hastily assembled and scribbled with his opening remarks before the camera. The producers understood and time thereafter was duly spent on proper scripts, mostly by Bruce MacDonnell.

After a few shows, all the bugs were vetted and Don could relax into his role as smiling, hard-traveling guide. The first few episodes reminded him, painfully, of the beginnings of his Hollywood career when notes and scripts were quickly changed the night before. But the intense workload didn't stop with smoother runs. Every circus performance was a full night's work, about three hours or more. Don would arrive in each circus town three days before shooting, watching the circus the first day, receiving his script and rehearsing the second day, and taping the show on the third. It required a crew of 35 to film each *IS*, including nine American technicians. Two of the show's agents spoke ten languages between them, enabling an easier European crossing.

Unlike the official ringmaster of the circus, Ameche did not dress up formally in a tuxedo for his emcee duties but kept to a jacket, shirt and tie, even in the hottest of spots—such as Holstebro, in northern Denmark on the Jutland Peninsula, where everyone else in the crew stripped down to T-shirts. It was sometimes intensely difficult to keep himself and his clothes as clean and fresh as he would've liked, but Don was a thorough professional who conducted himself with dignity all the way. Though various European laundries usually sent back his shirts starched beyond comfort, Don had bought himself three wash-n-wear shirts which he nightly laundered himself in his hotel room.

Riding in Copenhagen with Kiki, the dwarf clown, in 1962.

TV Guide's explicit December 22, 1962 article on the series gave rare insight into *IS*'s inner workings, and boasted that in less than two years Ameche had crossed Europe eight times, visiting eight countries and twenty-one cities/towns.

In the episode "Circus and Ice from Europe," in the Spring of 1963, Don once appeared as part of the act in Circus Schumann in Copenhagen with a trained (of course) horse. The head of Circus Schumann knew of Don's love for horses and suggested the act. Ameche rehearsed diligently for a week and everything was fine. But during the performance, something happened. The horse acted oddly all the way through, and just would not jump through the big hoop and race out of the ring at the act's finale. The circus owner himself had to grab the bridle and force the horse through the hoop. The Ameche ego was bruised.

As the series progressed, a theme for every program was sought, be it the number of times a lion tamer had been hurt in the ring or humorous stories behind the acts (as in the cowgirl "Sigrid, Daughter of Texas," who had never been to Texas in her life, but learned her talents from a stepfather who toured as a cowboy in American circuses).

Eventually, European circuses were exhausted—there just weren't enough of them not to stay out of the rest of the world. At the end of the 1961-62 season, the last two or three programs were shot in Japan. There were plans the next year to expand into circuses of the Far East, which pleased the culinary spirit of Ameche who was day by day growing as a connoisseur of gourmet food and drink. On his time off he would frequent the best restaurants and the quaintest of family-owned pubs with charmed curiosity, daring to try new items.

The best wine, he was convinced during these travels, was found in France's Burgundy country near Lyon. There he could have dinner and wine for $20, including tip, which delighted his ongoing sense of frugality as well. Though he claimed prices were outrageous in Paris and Copenhagen, they still served his two favorite European dishes: Frog Legs a la Grenouille at La Grenouille in Paris, and flaskestee (a Danish pork delicacy) at the Seven Nations restaurant in Copenhagen.

In Munich with the Bronleys, a daredevil aerial act, in 1963.

He made the cover of *The Chicago Tribune*'s *TV Week* on July 27, 1963, which contained a small article about himself and the show: "1930s' 'Voice with a Smile,' Don Ameche, Going Strong on TV."

"*Showtime* is good entertainment," he stated, "and better quality than anything else on the air. The people who work with the circus have spent a lifetime perfecting their acts and then some of them lay their lives on the line every time they perform, whether for an audience of 100 persons or 2,000. They're a dedicated people who have put much time, effort, and thought into their work. The audience appeal of such a show is unlimited. You'd expect children would make up the bulk of our audience, but this isn't true. It's the middle-age men and women who watch, but refuse to admit it."

The great circus show played nineteen performances, including nine matinees, at the new Polar Dome (seating 4,000) in Dundee, Illinois from July 19 to 28, 1963. Acts from all over the globe came for their chance to show off on national television: the Aerial Hustrels from Germany, Mlle., Jeannine Divoteau from France, Rossell Troup from Mexico, the Les Romano trio from Italy, Pallenberg's Bears from Germany, Michael De La Vega's illusion act, Norbu the gorilla, Anden's (huge bundles of fluff) Poodles, and a barrelful of others.

Everything from chimps skipping rope and riding motorcycles to the Borjevas of Denmark spinning 32 plates was seen on Ameche's circus antics. From the Great Barton of Sweden, who balanced himself on his index finger, to Loni of Holland, who did a mean "risley" (or juggling with the feet), *International Showtime* was the ultimate vaudeville show.

By June 1963 it was reported that circumnavigator Ameche had filmed 95 circus shows. *The Washington Star* gave the show a rave review on August 6, 1963. Written on Don Ameche's own clipping of the review were the words, "Wonderful review. If this keeps up the show should be a smash but everywhere." The *Star* praised the Hustreis swaypole act (suspenseful swaying 120 feet in the air) done in the Carter Barron amphitheater.

The Washington Post was also enthusiastic, especially liking The Bizzarros, Italian clowns that shook out "Oh Susanna" with the bells attached to their feet, hands and heads. It called the vast set of acts, "a highly entertaining and very professional group." Don himself found that Europeans were much more impressed with circuses than Americans, clowns being the most popular, some receiving salaries of $2,000 a week.

"Most Americans are good travelers," he said, "once they learn that you won't find things in foreign countries like you do at home. They don't have the ordinary facilities that we do in the United States except at the very top hotels. My job takes me to many small cities and villages where the people don't think, act or behave like we do. And it is the American who must make the adjustment, not the natives."

Ed Youngman's column in *The Canadian Statesman* on September 4, 1963 praised the *International Showtime* performed on August 28 in the Memorial Arena in Peterborough, Canada. The audience was small for the Arena, seating that night around 1,500, but the review of acts from France, Germany, Norway,

Sweden, Denmark, England and the USA was entirely positive. "And, to top off a delightful evening, your scribe had the honour and pleasure of interviewing the master of ceremonies, Mr. Don Ameche, who is a handsome, well-groomed, urbane, gracious gentleman, dedicated to the best in show business, possessor of a splendidly flexible, resonant voice, and who uses impeccable English." He called Don a perfectionist and wrote at length on the show which began with a 2x2 bicycle act which balanced non-lightweights on the rider's shoulders. Tumblers, a balancing act of chimps in white boots and trousers, and a beautiful aerial act followed.

It may have seemed all glamour, but the constant trekking during those four *IS* years was long and hard. It was worth it to Don, who found himself with extra jobs because of it. When Hugh O'Brian was forced to cancel his star billing at an amusement park show in Boston, Don was called in as a replacement (a happening that would happily occur throughout his career). Knowing what emcee they had to work with, the producers of the show rounded up four circus acts and re-dubbed the gala as ***Don Ameche and His International Showtime Circus.*** It broke every record at the park, including the previous year's Ricky Nelson concert.

One of the many dog acts woofing it up on *International Showtime*.

One of Ameche's few films of the '60s was the *International Showtime* compilation movie, *Rings Around the World*, released in 1966, and again produced and directed by Gilbert Cates. Don had little screen time, but his rich, affectionate narration sparkled throughout, gluing the acts together. "Man has built himself many structures," he begins before the credits are shown and a tent is raised. "Homes, churches, theatres. But no building in the long history of man has housed such magic, so much fantasy and so much danger as a circus."

In his circus-dominated study, John Shawcross (Ameche) records his thoughts on the many circuses he has come across for a new book. He speaks not to camera, but for the benefit of a reel-to-reel tape recorder which captures his musings and bafflement at the various death-defying acts which comprise most of the picture. Much of it involves balancing acts, including the amazing Marco, who somehow manages to balance a glass tray with glasses full of wine, which is then balanced on a sword, which *then* teeters on the tip of a short sword which he keeps clenched in his teeth. If that wasn't enough, the brave man then climbs a ladder to the top at which point he bends all the way over so that if the sword were to fall, gravity would make it run him through.

Other incredible and incredulous performances included Tarzan, who let a great African elephant slowly walk over his six-year-old son. The most interesting lion act came from Pablo Noel, who had such control over the beasts that he commanded them all to lie down together, then jumped into the middle a few times as if they were huge stuffed animals. He also fearlessly put his face far into a lion's mouth. The other lion act, led by Gunther Gebel Williams, was not as lucky; the evening after his filmed performance of giving raw meat to his lion, he had his arm ripped off. Amazing top hat and etc. juggling from Rudy Cardenas, Mendez and Seitz on a tightrope with no net, and one lone clown act (Francesco Clowns) were other standouts of the 98-minute film. Not to mention the Mascott Sisters: one sister balancing the other on her head (head first) as she climbs a ladder.

"In the circus arena we see the glorious possibilities of man," says Shamcross in his closing narration. It was a delightful film, helped by a lengthy Disney-documentary-type score by Jacques Belasco, and interesting, though possibly dated, camera angles (point of view shots, for instance). "The Canvas Sky," sung by Neil Sedaka, played over the closing credits, which listed the circuses and where they were filmed: Smethport County Fair (Smethport, PA), the Circus Schumann (Copenhagen), the Circus Krone (Kiel), the Spanish National Circus (Munich), the Circus Scott (Stockholm), and the Circus Knie (Lausanne).

The Ameche girls had the sublime delight to spend an entire summer traveling with the TV show in Europe. "It was not only a fun summer, but an educational one as well," Connie recalled. "Bonnie and I traveled on our own for part of the time, staying in Youth Hostels, strange rented rooms, and generally sightseeing as much as possible. Joe Cates was the producer and he was always very nice to us. One of the fun times was holding a baby lion in my lap during the beginning a show.

"It is difficult to know whether or not Papa enjoyed doing the show, but he did it with grace and charm. I am sure that he had a good time in Europe and enjoyed the company of many of the crew. We did spend time with my father, but as you can imagine he was very busy. He did 21 circuses and I don't know how many magic shows. Bonnie and I saw about seven or eight circuses and three or four magic shows."

When the magic was over, Don slipped back into his old faithful stage work. Only this time, it wasn't Broadway.

Chapter Ten

The Lean Years

After the success of *International Showtime*, it's difficult to guess why Don Ameche hid himself in the constant touring of theatre companies. Yes, regional theatre meant he could command the top billing he deserved, but the hours were long, learning new shows, traveling to new cities. And he still had his investments: during *IS* his two-year-old horses "Mountain Dawn" and "Toujour L'Amour" were quartered at Belmont and were being considered for the Kentucky Derby. His filly "Crystal Classic" had recently won her first race.

Perhaps it was his restless nature creeping up on him again. Perhaps it was that he had simply fallen out of favor with television producers and audiences. One theory as to Ameche's downfall in pictures had been that, by the end of the 1940s, his dapper charm was not as hungrily sought as Hollywood's new leading man type: the tough, unshaven look of a Humphrey Bogart, or the youthful carelessness of a James Dean. Perhaps it was the lack of opportunities that failed to materialize: Alice Faye hoped that Don would be cast opposite her in the 1962 remake of *State Fair*, as Abel Frake, the hog farmer. Tom Ewell received the role instead.

But those who count the 1960s and 1970s as Don's "lost years" don't realize that he stayed in the public eye—even if those eyes were focused from middle-America—constantly. He would perform in many tours and regional theatres during these decades, appearing in plays such as *The Girl in the Freudian Slip, Father of the Bride, Champagne Complex,* and many musicals with the Kenley Players in Akron, Ohio. In December of 1960 he briefly went to work for Detroit's WXYZ-TV, hosting *Don Ameche's Hollywood Theatre*, which ran late showings of old Hollywood musicals.

When the odd movie role came around, however, he made time for it. On January 28, 1961, Warner Brothers released *A Fever in the Blood*, based on William Pearson's novel, starring Efrem Zimbalist, Jack Kelly, and Don Ameche.

Dynamo Senator Simon (Ameche) has dreams of the Presidency, but must first win the Governorship (of an unnamed state) and he's prepared to fight hard for it. So is District Attorney Dan Callahan (Jack Kelly), who uses a current sensational murder case to get his name in the papers. The thorn in both their sides is Judge Hoffman (Efrem Zimbalist), who would also like to be Governor, but not at the cost of his own integrity. Simon wants Hoffman to declare a mistrial so Callahan won't have a conviction to laud over everyone. Hoffman rejects the idea (and Simon's offhand bribe), ultimately allowing in some questionable testimony that soon convicts the actually innocent defendant (the opening scene shows the real murderer: a gardener who isn't part of the film's main plot). Thinking that he may have condemned an innocent man, Hoffman tells the truth about the bribe, which Simon angrily denies. Only when Simon is dying from a heart attack in the hospital does he admit the truth. Hoffman, at last, wins the nomination (and, it's implied, the Governorship), at the rousing political rally at the end.

A make-up session for A Fever in the Blood, 1961.

The Los Angeles Examiner called *A Fever in the Blood* "packed with action" and that Don Ameche gave "a delineation of such technical perfection that it should be studied by all young actors who aspire to greatness." Ameche showed his confidence and command as Senator, making one wonder why this role was so out of the blue. He would have to wait until 1970 to receive such an imperious character to portray again.

The press made much of the fact that it was his first film in a dozen years. "I'm glad no one said I'm making a comeback," he told *Screen Stories*. "Many roles were offered to me when I left 20th Century-Fox in 1946. Either the story wasn't right, or perhaps, foolishly, I wouldn't accept anything less than the lead at the time. Since then, I've starred on Broadway in plays and musicals, and also became interested in racehorse breeding on my Ohio farm. Yes, I've had a ball. But right now, I miss my wife. She's busy running our New York apartment, and couldn't come out. We were school-day sweethearts and have been inseparable since 1932, when we were married."

But by then the Ameche marriage was no longer functioning. The lonely and often estranged Honore had gone back to Iowa to be with her mother. As Connie Ameche remembered, "I never saw any overt 'falling out' between my parents. They were always polite and seemed to care about each other. If they ever fought, they did it far from me. I think that when they were upset, they just went their separate ways for a while. The last time they ever were in a room together was the day I got married. I didn't know that right away, because everyone in the family thought that I wouldn't take it well, so it was six months later that I found out that they had separated, although they never did it officially. Papa took care of her until she passed away and talked to her very briefly on the phone from time to time when she was sick. From what my mother said, I think she kept waiting for him to come back right up to just shortly before she died.

"My parents did not act any differently than when they were together. I would say that the separation was a long time in coming, but they kept it to themselves. My mother never even acknowledged it, although I know from neighbors of theirs in Arizona that she did drink quite a bit more. I went to see her a few months after I was married and she seemed okay to me. A lot of my father's clothes were still in the apartment, so it was hard to tell. She talked as if he were just on a business trip and would be home shortly. Since I didn't know about the separation yet, I was in the dark."

Radio may have been a fading memory in 1961, but Bickersons creator Philip Rapp was determined not to let the Bickersons fade with it. The arguing duo had never found lasting fame in the new medium of television, but it had kept the comedy team in the public eye enough to interest Columbia Records in doing an original album of its greatest quips.

Rapp flew to New York on March 6, 1961 to put everything in order to reunite Frances Langford and Don Ameche in the recording studio. A tentative date for recording 35 to 40 minutes worth of material at Perry Como's studio was set for June 6 and 8 of that year, to be recorded in front of a live audience. Rapp was adamant on keeping the live flavor, so that even if a line was partially obscured by laughter, the line would stay as is. Except for the fact that the production quality was better, and in stereo, it's often hard to tell the difference between the album tracks and *Old Gold Show* bits. Record executives wanted the record to be out for that Christmas, securing it a spot in the Columbia House Record Club.

The Bickersons was released in November of 1961 on the Columbia/CBS label. Don and Frances were shown arguing in their separate beds in several poses on the cover. In April of 1961 a royalty rate had been set for the record: the combined artist royalty (Ameche and Langford) was five cents per record, with Rapp receiving 15 cents a record for his copyrighted characters. A 45-single boasting "more from the hottest comedy record in the country!" was passed around to radio stations resulting in frequent airplay.

The record was such a hit (even ending up on airplanes), that Columbia decided to follow it up with a sequel recording. *The Bickersons Fight Back* was released the following August. A compilation of both albums, under the name *The Bickersons Rematch*, was put out in April 1971. Phil, Don and Frances received royalties on these for years afterwards. The trilogy of albums was to become one of Don's greatest legacies, prompting the actor to once explain that Bickersons work sometimes kept him working when all other avenues had dried up. Indeed, even a .025 royalty on a million-selling album was a good $25,000.

With the records as global hits, it also brought sponsor interest in seemingly unending supply, causing the Bickersons to hawk cars, air conditioners, refrigerators, and even a multitude of Coffee Rich, putting the caustic couple in a few odd surroundings.

SOUND:	RIPPLING STREAM. HOLD THROUGH COMMERCIAL.
JOHN:	Blanche, be perfectly still. I think I've got a bite.
BLANCHE:	Don't hurt him, John.
JOHN:	Oh, for Pete's sake, it's only a trout, Blanche. And besides, how do you know if a fish is a him or a her? Quick, open the creel.
BLANCHE:	What's the creel?
JOHN:	It's the wicker basket you're wearing over your shoulder.
BLANCHE:	He won't fit in there. It's full of Coffee Rich.
JOHN:	Coffee Rich!
BLANCHE:	Yes. You know how you love it in your coffee every morning. You always say Coffee Rich tastes better than cream and brings out the full-bodied flavor of even my coffee.
JOHN:	True.
BLANCHE:	And you like the lively new flavor Coffee Rich gives to your morning cereal.
JOHN:	I know, I know. And I like Coffee Rich on fruit, too. But we didn't need a whole creel full. We're only going to be here three weeks.
BLANCHE:	Well, Coffee Rich keeps three weeks in the refrigerator. And I'll use some to make a cream sauce for all the trout you catch. My mother gave me a recipe.
JOHN:	Your mother . . .
BLANCHE:	You never did like my mother, did you, John?
JOHN:	Oh, for Pete's sake. Here, put the trout in your pocket and let's get back to the lodge.
ANNCR:	That's Don Ameche and Frances Langford as the

Bickersons. They agree on only one thing . . . Coffee Rich, the new non-diary creamer that tastes better than cream, costs less and with less calories, too. In pints or quarts. In your grocer's frozen food section.

As much as he liked the regular work and rather consistent commercial royalties, Don also loved being back behind the microphone. "It really feels good to be doing radio again. In my very humble opinion, radio is a very distinctive medium, one all its own, with more prerequisites for actors, directors, producers, technicians and the fellow that foots the bill, than any of the related media.

"There can't, for instance, be anything but a perfect 'set' on radio, for every set is built by the listener in his or her own mind. There's none of the sweat and strain and staggering cost involved in building sets on movie and television sound stages. Furthermore, there can't be anything but very handsome men and very beautiful women on radio, for the actors, too, are conceived, presumably without fault, flaw or unfortunate camera angle, in the listeners' minds. On radio, you can remain forever young. Geographically, you can be, merely by saying so, in Tibet or on the moon, right here in New York. Radio is limitless, as limitless as the imagination."

Unfortunately, radio was limited by the almighty buck and jobs playing to the "mind" were few and far between. To pick up the slack, Don continued his regional theatre activities. At some point he appeared in *The Pleasure of His Company* with Jen Nelson in Avondale-on-the-Mall, Kentucky. He played the aging playboy who returns to the home of his ex-wife to supervise his daughter's marriage.

When *TV Guide* wrote its April 24, 1965 tribute to the one-time matinee idol, for *International Showtime* fans, the emphasis was on his age. The weekly magazine described Don as looking the same as his dapper 1930s image, with a bit of white speckling the pressed black hair and musketeer mustache. "The jawline's getting jowly, the face is heavier," but those were the only noticeable physical changes. The personality that was once described as fizzy was now called solemn, and the eyes that "sparkled like angel dust" are "now distant." Don attributed all these changes to age, and to a self-awakening that "I'm just not box office anymore." His constant thriving for success was a 24-hour-a-day job that was now laid off. Other personal revelations were equally as frank.

He admitted to at one time drinking a fifth of bourbon a day, and had gambled away, over time, close to a million dollars in all. "I've always loved horses. It's a great thrill to see a fine horse run. And I never drank because I was despondent." But around 1950, when Hollywood had fallen out of the picture, he stopped all that. He became serious.

Restaurateur Toots Shor, a friend for 30 years, was quoted as saying, "If I gave you a list of the people Don has helped financially over the years, it would rock you. He went through money faster than anybody I know, and it always went to others."

"I regret," Don stated, "that I didn't take the time when I was younger to go after the things that now give me so much pleasure, like great art, music and literature. I know so little and the great masters knew so much. Now that I've discovered what's important to me, I intend to find out all that I can. I still have energy and an active mind."

One of the least significant entries in the Don Ameche film cannon was 1966's *Picture Mommy Dead*, a gothic gaslight tale of murder among the rich.

The film begins with a little girl's hands taking a glittering necklace from Mommy's (Zsa Zsa Gabor) dead throat. The girl, played by Susan Gordon, sings as she watches flames run up Mommy's legs from the already afire room. After the credits, daughter Susan is retrieved from the St. Maria Convent and Hospital

Zsa Zsa and Don in *Picture Mommy Dead*, 1966.

by Daddy (Don Ameche) and his new wife (Martha Hyer) Francene, who used to be Susan's governess. Concerned father Edward Shelley (Ameche) is forced to sell off bits of the estate to pay for the previous extravagances of Francene, who is itching for money again. Mommy's will dictates that Susan is to receive the house and half a million dollars, but if Susan were to die or go back to the sanitarium, all would go to Edward. Francene wants that money and eventually kills someone for it who stands in her way. But after several twists in the plot, it turns out that Edward was indeed the killer, and kills Francene in almost exactly the same way as he killed Mommy. Susan helped cover up for Daddy once, and does so again. Father and daughter walk off into the driveway as the cops arrive. Is he going to recommit her, or will these tragedies unite them forever?

There is a Hammer horror flavor to this old mansion (filmed at Beverly Hills' Greystone Mansion) mystery which gave Don top billing, though the real work went to the terrified Susan who was afraid of losing her mind, and eventually does. Susan Gordon was the daughter of director Bert I. Gordon, famous for writing and directing *The Cyclops, The Amazing Colossal Man* and other fun B pictures of the '50s.

The following year Don toured with Robert Q. Lewis in Neil Simon's much-played *The Odd Couple*. It is difficult to believe that in a tour of the famed slob vs. neat freak play that Ameche replaced Dana Andrews as the messy Oscar Madison character, but apparently he did sometime between its October 16, 1967 Boston opening and the June 1, 1968 closing in Baltimore. Robert Q. Lewis remained Felix Unger for the complete run.

Then, back to New York.

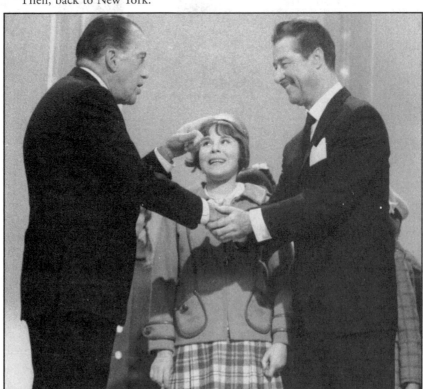

Playing a number from *Henry, Sweet Henry* for Ed Sullivan's TV show.

The Peter Sellers film *The World of Henry Orient* had a Broadway run as *Henry, Sweet Henry* for 80 performances and 12 previews, from October 23 to December 31, 1967, with Ameche in the title role. However, the stars of the piece were the 14-year-old girls who chased after him: Valerie Boyd (Robin Wilson) and Marian Gilbert (Neva Small). Henry is a smooth-talking, far-out conductor/composer who tries to woo women his age, but attracts the under-aged who pledge their devotion to the 'star' from afar. Standout moments include Alice Playten's belting number "Nobody Steps on Kafritz" and the opening of the second act: a timely hippie ballet.

Don only had two songs in the piece (and neither were solos), and, like Peter Sellers, his bits were small but memorable. As *avant garde* composer, he performs a concert "symbolizing man's emergence from primeval slime to 5:30 this afternoon," played on human bodies, not musical instruments. Poor Henry is also literally caught with his pants down at the end of the first act when cops mistakenly burst into his apartment thinking he's a dope pusher. The last seen of Henry Orient is deep in act two when he is professing eternal devotion to Valerie's mom in one phone and booking a flight to India on another line.

Based on the 1958 book by Nora Johnson, the score, with its beautiful ballad "Do You Ever Go to Boston," (sung by Robin Wilson) was by Bob Merrill (co-writer of *Funny Girl*), and book by Nunnally Johnson. Bittersweet reviews did not help Henry survive long on Broadway. The *New York Post* claimed it to be a "most disappointing musical . . . Although Don Ameche portrays [Henry] with the nonchalance he used to bring to his characterizations of famous inventors. Henry comes off as an oddly humorless and commonplace individual." *Women's Wear Daily* literally called Ameche a square. Except for a quick substitution in the late 1980s, after superstardom had come again, it was to be Don's last Broadway outing.

Then, back to Hollywood.

Though it was not based on a novel, the character-driven *Suppose They Gave a War and Nobody Came?* certainly seemed like it. This two-hour comedy, directed by Hy Averback, concerns the tussle between an Army base, run by Colonel Flanders (Ameche), and the nearby town that supports its soldiers.

Suppose They Gave a War and Nobody Came?, 1970.

Unfortunately for the military, Sheriff Harve (Ernest Borgnine) has extreme prejudice against the sometimes out of control soldiers who profane the streets with their drunkenness, foul language and other fun-loving sins. A new man, Officer Nace (Brian Keith), is brought in to improve community relations between the "warring" sides. Over a game of pool, Flanders explains that "the people of this town do not like us—very hard. I don't want trouble." Nace ultimately achieves the goal, in a way: in the film's last scene he drives a tank through the jail, thereby freeing a soldier/prisoner (Tony Curtis), and causing Sheriff Harve to be arrested after he refuses to give up the prisoners to Flanders and his men. When asked what he's proved by ruining the jail, Nace responds, "Not a Goddamn thing, sir."

The movie's tone was satirical, akin to other military parodies of the time (most notably *The Russians Are Coming! The Russians Are Coming!* and *MASH*), but even the strong cast failed to do much to raise it to financial or critical success. However, the film at least gave Don Ameche a major role in his leaner years. His world-weary performance of a Brigadier General, who wants to retire—soon, gave him a few of the best lines in Hal Captain and Don McGuire's script. Many of its location shots were filmed in Fort Huachuca, Arizona, which may have resulted in Ameche's being cast, as he began living in that state sometime in the 1960s. The movie opened in Philadelphia on May 20, 1970.

The Boatniks was not one of Disney's greatest films in their years after Walt's death, but it did give Don ample opportunity to shout in a non-Bickerson role in 1970. The plot follows klutz Ensign Thomas Garland (Robert Morse) in his quest to become a little like his war hero father. Commander Taylor (Ameche), a friend of his father's, applauds the boy's enthusiasm, but not his incompetence. But like Inspector Closeau, the luck of the stupid reigns supreme, allowing Garland to finally round up three jewel thieves (Phil Silvers, Norman Fell and Mickey Shaughnessy) before the hundred-minute film winds down. Stefanie Powers, Wally Cox, Vito Scotti and other familiar faces make the film worth watching, though it lacked the pace and humor of Disney's previous hit, *The Love Bug*. Location shots were filmed in Newport Beach, California, and movie opened on July 1, 1970 in New York.

This was also the year that Don tried his hand at directing: an episode of *Julia*, entitled "Call Me by My Rightful Number," written by Arthur Alsberg and Don Nelson.

Two years later *The Arizona Republic* reported that Don was honorary chairman of the March 1972 Bell Art Festival Ball, a combination art show & auction and dancing & dinner event at Mountain Shadows to aid the Maricopa Mental Health Association.

In 1973 he could be seen performing in *The Moon Is Blue* at Windmill Dinner Theater. He told *The Arizona Republic* that in one year (possibly 1971) he only worked five days—and nearly went crazy! So he had to make compromises (dinner theatre being one of them) in order to work. The review of the show was quite complimentary: "Don Ameche is jolly fun as the older man in a romantic triangle, and has the two biggest laughs of the evening—with a remark about governmental leadership (updated to reflect the Watergate mess) and his debonair way with mixing an ever so dry martini with but a whiff of vermouth."

In the mid-1970s Don appeared opposite Ruby Keeler in a tour of the hit Broadway revival, *No, No, Nanette*. Music director Bill Cox remembered the star. "Don was ever the gentleman, not chummy, but not unfriendly, very businesslike, and not prone to whimsy. Certainly not difficult. Most always the first one out of the theater during rehearsal and performances. Not one to chitchat. I also played a few rehearsals for *Henry, Sweet Henry* years before *Nanette*, and he was much the same then. To him theatre was a job.

"He enjoyed good Italian food after the show, and I enjoyed dining with him once or twice. He was always in a hurry to leave after the curtain came down. He either didn't wear makeup, or removed it before the curtain call and was ready to leave ASAP. It annoyed him that I had to stay until the end of the playout music, at which point he was waiting at the stage door.

"He was always concerned about hearing his musical entrances. I believe by that time he was somewhat deaf, however his intonation was great, diction perfect, and his sound, though not beautiful, was very pleasant.

"He was a rather private man, but our conversations were amusing with some fun stories about Hollywood. He was apparently a golf partner of W.C. Fields, and not a personal fan of Bogart."

When the telephone turned 100 in 1976 Don acted as "advance man" for a 90-minute TV special, *Jubilee*, broadcast on NBC on March 26 and repeated twice more that same year.

He had been seen sporadically in the '70s on such shows as *Columbo* ("Suitable for Framing"); *Alias Smith and Jones* ("Diamond Jim Guffy"); in 1971, *Ellery Queen* ("The Adventure of the Lover's Leap"); and sailing on a few *Love Boats*

"Suitable for Framing" episode of *Columbo,* **1972.**

(1979 & 1981). But for some of these and others (*McCloud, Quincy*), though the series were high profile at the time, Don was little more than a cameo, underused, with hardly any screen time. His roles may have been insignificant to the plots, but Don had always been just as concerned with quality as quantity.

In 1979 he appeared in *Life with Father* at Chicago's Drury Lane Theatre in McCormick Place, then had a summer tour as J.B. Biggley in *How to Succeed in Business Without Really Trying*. The run of ten or eleven weeks was the just right amount for him, at which point Don was living in a condo in Murrieta, California. Touring was a little harder now, as he told a local newspaper. "I love the travel. But being on the road, keeping yourself in shape . . . that's not always easy. I exercise. I walk quite a bit. I watch my diet. I vocalize. And I am keeping my weight at 155. I think that's the best insurance you can have, to keep yourself in shape."

Don didn't *have* to be aggressive in his quest for more work, since his investments (such as oil interests in Southwest Texas) brought in more than enough to live on. It was keeping occupied that seemed to be his greatest concern. In the last ten years he had only seen *The Godfather, Kramer vs. Kramer* and *E.T.*, all of which did not make him desperate for film work. But luckily, one extraordinary script landed on his lap that was soon to make the lean times a faded memory.

Chapter Eleven

Return of the Comeback Kid

The year Jim Ameche died—1983—was the year Don Ameche was reborn. The phenomenal hit comedy *Trading Places* was the year's third biggest moneymaker ($40.6 million), after *Return of the Jedi* and *Tootsie*, and launched Eddie Murphy as one of the hottest draws of the decade. Arguably Murphy's finest comedy, it was the ensemble casting of Dan Ackroyd, Jamie Lee Curtis and villains Ameche and Ralph Bellamy, led by *Animal House/Blues Brothers* director John Landis, that kept this adult *Prince and the Pauper* story a classic. Yet, if it weren't for a quirk of fate, Don might never have shined as a star again.

"Ray Milland was set for the part," he said, "but then he didn't pass the insurance physical. They sent me the script and I liked it, but my agent, Tom Corman, said they wouldn't meet the money. I thought, 'Well, I've waited twelve years, why cave in now?' We held out and they came through."

The film opens to the strains of Mozart (provided by Elmer Bernstein, who received the only Oscar nomination for the movie), with alternating scenes of the rich and poor and the great sights of Philadelphia. The Duke brothers, Randolph (Bellamy) and older brother Mortimer (Ameche), are ultra-rich bastards with a thirst for wealth mixed with their boredom and complacency. The only thing that shakes up their days in the conservative Heritage Club ("founded 1776—with liberty and justice for all—members only") is the argument of what money does to people. When Louis Winthorpe III (Dan Ackroyd) brings them payroll checks to sign (including a suspect one for someone who doesn't even work for them), the seeds of a bet are sown. Mortimer believes that "with his [Winthorpe] genes you could put him anywhere and he's bound to come out on top," while his younger brother believes that all human nature is a product of its environment. "Breeding," says Mortimer. When panhandler Billy Ray Valentine (Murphy) races through the Club chased by cops, Randolph suggests that this "Negro" can run the company as well as Winthorpe can. Mortimer is intrigued by the wager, so they bail Mr. Valentine out of jail, and set up Winthorpe by having their "investigator" plant marked, stolen bills and the drug PCP on him. He goes to jail, and loses everything.

Valentine fits into wealthy society just fine, while Winthorpe is shunned by all his rich "friends." Only the pity of hot hooker Ophelia (Curtis), who helped

Those nasty Duke brothers from *Trading Places*, 1983.

frame him, guides Winthorpe back to tolerating life. The villains are undone when Valentine overhears Mortimer paying off on the bet (a whole dollar) and planning how to reinstate Winthorpe after New Year's (when a big deal of theirs is going down). Prince and pauper team up to turn the tables on the Duke gods by snatching up their stock at the film's end, driving the old men to screaming bankruptcy. Mortimer's big scene and true colors emerge when he learns they're busted—Randolph is having a heart attack. "Fuck him!" screams Mortimer. "Turn those machines back on!" echo the hallowed halls of the Stock Exchange, where a Duke has been sitting since it was founded. Hooker and heroes then depart to a Caribbean island to sail into the credits.

Before use of the f-word in that infamous scene, director Landis recalled that Don called for the attention of the entire assembled crew and formally apologized for using such language. The man was a patrician—if traditional in his views. *Trading Places* gained an R rating for language and nudity; not Ameche's first choice to watch for an evening's entertainment, but he thought it a fine piece of work.

"Do you know what percentage of movies made per year are R pictures?" he asked an interviewer. "Over 50 percent. So that's over 50% of your product that you can't get a certain age group to see."

The Los Angeles Times wrote, "Part of what gives the film its expansive delight is that it isn't a two-actor comedy, but a six-actor one. Ameche and Bellamy are superlative, their work together has the touch of Lubitsch or Rene Clair." The film's style was often compared to Preston Sturges and Frank Capra, with *New York* magazine calling it "Eddie Murphy's movie." *Newsday* agreed, "Its most accessible pleasure is Murphy's pomposity-deflating funky wit."

Film offers did not flood in, but Ameche was still picky in choosing a follow-up to one of Hollywood's biggest comedies. What came next was a once-in-a-lifetime role. And yet another substitution.

Cocoon, directed by Ron Howard, became an archetype film, in much the same way the words *Star Wars* and Rambo conjure up an instant definition. The feel-good film of 1985 won Ameche the Oscar for Best Supporting Actor as well as Best Visual Effects for the Industrial Light & Magic team the following year. The ensemble unit of aging actors—Wilfred Brimley, Hume Cronyn, Jack Gilford, Maureen Stapleton, Jessica Tandy, Gwen Verdon—mixed well with the younger set—Steve Guttenberg, Tawnee Welch (Raquel's daughter), Brian Dennehy, and even briefly, the son of Don's old friend, Tyrone Power, Jr. Spreading the story among so much talent meant that there was no real star, and gave the film a very homey, family atmosphere set in contrasting realism with the fantasy provided.

When a UFO lands to collect cocoons from the ocean, a group of aliens (beings of light covered in perfect skin suits) store some in the pool of a house they have rented which is next door to an old folks' home. Three of the men— Art Selwyn (Ameche), Ben Luckett (Brimley) and Joseph Finley (Cronyn)—have been sneaking into the pool for a daily swim and see no reason to stop just because there's something weird in the water. Swimming among the cocoons stimulates them into rejuvenation, the likes they haven't felt since they were in their 20s. Passion for their wives, sport and life pulses back to them, even causing Art to improv a spirited breakdance in a club one night.

The aliens are upset at first with their trespassing, but these are healing, not destructive, beings who soon offer the group the hospitality of their planet, where no one is ever sick or grows old. The elders gratefully take the offer and through many tears of separation, are spirited off never to return again; unless the film makes enough money.

The sleeper hit of the summer won raves from the critics. Some were not overly enamored at the less-than-subtle ending, but no one discounted its charm and novelty in an era of ever-increasing teen-sex comedies. *The Los Angeles Times* wrote that "the movie is about treasure. Treasure wasted: the experience of our older people" and its "view is rosy but not mawkish," with "wit, against-expectation situations, tenderness, humanity, a collection of brilliantly fine actors" and "the energy it generates is probably enough to raise the Titanic."

The New Leader was certainly correct in calling *Cocoon* "the first, and will almost certainly be the only, smash hit set in a retirement community." *The New York Post* called it "*E.T. On Golden Pond*. It's funny and touching and spirited and imaginative and never boring" and though it's "preposterous beyond belief on every level, this is nevertheless a charming, humorous, and very entertaining little concoction." *The Village Voice* singled out Ameche: "*Cocoon's* greatest stamp-and-cheer thrill belongs to Don Ameche, who passed 70 a while ago: elegant in his white suit and combed mustache, he awes a room full of cynical disco youth as he moonwalks and yes! breakdances! so spectacularly that he makes John Travola's *Saturday Night Fever* triumph look like just another gym class."

"I'd never seen breakdancing prior to this film," Don admitted. "I didn't know what it was." According to *The New York Times*, he worked with a 19-year-old professional dancer for four weeks to do roughly 50% of the breakdancing seen in the film. A stunt double wore an Ameche mask during the more difficult maneuvers of the scene. An elder swimmer, who looked a *lot* like Don, also doubled for him in one particular dive scene into the pool.

Cocoon, 1985.

But, as usual, Don kept in shape during shooting, taking his four-mile walk up and down the beach every morning before the cameras rolled. He told interviewer Michael Stein, "How do they make us look young again? The make-up is changed, and the dialogue. But most of it is in the acting—there are differences, highs and lows.

"Has it been fun? Yeah. It's hard to have a perspective on what has or hasn't happened, though. There are no sustained scenes in this picture. They're all short. Maybe one or two longer scenes in the whole picture. Vignettes everywhere. Which is probably good for today's kind of picture making. They want to keep things moving. It's different from the old days."

He chose the film, he said, because he thought that science fiction could mean a big box office success that might prompt more work. He admitted too few film offers after *Trading Places*, but like the previous hit, even this one was a replacement role. Buddy Ebsen had originally been cast but then became "unavailable," as did several actors (including Red Buttons). "As an actor, I seem to be a replacement these days, which is fine with me."

Even though they had to shoot through the tail end of hurricane Isadora, at one point with rain pouring down through the roof of the pool house, optimism was high about the picture. Producer Richard Zanuck, Jr. had been attracted to the film because of Fox's previous sci-fi hits (*Planet of the Apes* series, *Fantastic Voyage*) and found *Cocoon*'s script "appealing to a broad audience of all ages." He also thought it had "heart," which a sensitive person/director like Ron Howard could make a hit out of. Ron's not "afraid to be 'sentimental' or show too much emotion." The screenplay by first-time author David Saperstein had been submitted in 1980, but three changes of 20th Century-Fox administrations kept the film from moving ahead. Either the new people hated the script or loved it. Zanuck almost took the project to another studio.

What most of the country took to heart was the fact that over-60s shouldn't be counted out as regular people or matinee stars. Gwen Verdon played an ex-showgirl who teaches the old folks aerobics to keep in shape, but once she's revitalized with the "vitamins" in the pool water, she moves on to more courageous teachings of old showgirl routines. She admitted to chasing Don's character all the way through the film. "I hope teenagers will stop chewing their popcorn long enough to learn that older people still have the same feelings they do. We are erotic human beings, even at 70." (Shortly after *Cocoon*, *Playboy* named Don one of America's 10 sexiest men.)

Ron Howard had always wanted to make a film that dealt with retirement-age actors, and felt that with this project "the fantasy element really serves the characters, and not the other way around." One of the main lures was the cast. The producers had already conferred with Maureen Stapleton, Hume Cronyn and Jessica Tandy, and Howard began making a cast list on the back of his first draft script after he'd read it. He knew it needed a rewrite, but felt the foundation of the film was solid. The main thing Howard was concerned about was that regaining youth shouldn't be a completely wonderful thing; that in any situation, there is a down side.

Winning the Oscar meant a lot to Don. With the award in hand, he merely said, "For all you members of the Academy, this esteemed gentleman [the Oscar] says that you have given me your recognition. You've given to me your love. I hope that I have earned your respect." The ovation of applause lasted a good thirty seconds. He later admitted that it took him a year to understand that he got the award for his career, his body of work, not for his portrayal in *Cocoon*, a practice the Academy often engages in to reward legends. But Don appreciated it nonetheless. Irving Berlin was the first to phone him after he won, because of his part in ***Alexander's Ragtime Band***. Don asked the old songwriter how he was, to which the composer replied, "Mentally, I feel 45. Physically, I'm 180."

One of the things (aside from breakdancing) that may have secretly helped Don gain the coveted Oscar was the large amount of public relations he did for the film, at the studio's request: interviews galore, taking journalists to dinner, appearances in England to promote the film, etc., etc. An October 8, 1985 letter from Fox's Joel H. Coler illustrates the studio's stress on Ameche's relation to the cross-genre title.

Dear Don,

Now that you have returned from your around-the-world trip on behalf of *Cocoon*, I want to extend our sincere congratulations and thanks for all your hard efforts.

It is very rare indeed that a person of your skill and stature works as hard and as efficiently on a tour.

Your efforts have not gone unrewarded. As you are aware, *Cocoon* has opened very big in almost all the territories we have opened so far, and your help has been one of the contributing reasons.

Thanks again. We sincerely appreciate it.

He actually circled the globe once more, in 1986, to push the film's opening, and was honored at the Deauville Film Festival, and met Prince Philip and Queen Elizabeth in London.

The most publicized event was perhaps the lengthy Scottsdale Film Festival, which ran May 1-18, 1986 at the Scottsdale Center for the Arts. It was Arizona's second major film festival, highlighting "New Technologies and Movie Magic . . . the Art of Special Effects." In association with The American Film Institute, the festival screened nearly 60 new/recent films from Hollywood, China, Germany, Russia, Canada, Australia, France, student films, winners of the Scottsdale Film Festival National Competition, and more during its first fifteen days. On Friday the 16th a Gala Festival Tribute was held, screening the Zanuck/Brown Company's big hits: *Jaws, The Sting, Cocoon* and others. Lili Fini Zanuck was Honorary Chairperson.

For $117 one could attend the Gala and Tribute (complete with champagne reception), all nine seminars plus a choice of ten "Movies Galore." The picture on the front of the Festival program was Don and Gwen Verdon in a dancing pose from *Cocoon*. Day one's program was "The Art of Special Effects," which

Don Ameche and Gwen Verdon share a wonderful moment in the motion picture "Cocoon"

1986 Scottsdale Film Festival

highlighted the making of *Cocoon*. Don was among special *Cocoon* guests, including co-producer Lili Fini Zanuck; winner of the Oscar for Best Visual Effects, Ken Ralston; Greg Cannom, creator of the alien creatures; and Robert Short, creator of the cocoons themselves and the mechanical dolphins.

Cocoon was heavily promoted that night. After the festival, guests, including Don, arrived at the cinema entrance at 7:30 p.m., and the celebrity audience was seated. At 9:25 Arthur Loew introduced Don Ameche, directly after Wilford Brimley's talk, both speaking of their *Cocoon* roles and relation to Zanuck/Brown. Don then introduced the Zanuck/Brown company and honored guests: David Brown and Lili Fini Zanuck, after which the guests departed to the private reception.

Don just enjoyed the work, whether it was in front of the camera or plugging what was in the can to new audiences. "He was never impressed with being an entertainer," says Don Ameche, Jr., "or being somebody of importance. I remember the night when he won the Oscar. It meant a great, great deal to him. My wife and I had spent the day with him, and that night we got in the limousine. It was very quiet. I asked him, 'What are you going to say if you win?' He said, 'Oh, I don't worry about that.' Then he walked up there, with no notes or anything, and made one of the finest acceptance speeches I've ever heard. Afterwards, we ended up going to dinner at a little Italian restaurant in Van Nuys, just my wife, myself, my dad, and one of his brothers and sister-in-law, and his agents. It was totally away from the parties or the rest of Hollywood. That was the way he wanted it, and that's the way he always kind of was. Yet, he was thrilled to win. It meant everything in the world to him."

The resurgence of his career and name value also gave Don the confidence to reestablish ties with his own family, something he felt strongly about, yet was inherently difficult for him. Perhaps he needed his children to see him as a success, with something more than himself to give them. Whatever the reason, the last decade of his life was a definite homecoming to Papa Ameche.

"The majority of my time with him was in the last ten years of his life," says Tom Ameche. "I don't remember much about the early days. I can remember coming home from boarding school on the weekends. We spent a summer on the beach in Malibu. We spent one summer in Pennsylvania, and one in Shawnee, Illinois. We flew to New York for Christmas one year, in the '40s.

"They sent me to Brophy Preparatory College in Phoenix, Arizona, so I spent five or six or seven years there before I went in the Navy. I came back here to Kentucky in 1966 because Dad was always into thoroughbred horses, and when I was in Arizona I was with his quarter-horses all the time. I was the only one at that time who was involved with them, as far back as the '50s. Dad was talking about getting a place in Arizona and getting some broodmares, but he wanted me to come back here [Kentucky] to learn what they do with thoroughbreds. I couldn't convince him that they're all handled the same until they go into training. There's no difference in the way you handle them. But he just chucked the idea, like he did with a lot of things.

"Somewhere in the '70s I got to talking with Dad about mares and what have you, and he bought one. I kept her on my place. We got three or four folds out of her. He ended up getting rid of her and bought a mare called Arctic Swing, then several after her. I kind of watched everything back here for him. All the breeding of the mares, what they were doing, what the babies were doing. He got back into horses then. What kept him alive during his last years was his horses. Meech [Don, Jr.] got involved with them about eight or ten years ago, too.

"Dad was involved with horses in the '30s with Bing Crosby, who built Del Mar. Dad was there all the time. That was his love, what he really enjoyed. That's what I do too. I transport them for a living. Meech and I, along with one of his sons and daughter, have a broodmare back here.

"Dad and I got together again in the '80s. He had a colt by 'I'm Glad' in California that was kind of an outlaw. Once you showed him that you were on top and he wasn't going to get you, he was a piece of cake. But they were afraid of him, and when a horse knows you're afraid of him, he'll eat you alive. That's just their way. Dad called Dr. McGee, part of a famous veterinarian clinic; I'd worked on several farms where he was. Dad asked who he could get to break his horse, get him straightened out where they could break him. Dad didn't really *know* that much about me. Dr. McGee said, 'What's the matter with your son?' 'Who?' 'Tom!' 'What the hell does he know about a horse?' McGee said if he were to send someone, I'd be who he sends. So he picked up the phone at 10 o'clock one night. Dad was a very strict, strict person. It was 'Yes, sir,' 'No, sir,' no 'Yeah' or anything. He said, 'I want you out here in California in the morning at 9 o'clock.' He told me about the colt, but said I'd find out about it when I got out here. I said, 'Dad, how am I going get reservations at this time of night?' He said he'd take care of that. So, I jumped a plane to California and was out there at 9 o'clock.

"I got in the car with him, and that's the worst mistake I ever made. He's on the freeway driving like 90 or 100 miles an hour. That's the way he was, flying in and out of traffic. We got down to San Diego, in that area. He pointed out the horse and said, 'Fix him.' He stayed for a minute. I worked with the colt for about an hour and a half and when he came back, I had the colt walking right alongside of me. Didn't even have a shank on him. He followed me wherever I'd go. Dad looked at me and said, 'Where in the hell did you learn how to do that?' I didn't say anything. I was out there about a week. That's what really broke the ice. He had no idea that I could handle a horse. But he didn't know me. And I didn't really know him. From there it graduated to working more with the horses and getting him involved.

"In all the years that he had horses, he never saw a baby born. I had a mare here for him that I bought called A Girl Named Sam. I talked him into coming back here just before she was due to fold, which was just before he got his Oscar. I had an army cot down in the barn, but I was in contact with my wife in the house by way of a CB radio. I would sleep in the barn watching her all night, driving horse vans all day long. When that horse gave birth, I called Dad to see it. I don't know if he was frightened, but it blew his mind. When he was in the field with me, he was very at ease around the horses, though.

"He called me one day when he'd bought Arctic Swing, who produced a colt called Ferrara, and he wanted to sell her. He'd bought her because of a good pedigree. I said if it was mine I wouldn't sell her. 'Okay,' and he slammed the phone down. Twenty minutes later I got a call from Meech. He said, 'What the hell did you say to the old man?' I said, 'I told him I thought he was making a mistake, but it's his mare, he can do whatever the hell he wants with it.' From that day forward, we were at a level we'd never been at before, and it continued for about ten years. He'd call and ask questions and want to know what I thought.

"We once sent him a little horse—Arezzo (all of his horses were named after Italian cities). We called him the little engine that could. He was a crooked son of a gun and probably shouldn't have been a racehorse. But he won four or five races. From there on, Dad and I could talk like we were never able to before. You might say he started believing in me. I hadn't seen him for ten or fifteen years, not even when I got married. Mom came but he didn't. I hadn't even really spoken with him, because I never knew where he was. If he wanted you to know where he was, he'd tell you. After we got going with these horses, he and I got real close. We had something in common.

"I had learned all about horses from the cowboys out in Arizona. Roy Patton was in his 60s and was a hand with the horses like you've never, ever seen in your life. When I wasn't working in Arizona, I'd go out to his place every weekend. He taught me things like you wouldn't believe. And of course Dad didn't know that.

"He had an incredible memory. Pedigree was his cup of tea, not mine. But that's all he knew. He didn't know confirmation or disposition, or what they meant in a horse. That's when we got together and I got to explain it to him. He'd come back here five or seven times a year. He'd look at the horses and I'd tell him what we'd have to do. It just blew his mind that someone would know that, but he began to see what I was saying. I enjoyed the last ten years immensely."

A Masterpiece of Murder was Bob Hope's first outing into TV movies and could have been a lot better, given the wealth of Hope's joke file and gag writers. It also wasn't the best follow-up Ameche could have picked after winning the Oscar, but the temptation to play opposite an old radio crony was too great. Hope emulated a downtrodden PI who likes to bet on horses that don't like to win. Long ago, when he was a cop, he nabbed a cat burglar (Ameche) who spent his time in jail learning the finer points of real estate. Now the thief-turned-businessman is incredibly wealthy and is set to the task of recovering paintings that were stolen from his rich friend (Kevin McCarthy). But along the way the supposed thief is murdered and Hope and Ameche, for some reason joined together by McCarthy, have to solve the case and retrieve the art.

As *Variety* rightly stated, "One has the feeling all this has been seen before, and it has, many times, but with more polish and vigor. The dialog is old-hat, like the vehicle. Hope and Ameche go through their paces, but are let down by the confusing, uninspired script." Indeed, there was no real reason for Hope to be in the film, plot-wise, except for dotting the scenes with mildly funny quips.

The '80s and television were shaping up to be pure nostalgia for Don Ameche. He filmed his greetings for Alice Faye's hour-long *This Is Your Life* in 1985 produced by the BBC and broadcast in Britain. They also did a "Hollywood Musical" charity event in 1986 before Queen Elizabeth, where Don proclaimed Alice his favorite leading lady.

Pals was a quaint TV-movie comedy starring George C. Scott as Jack Stobbs, Don Ameche as Art Riddle and Sylvia Sidney as Jack's mother, Fern. On coming back from claiming a TV left to Fern in a friend's will, the trio stumbles upon an abandoned car containing payoff money for cocaine. They get away with the 3.6 million dollars, but the hitman involved in the deal is on their trail. On the way they pick up young Certainty Dowd (Susan Rinell), who has just tried to steal

Bob and Don in *A Masterpiece of Murder*, 1986.

their car but quickly fits in as one of the misfits.

Just the other day Jack and Art were talking with their good friends who want to sell their boat charter business for fifty grand. Now they cannot only buy the business, but buy their house (to hide out from whomever they stole from), too. They think up interesting names, get new identities and list their old selves as "dead" to the government. They open 129 bank accounts all over town and start spending the dough by fixing up their business. Stupidly, dreamily, Jack buys a huge estate for himself and is beginning to lose himself in his newfound wealthy mind set. It eventually drives Jack and Art apart, but Certainty ruins Jack's social status very publicly by wearing her proper punk clothes to a fancy do. Jack is forced to own up to all the blue blood lies he's been telling, and goes back to Art, hoping they can start again. They decide to sell the house and give the remaining millions to charity.

Unfortunately, the hit man catches up with them and forces them to do an accounting. They'd spent $689,000. They manage to get away from him (Fern zaps him with a TV remote, causing his pacemaker to short out), only to wind up in the hands of the Feds who assume Jack and Art's money is drug-related. In court, all criminal charges are dropped against them, and they're allowed to keep the money. But only after taxes whittles it down to a mere $4.50. They give the judge fifty cents, take their five bucks and go back to the trailer park.

Pals, broadcast on February 28, 1987, was a charming story, more to the credit of George C. Scott than any buddy film formula. The title was rather deceptive, but a good entry for Don's elder *Cocoon* crowd. *Variety*, usually a tough critic to win over, called it a "delightful comedy . . . Scott and Ameche are superb," and surprisingly praised its script and direction equally as well.

Later that month Don found himself in the literally huge Universal comedy, *Harry and the Hendersons*, starring John Lithgow as the head of the Henderson family who happen to hit Bigfoot while returning from a hunting trip. The sitcom-like plot involved the family's making amends by nursing it back to health and keep it safe from the cops and a deranged French Bigfoot hunter (David Suchet). Don Ameche appears as Dr. Wallace Wrightwood, who had once seen the legendary hairy creature and now runs a Bigfoot souvenir stand. Critics admired a few gags and often singled Lithgow and Ameche out for their attempts, but found the film as a whole uninspired and tiring.

Eddie Murphy's hit, *Coming to America*, was a different matter. Some have called the *Crocodile Dundee*-like, fish-out-of-water comedy one of Murphy's funniest outings, while other critics were ready and willing to be disgruntled after previous disappointments of *The Golden Child* and *Beverly Hills Cop II*. What *Coming to America* had, however, was John Landis back at the helm, and by association, Don Ameche again. He and Ralph Bellamy appear briefly in a scene in which Prince Akeem (Murphy) plunks down a large wad of bills into a bowl before a dirty cardboard box on the riverbank. The Duke brothers, freezing and poor as dirt, rejoice to the world that they're in the money again and start plotting their path toward world domination.

John Landis recalled, "Don and Ralph's cameo in *Coming to America* was shot one very, very cold night by the Brooklyn Bridge. I don't recall what they were each doing at the time, but they were both constantly working so I'm sure we scheduled their work at their convenience. I just called both of them and asked them to do it. The Dukes were not in the screenplay, I just made that up. When I told Eddie of my idea, he thought it was funny. People responded so strongly to Don and Ralph in *Trading Places* that it just amused me to bring their characters back the next time I worked with Eddie. They were so thoroughly crushed at the end of the first movie, I felt that maybe we could redeem them in the second."

Luckily for Ameche *Things Change*. It was award-winning playwright David Mamet's second film and Ameche's second most critically acclaimed film of later years. The character-driven comedy starred Joe Mantegna as mob man Jerry whose job it is to keep shoeshine man Gino (Ameche) occupied for a weekend before Gino willingly takes a murder rap for a guilty mobster. The prize: what he cherishes most in the world, his own fishing boat in Sicily if/when he gets out of prison. Gino is intensely humble, from the old world, and is a simple man whom Jerry pities enough to take out for a first-class weekend before his jail time. The two bond like father and son, but when "things change" and Jerry is forced to kill the old man, Jerry realizes he doesn't have the heart to be a mobster. Luckily, Gino calls in the one mafia favor he has in the world in order to save both their lives. They are both demoted to shining shoes at the end of the film, collectively shrugging—it could've turned out much worse.

Things Change, **1988.**

When Don was in Seattle filming *Harry and the Hendersons*, he was eating alone in a restaurant when David Mamet's wife, Lindsay Crouse, walked over and introduced herself. She was doing Mamet's debut film, *House of Games*, also now shooting in Seattle. Don had done a *Life with Father*, written by her father, Lindsay Crouse, so conversation was easy for Don. When Mamet came in to say hello, Don nearly fell out of his chair. It was a good thing Don was hungry that day.

Mamet and the producers of his next film, *Things Change*, wanted a real Italian actor for the lead but that actor didn't want to leave Europe. Don was originally signed to play a Mafia bigshot in Lake Tahoe, the part Robert Prosky got. Joe Mantegna explains: "Then one day, David set up a lunch with Don. At the lunch, Don was telling us about his immigrant father, and all of a sudden David asked Don if he'd play Gino. He caught us both by surprise, and then he left the table. So Don leans over to me and says, 'If I agree to do this, will that be okay with you?' And that's when I knew this guy had to play the part. Because that was so much the character anyway. I mean, Don Ameche is Gino." Don had never read anything by the playwright before, but took the script home and loved it.

"I have never played a character like Geno before," Don said at the time. "But I knew I could do it because I understand the Italian mentality. I was around Italians all during my childhood. My father was from Italy. The accent I used for Gino is totally my father's and he had that until he died. And like Gino, he was a man of integrity, according to his standards."

Mamet went into great detail for all scenes, explaining away anything that didn't make sense to the 80-year-old actor. Back at Fox, Ameche did a lot of questioning of characters and relationships when directors were working with properties written by others. But as Mamet was the writer as well (along with Shel Silverstein), Don knew exactly who to talk to. "I really loved the writing, even those unfinished sentences. I was totally trying to give him what he wanted. You see, I had watched David's first film, *House of Games*, before I took the part. I just thought it was wonderful. I would've done anything he asked me to do, truthfully, after seeing that."

He told the *Chicago Tribune*, "I've never known a good director yet who wasn't meticulous to the nth degree in every detail. And what a joy it is for an actor to work with someone who knows exactly what he's doing. All you have to do is know your lines, and you can trust your director, because he has the whole movie figured out. David is like that. He knows every camera angle, and he knows exactly what he wants, because he wrote it."

In another interview, he stated, "I didn't feel strange on the set being with all these people David had known, but I never ever got into the circle. Because I knew I didn't belong, and I never did try to get involved in it. If that happens, it has to be of its own volition. This is a really tight thing, and it goes back a long way, to the Goodman Theater 15 years ago. So it never entered my mind that I would be a part of that. Never."

As usual, what was most important to Ameche wasn't the socializing, it was the work. Master playwright and stars were praised highly for *Things Change*. *Films in Review* wrote that both leads "deserve Best Actor Oscar nominations" and *The Los Angles Times* admitted it was "probably the subtlest movie acting Ameche has done since his hellbound roue in Ernst Lubitsch's 1943 *Heaven Can Wait*. Radiating graciousness and serenity, Ameche swallows himself inside the skin of this self-effecting man—with his measured, broken English, his neat old clothes and poised maestro movements." *The Miami Herald* wrote that "Ameche

Things Change, 1988.

gives a very still, dignified performance" and "Mantegna, the perfect Mamet actor, has never been better. He can do more with the arch of an eyebrow than some actors can do in an entire film."

Ameche and Mantegna did end up sharing the Best Actor prize (Volpi Cup) at the Venice film festival. When it screened there, Don said, "I had a huge emotional reaction. The audience got every joke, caught every inflection in the movie, and when it was over, the crowd didn't stop cheering and applauding until 10 minutes had gone by. I just broke up into a million pieces."

"Don was the nicest person I ever worked with," stated Mamet. "I did not see him after *Things Change.* We corresponded for the year or so before his death. I remember Don saying that, after Tyrone Power, he had more fun working with Joe [Mantegna] than with anyone. I remember asking him about Carmen Miranda. How did she get that way, I asked, and was it all an act? He said that no, it was not an act. She took a mug and filled it halfway with sugar, and topped it off with espresso, and when it was empty, filled another one, and she drank them all day and that is how she got 'that way.'"

Chapter Twelve
The Final Years

Now sharing time between living in Santa Monica, California and Phoenix, Arizona, life was good to Don Ameche. He kept up with his extended family: six children, thirteen grandchildren and three great-grandchildren. He was still a loner, living by himself in a beautiful Santa Monica apartment with its gorgeous view of the Pacific Ocean. He said simply, "A man who cannot be alone cannot be a happy man."

His career was at its greatest peak in 50+ years. "I just can't retire. I guess I'm still too restless." He hardly had time for daily exercise, so full was his schedule after *Things Change*. But some things he would *not* let change. "There are places where I can take walks in Santa Monica that are serene. The trees are beautiful, there's no need to worry about what's going to happen to you, and there's the beauty of that ocean. In the last two weeks, the blue of the ocean varied every single day, and on three different occasions I said to myself, this is the most beautiful day over the ocean that I have ever seen.

"The walks are very precious to me. If I had to walk with somebody else, I wouldn't enjoy it half so much. You can't walk at your own pace, you can't think of the things you want to think about. It's an hour and forty-five minutes that are very precious to me. And throwing back my head and seeing that blue sky through the trees . . . ! I pass a lot of regulars on my walks, but very few do I say hello to. One man, he runs on the median, I walk on the sidewalk, we talked for two minutes one day, and he seemed like such a nice person. I wave to him every day. But very few people do I speak to. And the women. A lot of women walk, but they never look at anybody. They look straight ahead."

He boasted the same 31-inch waistline that he had in his early films. He needed to keep in shape to reprise his Oscar-winning role in *Cocoon: The Return*, which producers refused to call *Cocoon II*. He had mixed feelings about the project, but agreed to return with the original ensemble cast for several personal reasons. In the first place, he trusted Richard Zanuck's judgement. Initially, Zanuck really didn't want to do a sequel, but then found a script he liked, which made Don think it was worth doing. Don wasn't pleased with the *Cocoon* sequel script, concerned about what his character had to do. He thought it was crazy. But he also thought what a horrible thing it would be to turn down the sequel after he'd won the Oscar for the original. As he publicly stated 60 years ago, an actor had to be dependable, or he was not worthy of the label "actor."

Rather than simply remaking the first one, *Cocoon: The Return* examined new problems for the frisky couples who hitch a ride with the returning aliens who must collect their oceanic cocoons before seismic activity can disrupt the sleeping life forms. But they aren't quite quick enough; one cocoon is salvaged by the St. Petersburg Oceanographic Institute, and needs to be rescued before the spaceship

An older, but in great shape, Don Ameche.

returns in three days' time. Meantime, the old folks mingle with friends and family who never expected to see them again. While on Earth, age and illness reassert themselves, but not before the old guys challenge some overconfident young punks to a game of basketball in one of the film's liveliest scenes. The geezers win, of course.

There is regret, death and rebirth in *The Return*. Hume Cronyn's leukemia regenerates, so when his wife is in the hospital after being hit by a car, he gladly gives his life force to her so she can stay and take the job she wanted (looking after children). Wilford Brimley and "wife" Maureen Stapleton also elect to stay on Earth, thinking it more natural that parents shouldn't outlive their children. The only ones returning to the planet of everlasting life are Don and Gwen Verdon, who is now with child; they realize if they stayed, she probably wouldn't survive the pregnancy and they'd never live to see their child grow up. Even complainer Jack Gilford, who starts the film trying to kill himself, finds delayed euphoria in the arms of earthy, scene-stealing Elaine Stritch who doesn't need to change planets get a kick out of life.

Emotionally, some of its scenes were as effective as the original, but reviews were mixed for *Cocoon: The Return*. *The Los Angeles Times* was it greatest champion, calling it "the best kind of sequel: it doesn't merely cash in on the success of the original but actually continues its story in new directions, eliciting fresh meaning and emotion. It has also the charm, imagination, humor and originality of *Cocoon*, but even more poignancy." *The New York Post*, on the flipside, asked, "Do you really crave another turn with the sprightly geezers of *Cocoon*, who have no reason for coming back to horrid old Earth except that someone in Twentieth Century-Fox's marketing department thought there were more bucks to be squeezed out of your fat Christmas wallet?" Several papers lamented the fact that the sequel did nothing to earn the attention and sentiment that the original did. "Sequels," wrote *The Village Voice*, "like this exist for pretty much the same reason dogs lick their own balls—because they can."

The film did well financially, though certainly not on the scale of the original, grossing a healthy $18 million at the box office.

Immediately thereafter, Ameche took over the pivotal role of the Stage Manager in *Our Town* on March 21, 1989 at New York's Lyceum Theater. The Thornton Wilder play had begun on December 4, 1988, but Don saw it through to its end on April 2, 1989 by which point it had won the 1989 Tony for Best Revival.

Between films, he filled up the odd gaps with a few commercials, once collaborating with *Cocoon* cohort Wilfred Brimley in a Chrysler commercial, shouting to his chubby golfing partner, "Come on, get the lead out!" In the 1990s he richly intoned narration for at least seven Club Med vacation TV commercials. He had also been approached to make senior citizen fitness videos but was not interested. There were rumors that he tried to get a sitcom in later life, and though he did appear as "Papa" McGuire in 1991's *Our Shining Moment*, an hour-long family drama starring Max Gail and Cindy Pickett, feature film work kept him busy enough.

In a way, Don's last years seemed to be back in Fox mode: taking any role that came his way, the good and the bad both. One of his weakest and most puzzling venues came in the form of *Oddball Hall*, a promising title that refused to deliver.

Don, Burgess Meredith and two other crooks are hiding out in a small South African village until the heat blows over from their jewel heist. They have taken over the local Oddball fraternity, which promises to do good deeds in return for the right to act weird (both of which they seldom do in the picture). On the eve of their meeting up with a fence who will trade a fortune in cash for their sparkling booty, they learn that the Oddballs' Grand Wizard is coming to visit. As he is supposed to be recognizable to all Oddballs after giving the password (which they don't know), they've no idea who this man will be. Metoo-U (Tiny Skefile), having traveled far from his desert village in order to have a washer mended that will repair his people's device for supplying their fresh water, is mistaken for the Grand man. Meanwhile, two other crooks find the Oddballs and try to steal the jewels at the same time that the real Grand Wizard enters to unveil the imposter. Chases ensue, and though the good-bad guys escape with their treasure in tact, they are forced into hiding out in the desert, among Metoo-U's people, where they find they are happiest, living the hot but simple life.

Ameche was certainly the star of this not-odd-enough comedy, though Burgess Meredith was terribly underused. It had elements of *The Gods Must Be Crazy*, but contained little in the way of gags, character development or sustained farcical plot that could have made it at least as madcap as the premise alluded to.

Taking off a little time between pictures, on August 9-11, 1991 the average man in the street could have "A Weekend with Don Ameche In-Person," sponsored by the American Cinematheque which at the time was having its permanent home built adjacent to Mann's Chinese Theater. Meantime, the nonprofit, viewer-supported cultural organization was housed at the Directors Guild, where it offered monthly film festivals throughout the year. This time, Don's greatest hits: Friday—*Heaven Can Wait*, followed by a double feature of *Down Argentine Way* and *Moon Over Miami*. Saturday—*Midnight*, *The Three Musketeers*, *In Old Chicago*, *The Story of Alexander Graham Bell*. Sunday—*Wing and a Prayer*, *The Magnificent Dope*, a repeat of two TV features, and *Things Change*. Don appeared for discussions with the audience of all ages and charmed them graciously.

Oscar, starring Sylvester Stallone as a mobster who promises his dying father (Kirk Douglas) that he will go straight, easily erased the memory of *Oddball Hall*. Directed by John Landis, the farcical plot, based on the French play by Claude Magnier, might take a whole other chapter to relate, but as Landis explains, "The original Magnier play was set today in Paris and was about a wealthy executive. The plot machinations about the fake daughter and fiancé mix-up are from the original. The Charles bothers (who created the TV shows *Taxi* and *Cheers*) wrote the first pass of an American script, changing the lead into a contemporary Mafia Don. I thought it would play better in period and wanted to make it a Damon Runyonesque gangster movie. Jim Mulholland and Michael Berrie wrote the shooting script. Don was my first choice for the priest and he was available."

Don's scenes as the priest who marries Stallone's daughter off at the end weren't long, but certainly more memorable than some of his other later comedies. Critics weren't thrilled to see Stallone in another comedy, but some were kinder than others. *Newsday* reported, "Stallone genuinely appears to 'have fun with it,' and Landis surrounds him with such capable supporting players . . ." *The Los Angeles Times* took it a bit too seriously: "As honorable as Stallone acquits himself here, simply getting out of his way is not enough to make anyone laugh very hard." *The New York Post* got it, and especially loved Tim Curry's scene-stealing

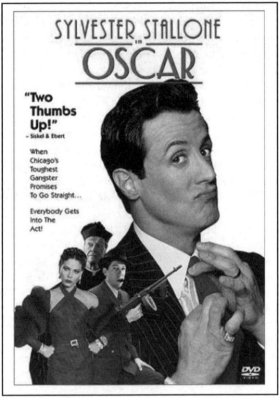

as the elocution teacher. "Stallone good-naturedly allows the script to poke fun at him. (It worked for Schwarzenegger, after all.) As a gangster (read: actor) trying to clean up his image, he learns a word a day and takes elocution lessons, a Rambo Doolittle on the rocky road to social standing. It wins you over." It also won $23.5 million in ticket sales.

Folks!, on the other hand, is a difficult film to watch if you're seeking likeable characters, and seems to progress the noxious notion that you shouldn't be a nice guy or you will get severely beaten.

Stockbroker Jon Aldrich (Tom Selleck) has the perfect life, until his senile father Harry (Ameche), his sister (Christine Ebersole) and her abominable children invade his life and cause untold physical wreckage to his bank account and person. Eventually, father and son reunite, though Harry's condition is obviously irreparable, and all financial worries are wiped out with the discovery of a fantastic stock certificate at the end. Luckily, the ever-optimistic Jon seems to feel the entire, painful journey was somehow worth it.

John Harkness of *Sight and Sound* rightly described the film in his review thusly: "*Folks!* is a feel-good movie about having your father come down with Alzheimer's; a light comedy about trying to kill your parents; a laugh-fest where the hero is more abused than Wile E. Coyote, at various junctures receiving a serious eye injury, being half-deafened by a gunshot, losing a testicle and a toe, and incurring minor arm and leg injuries."

Don and Tom Selleck in *Folks!*, 1992.

As usual, reviews were kind to Ameche, who claimed he was caught up in an idea that the average person would just not care to watch. *The Los Angeles Times* had "a slight problem with this premise: senility isn't inherently funny," admitting that Ameche "is such a sympathetic actor that you feel too much pity, both for his character and him as a performer, to enjoy laughs at his expense." It awoke from its ranting long enough to state, "Ameche is both the best thing about this film, and the worst. That is its main problem: He gives a solid performance in a highly questionable role, that of a man who's losing his mind. Is this funny?" After more flaws: "There are moments in the film that are funny, and there are some that are actually touching: When Harry experiences a rare moment of lucidity, and explains to Jon that the senile life is not worth living, *Folks!* rises well above its usual slapstick style. But there are too few moments like this."

Even Connie Ameche found the movie difficult. "*Folks!* was hard to watch, because of the role he played almost too well." The shoot itself was even hard for the aging actor, requiring numerous takes for a month in the heat and humidity of Ft. Lauderdale, then two months in Chicago.

Living in Arizona may have made Don handy for casting in sexy Jane Seymour's made-for-TV thriller, *Sunstroke*. Seymour (also co-executive producer) plays sultry Georgia mother Teresa Winters whose only goal in life is to find her daughter, taken from her by ex-husband Larry (Ray Wise). She follows the trail to sweltering Scottsdale, Arizona in the summer, and finds herself trusting the wrong man to help her, Greg Foster (Stephen Meadows). Most of the action takes place in and around "a quiet, family motel" run by Jake (Ameche), who provides the comic relief in the film. Jake has definite ideas about the law, privacy and how to run a "proper" motel; he does not give the sheriff any help unless his search warrants are correct and believes firmly in his Constitutional rights. But for all his authoritative airs, he's forced to take anyone that comes in during the too-hot summer months, which ultimately results in his getting shot (not fatally) at the end of the picture.

Though the thriller did not break any new ground in an era saturated with this steamy formula, it gave Ameche one of his biggest roles of the 1990s, now and then even weaving him into the plot. His intense stares, frequent smiles and energetic stature balanced the heaviness of the rest of the film in a much-needed way. It was broadcast on September 23, 1992.

It was around this time that Don was diagnosed with prostate cancer. It had spread throughout his body. But he was not about to sit back and undergo treatment that would rob him of the very independence and activity that kept him satisfied and dynamic his whole life. Instead, he buried his mind in films, horses and family.

"I was very fortunate to be very close to him in the latter years," says Don Ameche, Jr. "In fact, I was his financial guy, and I helped him tremendously with thoroughbred racehorses which was his passion for the last 10 years of his life. But it was only at that point that we got close at all. And shared so many things.

"The last couple of years of my father's life, I finally got him to move from California over here to Phoenix where I live, so I could keep an eye on him and take care of him. In the later part of his life, he didn't even have a checkbook. He was in his mid-80s by this point. I was taking care of his finances, and after being here for about a month, I would go every day and we would visit. I said to him, 'Where's your mail? Where are your checks? You must be getting social security checks, and I know there's some Medicare checks that I'm looking for that have to come in. Where's your mail?' He said, 'I don't have any mail.' Well, it turned out every day when the mailman would put the mail in the box, he'd go out and pick it up and throw it all in the garbage! He never opened a thing! So finally I told him to just leave it alone, that I'd take care of the mail. It was much easier than replacing Medicare checks and social security checks! That's the kind of character he was."

Connie Ameche: "I can't say if I was any closer to Papa during the last 10 years. I made a special visit to the West Coast in 1987, and we spent a great deal of time together, talking and walking because I, like my brothers, had had a time of estrangement from him, but for different reasons. It was during 1987 and during the week before he died that we were the closest.

"I don't dwell in the past, so dredging up memories is hard to do. My father was a very important person in my life, but as I mentioned, he was complex—difficult to figure out and certainly not easy to describe or explain. He was very disciplined with himself first, and with others second. He had extremely high standards and we children fell short—I more than most. I learned a tremendous amount from him and tried to be like him in many ways, but thankfully, I am who I am, as are my sister and brothers. Papa was a taskmaster, who wanted or needed to control people and situations. He said to me, more than once, that he had lost control of me when I was 14 and he regretted that.

Forever Bell.

"We had a family reunion in Iowa to which he did not come, so my family and I met him in Ohio, on our way back to Virginia. I must say that I was really surprised that he showed up in jeans and driving a VW—most unlike him. He had a woman with him and although he said they were working together, I noticed that she had his emerald ring on her left ring finger. When I mentioned it to her, while he went to the men's room, she acknowledged that he had given it to her. The family never saw it again. When I asked him about it, he said he had tried to get it back. In 1987, I brought it up again, but he was not interested in talking about it."

Don earlier told *TV Guide*, "I'm afraid I didn't take the time to show my children how much I loved them." And the selfish side of Hollywood didn't help much. "When you're an actor, trying to live for others is a great strain."

Perhaps that is why he felt such solace in horses: they required only the love of winning, and worked as nonstop as he did. Richard Frank: "Don Ameche did not find the need to retire. He was too busy with his love for horses. He had a stable of race horses (two) that he wanted to be near and to watch them race. It was down in Del Mar that I said my final goodbye to him. He was there to watch his horse run."

Tom Ameche also agreed that the horses kept *Don* running for those last months. "In the last year of his life, he knew he had prostate cancer but he never told any of us. He literally lived at the track every day. I don't think he was in a lot of pain until the last week. He was on medication.

"He lived for horses. L'Aquila (an Italian city which means "the Hawk") Ltd. was his company. Making money was not his primary concern. He would've liked to have had stakes winners. He had two horses that were early stakes winners, Sir Bim and Son of Chance." He boarded his horses at Nick Lotz' Briarbrooke Farm near Paris, KY, where, at the time of his death, he was grooming a new colt for the 1994 Kentucky Derby.

Early in 1993 Disney released its G-rated remake, *Homeward Bound: The Incredible Journey*, which *The Los Angeles Times* wrote "improves vastly on the original." The story involves two dogs and a cat trekking across Canadian High

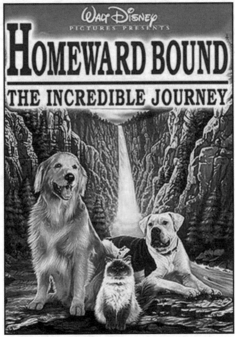

© Disney Enterprises, Inc.

Country in search of their human family whom they think has left for good. Actually, father Bob (Robert Hays) has a temporary job somewhere and moves his children and stepchildren and wife Laura (Kim Greist) to San Francisco. The family and family pets have not been together long, so the separation from what they know strenuously hurts all of them. Led by energetic bulldog pup Chance (voiced by Michael J. Fox), Himalayan cat Sassy (voiced by Sally Field) and kindly old golden retriever Shadow (voiced by Ameche) follow on a series of adventures that blend reality and fantasy quite well. The insults between Sassy and Chance might become somewhat annoying at times(some reviews nearly refer to its Bickersons roots), but Shadow is there to lend a quiet, respectful dignity to their travels. Ameche's low, semi-husky voice sounds tired and blends perfectly to the character.

Animal trainer Joe Camp and colleagues turn in some amazing scenes for the stars: plunging waterfalls, trysts with mountain cats. For a kid's film, the reviews were amazingly and almost universally positive. *The New York Post* wrote, "The sentiment teeters between touching and syrupy—but bring a hankie, since even adults might shed a tear or two at the shamelessly heart-tugging ending."

It would be the last movie released in Don Ameche's lifetime. If Don told anyone in Hollywood about his terminal prostrate cancer, it's difficult to understand how he would have been insured (a common practice by studios to make sure their stars can complete a picture) before filming his last movie, *Corrina, Corrina*, in the fall of 1993. It was arranged to get Don's part finished as quickly as possible, so his scenes were shot first. Producer Steve Tisch said, "In an ironic way he was playing himself."

Corrina, Corrina takes place in 1959's Los Angeles, where single dad Manny Singer (Ray Liotta) has the difficult job of raising his mute daughter Molly (Tina Marjorino). Only after new nanny Corrina (Whoppi Goldberg) is hired does Molly start to show signs of progress and a love of life. Because of that, the unthinkable happens: white man and black woman begin to fall in love, ultimately alienating some friends and family, but making their own family unit a whole.

Based on director/producer/writer Jessie Nelson's own childhood experience as the little girl, it was a gentle, touching comedy, and an elegant way for Ameche to end his exemplary film career. His few scenes as Manny's father, who never speaks and dies in the film, make a touching final performance and underlines his own final year. Little Tina was quoted in the press as saying that she could see angels around Don during filming. The picture was released on August 12, 1994, nine months after Don's death.

While some called *Corrina, Corrina* flawed, it still gathered much applause. "The movie is filled with such moments of insight," wrote *The New York Post*, "and it boasts Whoopi Goldberg's finest dramatic performance since *The Color Purple*." *The Village Voice* thought it a moving drama of wonder: "In less than two hours, the audience not only learns something about Manny, Corrina and Molly, it learns something from them—and that is what makes *Corrina, Corrina* worthwhile."

Don Ameche chose how to end his life: in the saddle. Don, Jr. agreed that it was his best therapy: "Until the day he died, he'd wake up in the middle of the night and say to me, 'What time do I have to go to work? What time are they picking me up?' He just loved it."

The Mayor of Scottsdale, Herb Drinkwater, said Ameche was liked around town because of his friendly personality. "He always had a good word for everybody. I saw him in a restaurant only a couple of months ago, and he came over and talked. It was obvious he wasn't feeling real well, but he stopped and talked to anybody who wanted to say something to him. He was just a kind, nice person."

Even in his final weeks, he would walk daily to Mass at Our Lady of Perpetual Help Catholic Church. Rev. Eugene Maguire remembered, "Even though there were times he was in pain, he was there. He was a real gentleman and practiced his religion almost to the end." He was often seen in Italian restaurants in Scottsdale. In his last months, with cancer having spread to his esophagus, all he could eat was pasta.

All of his children had visited Don in his last three weeks, allowing everyone to make their peace. Honore had died in 1991, buried in Dubuque, Iowa at the

The Ameche family in the 1990s.

Resurrection Catholic Cemetery. Don passed away at 6:00 p.m. on Monday, December 6, 1993, from prostate cancer, the top cancer killer of men (second only to lung cancer), which also claimed the deaths of Bill Bixby, Stewart Granger and Frank Zappa that year alone.

Don was cremated and buried next to his beloved Honore. A Memorial Mass was held the following Monday at 11:00 a.m. at Our Lady of Perpetual Help Catholic Church at 7655 Main St. in Phoenix. Contributions in his name were asked to be sent to Hospice of the Valley in that city. Rev. Frank Fernandez officiated at the service of 600 mourners, calling Don "a man with a tremendous sense of spirituality. So much of what we once were was carried in this man. With him went an era, an era more innocent than the one in which we live today."

Ameche's family attended Mass in the presence of the Most Rev. Thomas O'Brien, bishop of the Phoenix Roman Catholic Diocese. No Hollywood celebrities were expected to attend, though a more public memorial service was held in Los Angeles on Friday the December 17. It was the way he would have wanted it—separate from Hollywood, yet respectful to it.

Don Ameche's career lasted a sturdy 60 years, an impressive feat that was only strengthened into longevity by his eager, often perfectionist versatility. Even today, whenever a *Cocoon* shows up on cable, or a Bickersons CD is sold to someone who was not even born before Don died, the work he tried so hard to perpetuate into something *good* and meaningful will continue to live, cheer, sing and smile.

Credits

STAGE

1922	SHEPHERD IN THE DISTANCE (COLUMBIA COLLEGE)
1923	DRESS REHEARSAL (COLUMBIA COLLEGE)
1924	CAPTAIN APPLEJACK (COLUMBIA COLLEGE)
1924	THE LAMP WENT OUT (COLUMBIA COLLEGE)
1925	FINDERS KEEPERS (COLUMBIA COLLEGE)
1926	GAME OF CHESS (COLUMBIA COLLEGE)
1929	JERRY FOR SHORT (BROADWAY)
1955	SILK STOCKINGS (BROADWAY)
1957	HOLIDAY FOR LOVERS (BROADWAY)
1958-59	GOLDILOCKS (BROADWAY)
1961	13 DAUGHTERS (BROADWAY)
1967	HENRY, SWEET HENRY (BROADWAY)
1968	THE ODD COUPLE (TOUR)
1968	THERE'S A GIRL IN MY SOUP
1970S	GOOD NEWS
1973	THE MOON IS BLUE (KENLEY PLAYERS, WITH KAREN VALENTINE)
1976	ONCE MORE WITH FEELING
1979	SUGAR (PARKER PLAYHOUSE, MIAMI BEACH THEATER OF THE PERFORMING ARTS; NOMINATED FOR THE CARBONELL AWARD)
1981	HOW TO SUCCEED IN BUSINESS WITHOUT REALLY TRYING (3RD KENLEY PLAYERS SHOW, WITH FRED GRANDY)
1989	OUR TOWN
(UNKNOWN)	CHAMPAGNE COMPLEX
(UNKNOWN)	FATHER OF THE BRIDE
(UNKNOWN)	THE GIRL IN THE FREUDIAN SLIP
(UNKNOWN)	I MARRIED AN ANGEL
(UNKNOWN)	MAME (KENLEY PLAYERS, WITH KITTY CARLISLE)
(UNKNOWN)	ONCE MORE WITH FEELING

RADIO

(UNKNOWN)	THE NATIONAL FARM AND HOME HOUR
1930–1933	RIN-TIN-TIN
1930–1936	THE FIRST NIGHTER PROGRAM
1930–1933	GRAND HOTEL
1932–1936	BETTY AND BOB
DEC. 6, 1935	FIRST NIGHTER (THAT'S MY BABY)
DEC. 15, 1935	GRAND HOTEL
MAY 9, 1937–SEPT. 12, 1937	THE CHASE AND SANBORN HOUR (AS MC)
OCT. 10, 1937–JULY 3, 1938	THE CHASE AND SANBORN HOUR (AS MC)
NOV. 1, 1937	LUX RADIO THEATER (A FREE SOUL)
APRIL 25, 1938	LUX RADIO THEATER (DANGEROUS)
SEPT. 4, 1938–NOV. 5, 1939	THE CHASE AND SANBORN HOUR (AS MC)
OCT. 17, 1938	LUX RADIO THEATER (SEVENTH HEAVEN)
JULY 3, 1939	LUX RADIO THEATER (BORDERTOWN)
DEC. 17, 1939–DEC. 31, 1939	THE CHASE AND SANBORN HOUR (AS MC)
FEB. 5, 1940	LUX RADIO THEATER (THE YOUNG AT HEART)
MAY 20, 1940	LUX RADIO THEATER (MIDNIGHT)
SEPT. 9, 1940	LUX RADIO THEATER (MANHATTAN MELODRAMA)
JAN. 6, 1941	LUX RADIO THEATER (VIVACIOUS LADY)
JUNE 23, 1941	LUX RADIO THEATER (SHOP AROUND THE CORNER)
JUNE 26, 1941	KRAFT MUSIC HALL
OCT. 6, 1941	LUX RADIO THEATER (UNFINISHED BUSINESS)
MARCH 23, 1942	LUX RADIO THEATER (THE STRAWBERRY BLONDE)
APRIL 12, 1942	THE CHARLIE MCCARTHY SHOW
JUNE 11, 1942	COMMAND PERFORMANCE
JUNE 22, 1942	LUX RADIO THEATER (BEDTIME STORY)
SEPT. 3, 1942	MAIL CALL
SEPT. 6, 1942– MAY 30, 1943	THE CHASE AND SANBORN PROGRAM
SEPT. 22, 1942	COMMAND PERFORMANCE
SEPT. 28, 1942	LUX RADIO THEATER (THE MAGNIFICENT DOPE)
1943–1944	WHAT'S NEW?
SEPT. 5, 1943– JUNE 4, 1944	THE CHASE AND SANBORN PROGRAM
OCT. 2, 1943	COMMAND PERFORMANCE
OCT. 11, 1943	LUX RADIO THEATER (HEAVEN CAN WAIT)

RADIO (CONTINUED)

MARCH 25, 1944	COMMAND PERFORMANCE
APRIL 10, 1944	LUX RADIO THEATER (HAPPY LAND)
JULY 4, 1944	LUX RADIO THEATER (IT HAPPENED TOMORROW)
SEPT. 3, 1944–JUNE 3, 1945	THE CHASE AND SANBORN PROGRAM
SEPT. 20, 1944	MAIL CALL
SEPT. 25, 1944	LUX RADIO THEATER (LUCKY PARTNERS)
NOV. 13, 1944	LUX RADIO THEATER (MAGNIFICENT OBSESSION)
NOV. 26, 1944	THE CHARLIE MCCARTHY SHOW
SEPT. 2, 1945–MAY 25, 1946	THE CHASE AND SANDBORN PROGRAM
SEPT. 16, 1945	THE CHARLIE MCCARTHY SHOW
DEC. 10, 1945	LUX RADIO THEATER (GUEST WIFE)
1946–47	THE DON AMECHE SHOW
OCT. 14, 1946	PARADE OF STARS
OCT. 25, 1946	LOVE STORY THEATER (CONCERTO IN C MINOR)
SEPT. 1, 1946–MAY 25, 1947	THE CHASE AND SANDBORN PROGRAM
SEPT. 8, 1946–JUNE 1, 1947	DRENE TIME
DEC. 14, 1946	THIS IS HOLLYWOOD (SO GOES MY LOVE)
1947	COMMAND PERFORMANCE
JAN. 1, 1947	(GOOD HEALTH SHOW FROM NORTH CAROLINA STATIONS. PUBLIC SERVICE 30-MINUTE TRANSCRIBED SHOW)
JAN. 17, 1947	STORY THEATER (LIP SERVICE)
JAN. 19, 1947	THE CHARLIE MCCARTHY SHOW
FEB. 13, 1947	FAMILY THEATER (A ROSE BY ANY OTHER NAME)
FEB. 17, 1947	SCREEN GUILD PLAYERS (YOU BELONG TO ME)
APRIL 6, 1947	THE CHARLIE MCCARTHY SHOW
APRIL 14, 1947	CAVALCADE OF AMERICA (THE PEANUT VENDOR)
MAY 25, 1947	THE CHARLIE MCCARTHY SHOW
SEPT. 7, 1947–MAY 30, 1948	THE CHASE AND SANBORN PROGRAM
SEPT. 24, 1947–1948–1949	YOUR LUCKY STRIKE (A.K.A. DON AMECHE SHOW)
OCT. 5, 1947	THE CHARLIE MCCARTHY SHOW
FEB. 1948	TWO HOURS OF STARS (M.C.)
FEB. 2, 1948	THE CHARLIE MCCARTHY SHOW
FEB. 10, 1948	MAIL CALL
FEB. 24, 1948	MAIL CALL
MAY 9, 1948	THE CHARLIE MCCARTHY SHOW

RADIO (CONTINUED)

JUNE 25, 1948	THE OLD GOLD SHOW
OCT. 3, 1948–DEC. 19, 1948	THE CHASE AND SANBORN PROGRAM (BICKERSONS)
DEC. 6, 1948	YOUR LUCKY STRIKE
1949-50	THE JIMMY DURANTE SHOW
MARCH 21, 1949	LUX RADIO THEATRE (THAT WONDERFUL URGE)
JUNE 25, 1949	THE SPIKE JONES SHOW
OCT. 2, 1949–MAY 28, 1950	THE CHARLIE MCCARTHY SHOW
NOV. 5, 1950–JUNE 3, 1951	THE CHARLIE MCCARTHY SHOW
OCT. 7, 1951–JUNE 1, 1952	THE CHARLIE MCCARTHY SHOW
OCT. 5, 1952–MAY 31, 1953	THE CHARLIE MCCARTHY SHOW
OCT. 11, 1953–JUNE 20, 1954	THE CHARLIE MCCARTHY SHOW
SEPT. 12, 1954–FEB. 20, 1955	THE EDGAR BERGAN AND CHARLIE MCCARTHY SHOW
OCT. 2, 1955–JULY 1, 1956	THE NEW EDGAR BERGEN HOUR
NOV. 15, 1964	THE CHASE AND SANBORN 100TH ANNIVERSARY SHOW
1979	THE JEWELER'S SHOP

FILMOGRAPHY

1933	BEAUTY AT THE WORLD'S FAIR
1935	CLIVE OF INDIA (20TH CENTURY-FOX)
1935	DANTE'S INFERNO (20TH CENTURY-FOX)
1936	SINS OF MAN (20TH CENTURY-FOX)
1936	RAMONA (20TH CENTURY-FOX)
1936	LADIES IN LOVE (20TH CENTURY-FOX)
1937	ONE IN A MILLION (20TH CENTURY-FOX)
1937	FIFTY ROADS TO TOWN (20TH CENTURY-FOX)
1937	LOVE IS NEWS (20TH CENTURY-FOX)
1937	LOVE UNDER FIRE (20TH CENTURY-FOX)
1937	SCREEN SNAPSHOTS #8 (COLUMBIA) (SHORT)
1937	YOU CAN'T HAVE EVERYTHING (20TH CENTURY-FOX)
1938	JOSETTE (20TH CENTURY-FOX)
1938	IN OLD CHICAGO (20TH CENTURY-FOX)
1938	ALEXANDER'S RAGTIME BAND (20TH CENTURY-FOX)
1938	GATEWAY (20TH CENTURY-FOX)
1938	HAPPY LANDING (20TH CENTURY-FOX)
1939	HOLLYWOOD CAVALCADE (20TH CENTURY-FOX)
1939	THE STORY OF ALEXANDER GRAHAM BELL (20TH CENTURY-FOX)
1939	SWANEE RIVER (20TH CENTURY-FOX)

FILMOGRAPHY

1939	THE THREE MUSKETEERS (20TH CENTURY-FOX)
1939	MIDNIGHT (PARAMOUNT PICTURES)
1940	FOUR SONS (20TH CENTURY-FOX)
1940	DOWN ARGENTINE WAY (20TH CENTURY-FOX)
1940	LILLIAN RUSSELL (20TH CENTURY-FOX)
1941	CONFIRM OR DENY (20TH CENTURY-FOX)
1941	LAND OF LIBERTY (MOTION PICTURE PRODUCERS & DISTRIBUTORS OF AMERICA, INC.)
1941	MOON OVER MIAMI (20TH CENTURY-FOX)
1941	THAT NIGHT IN RIO (20TH CENTURY-FOX)
1941	THE FEMININE TOUCH (MGM)
1941	KISS THE BOYS GOODBYE (20TH CENTURY-FOX)
1942	GIRL TROUBLE (20TH CENTURY-FOX)
1942	THE MAGNIFICENT DOPE (20TH CENTURY-FOX)
1943	HAPPY LAND (20TH CENTURY-FOX)
1943	HEAVEN CAN WAIT (20TH CENTURY-FOX)
1943	SOMETHING TO SHOUT ABOUT (20TH CENTURY-FOX)
1944	GREENWICH VILLAGE (20TH CENTURY-FOX)
1944	WING AND A PRAYER (20TH CENTURY-FOX)
1945	GUEST WIFE (GREENTREE PRODUCTIONS)
1945	IT'S IN THE BAG (MANHATTAN PRODUCTIONS)
1946	SO GOES MY LOVE (SKIRBALL-MANNING PRODUCTIONS)
1947	SLEEP, MY LOVE (TRIANGLE PRODUCTIONS)
1948	THAT'S MY MAN (REPUBLIC PICTURES)
1949	SLIGHTLY FRENCH (COLUMBIA PICTURES)
1952	HOLLYWOOD NIGHT AT 21 CLUB (COLUMBIA) (SHORT)
1954	FIRE ONE (PRINCESS)
1954	PHANTOM CARAVAN (PRINCESS)
1961	A FEVER IN THE BLOOD (WARNER BROTHERS)
1966	RINGS AROUND THE WORLD (CAAM COMPANY)
1966	PICTURE MOMMY DEAD (BERKELEY PRODUCTIONS)
1970	THE BOATNIKS (WALT DISNEY PRODUCTIONS)
1970	SUPPOSE THEY GAVE A WAR AND NOBODY CAME? (ABC PICTURES)
1976	WON-TON-TON, THE DOG WHO SAVED HOLLYWOOD (PARAMOUNT)
1983	TRADING PLACES (PARAMOUNT PICTURES)
1985	COCOON (20TH CENTURY-FOX)
1987	HARRY AND THE HENDERSONS (UNIVERSAL PICTURES)
1988	COMING TO AMERICA (PARAMOUNT PICTURES)
1988	THINGS CHANGE (COLUMBIA PICTURES)
1988	COCOON: THE RETURN (20TH CENTURY-FOX)
1990	ODDBALL HALL (RAVENHILL PRODUCTIONS)

1992	OSCAR (TOUCHSTONE PICTURES)
1992	FOLKS! (PENTA PICTURES)
1992	SUNSTROKE (WILSHIRE COURT PRODUCTIONS)
1993	HOMEWARD BOUND: THE INCREDIBLE JOURNEY (WALT DISNEY PICTURES)
1994	CORRINA, CORRINA (NEW LINE CINEMA)

TELEVISION

REGULAR

1950S	PACKARD VARIETY SHOW (EMCEE) (ABC)
1950	TAKE A CHANCE (HOST) (NBC)
1950-51	HOLIDAY HOTEL (HOST) (ABC)
1951	DON'S MUSICAL PLAYHOUSE (ABC)
1951-52	THE FRANCES LANGFORD-DON AMECHE SHOW (ABC)
1953	COKE TIME WITH EDDIE FISHER (EMCEE) (NBC)
1957-59, 1961, 1964	TO TELL THE TRUTH (CBS) (REGULAR AFTER 1957)
MAY 14, 1959–JUNE 25, 1959	TOO YOUNG TO GO STEADY (NBC)
SEPT. 15, 1961–SEPT. 10, 1965	INTERNATIONAL SHOWTIME (HOST) (NBC)

GUEST

NOV. 1949	THE LASSIE SHOW ("HIS MASTER'S EYE")
NOV. 23, 1949	TEXACO STAR THEATER
NOV. 28, 1949	CHEVROLET TELE-THEATER ("THE DOOR") NBC
DEC. 23, 1949	CELEBRITY TIME
1950	THE TRIUMPHANT HOUR
1950	THE MOST IMPORTANT PEOPLE (DUM)
FEB. 15, 1950	THE KEN MURRAY SHOW
MARCH 4, 1950	SATURDAY NIGHT REVUE (JACK CARTER SHOW)
1951	CELEBRITY TIME (CBS)
1951	THE FOUR STAR REVUE (NBC)
1951	THE FRANK SINATRA SHOW
1951	THE KEN MURRAY SHOW (CBS)
1952, 1953	TEXACO STAR THEATER
1954	THE BUICK BERLE SHOW (NBC)
1954	FIRE ONE (EXCLUSIVE/PRINCES PICTURES)
1954	THE MARTHA RAYE SHOW (NBC)
1954-55	THE JACK CARSON SHOW (NBC)

TELEVISION (CONTINUED)

<u>GUEST</u>

1955	THE TRIUMPHANT HOUR (SYNDICATED)
OCT. 24, 1956	I'VE GOT A SECRET (CBS)
NOV. 24, 1956	SATURDAY SPECTACULAR: HIGH BUTTON SHOES (NBC)
DEC. 21, 1956	PERSON TO PERSON (CBS)
1956	CHRISTOPHERS: KEEPING OUR HERITAGE STRONG (SYNDICATED)
1957	ART LINKLETTER'S HOUSE PARTY (CBS)
1957	THE ED SULLIVAN SHOW (CBS)
1957	ARTHUR MURRAY PARTY (NBC)
1957	FRONT PAGE CHALLENGE (CANADIAN SERIES)
1957	GENERAL MOTORS 75TH ANNIVERSARY
1957	THE POLLY BERGEN SHOW (NBC)
1957	STRIKE IT RICH (CBS)
JUNE 16, 1957	GOODYEAR TELEVISION PLAYHOUSE ("YOUR EVERY WISH") (NBC)
DEC. 20, 1957	DUPONT SHOW OF THE MONTH ("JUNIOR MISS") (CBS)
FEB. 19, 1958	SUNDAY NIGHT AT THE (LONDON) PALLADIUM
FEB. 27, 1958	CLIMAX! ("ALBERT ANASTASIA: HIS LIFE AND DEATH") (CBS)
1960	CHRISTOPHERS: MAKING GOVERNMENT YOUR BUSINESS (SYNDICATED)
MAY 1, 1960	FRANCES LANGFORD SHOW (SPECIAL) (NBC)
1960	PAT BOONE CHEVY SHOWROOM (ABC)
1961	MAIN EVENT
1961	OUR AMERICAN HERITAGE ("WOODROW WILSON AND THE UNKNOWN SOLDIER") (NBC)
1961	PASSWORD (CBS)
1961	PERRY COMO'S KRAFT MUSIC HALL (NBC)
MARCH 17, 1962	THE HY GARDNER SHOW (NBC)
SEPT. 11, 1962	THE TONIGHT SHOW
JAN. 27, 1964	THE MATCH GAME (NBC)
MARCH 31, 1964	THE GREATEST SHOW ON EARTH: THE GLORIOUSDAYS OF USED TO BE (ABC)
APRIL 10, 1964	BURKE'S LAW ("WHO KILLED ANNIE FORAN?") (ABC)
DEC. 28, 1964	THE MATCH GAME (NBC)

1966	THE MERV GRIFFIN SHOW (SYNDICATED)
DEC. 30, 1967	THE ED SULLIVAN SHOW ("HENRY, SWEET HENRY") (CBS)
1968	ADVENTURES A LA CARTE (SYNDICATED)
MARCH 5, 1968	SHADOW OVER ELVERON (NBC)
JUNE 29, 1968	HOLLYWOOD PALACE (ABC)
NOV. 25, 1969	JULIA (NBC)
JAN. 31, 1970	PETTICOAT JUNCTION ("STEVE'S UNCLE GEORGE") (CBS)
FEB. 17, 1970	JULIA (DIRECTOR) (NBC)
1971	COMEDY PLAYHOUSE ("SHEPHERD'S FLOCK") (CBS)
AUGUST 29, 1971	SHEPHERD'S FLOCK (PILOT) (CBS)
NOV. 17, 1971	COLUMBO ("SUITABLE FOR FRAMING") (NBC)
NOV. 18, 1971	ALIAS SMITH AND JONES ("DREADFUL SORRY, CLEMENTINE") (ABC)
JAN. 12, 1975	MCCLOUD ("THE MAN IN THE GOLDEN HAT") (NBC)
SEPT. 18, 1975	ELLERY QUEEN ("THE ADVENTURE OF THE LOVER'S LEAP") (NBC)
1976	GOOD HEAVENS ("SUPERSCOOP") (ABC)
SEPT. 28, 1978	QUINCY ("DEATH CHALLENGE") (NBC)
MARCH 3, 1979	BOSTON AND KILBRIDE (PILOT) (CBS)
OCT. 13, 1978	THE LOVE BOAT ("ONE ROSE A DAY") (ABC)
DEC. 6, 1980	FANTASY ISLAND (ABC)
MARCH 14, 1981	THE LOVE BOAT ("AUNT HILLY") (ABC)
DEC. 16, 1983	MR. SMITH ("MR. SMITH GOES PUBLIC") (NBC)
MARCH 3, 1984	THE LOVE BOAT ("THE LADY AND THE MAID") (ABC)
JUNE 16, 1984	NOT IN FRONT OF THE KIDS (PILOT) (ABC)
1985	MAGNUM P.I.
MARCH 22, 1985	DETECTIVE IN THE HOUSE ("FATHERS AND OTHER STRANGERS") (CBS)
1986	14TH AMERICAN FILM INSTITUTE ACHIEVEMENT AWARD: A SALUTE TO BILLY WILDER
FEB. 1986	HOLLYWOOD VALENTINE
SEPT. 29, 1990	THE GOLDEN GIRLS ("ONCE IN ST. OLAF")
1991	OUR SHINING MOMENT (PILOT) (NBC)
1991	PROS & CONS ("ONCE A KID") (ABC)
1992	THE ARSENIO HALL SHOW (SYNDICATED)

Television (continued)

<u>Guest</u>
1992   Reflections on the Silver Screen with Prof. Richard Brown (AMC)

TV Movies

1968   Shadow Over Elveron (NBC)
1972   Gidget Gets Married (ABC)
1986   A Masterpiece of Murder (NBC)
1987   Pals (CBS)
1992   Sunstroke (USA)

Recordings

1955   Silk Stockings (Original Broadway Cast, RCA, 1102-2-RG)
1958   Goldilocks (Original Broadway Cast, Sony, SK 48222)
1961   The Bickersons (Columbia CL-1692/CS-8492)
1962   The Bickersons Fight Back (Columbia CL-1883/CS-8683)
1967   Henry, Sweet Henry (Original Broadway Cast, ABC ABCS-OC-4)
1971   The Bickersons Rematch (2-Columbia G-30523/Columbia CS-8492, CS-8683 RI)
Unknown   Co-Star with Don Ameche (OSTARCS112)

Index